Challenge Math

*For the Elementary and
Middle School Student*

(Second Edition)

Edward Zaccaro

Hickory Grove Press

About the Author

Ed lives outside of Dubuque, Iowa, where he has taught students of all ages and abilities. He has been an advocate for gifted education as a parent, teacher, school board member, and consultant, and is a popular presenter at education conferences around the country. His students will testify to his ability to make math fun and challenging for them and both students and fellow teachers appreciate his unique sense of humor which comes through in his classes, books, and workshops.

Ed has an undergraduate degree from Oberlin College, a Masters degree in Gifted Education from the University of Northern Iowa, and is the author of four math books for mathematically gifted students:

- *Challenge Math for the Elementary and Middle School Student*
- *Primary Grade Challenge Math*
- *The Ten Things All Future Mathematicians and Scientists Must Know*
- *Real World Algebra*

Ed credits his interest in math to his father, Luke N. Zaccaro, who was a college math professor for his entire career.

Cover designed by Wilderness Graphics, Dubuque, Iowa.

Phone: 563-583-4767
E-mail: challengemath@aol.com
http://www.challengemath.com

Library of Congress Card Number: 00-108667
ISBN: 0-9679915-5-2

This book is dedicated to my students, whose passion for math and science is the reason that I teach.

Acknowledgements

I would like to thank my family for their support and patience during the seven years it took to develop "Challenge Math". Thank you to my daughter Rachel for her art contributions and for her understanding when Mr. Math did not get picked for a starring role. Thank you to my son Luke for double-checking the solutions. I hope the probability chapter did not cause any permanent brain damage. Thank you to my son Dan for all his work on this book. I also want to thank him for his attempts to remain patient and for his willingness to teach a computer illiterate father the skills he needed to put "Challenge Math" into print. Special thanks to my wife Sara for her love and support and her willingness to do my share of the dishes during this long process. I also want to thank Sara for her willingness to proofread a book whose subject area is not her passion. Special thanks to Lyn Zaccaro for her support and encouragement.

To my colleagues, Cheryl and Dorothy, I appreciate your continued support and encouragement. Your dedication to children who are gifted in mathematics is truly appreciated.

Mr. Math

Contents

Introduction

When children first see the wonders of math and science, it is as if they stepped into a room that they didn't know existed. When they are provided with the opportunity to work with algebra, trigonometry, and physics, children are in awe of what mathematics allows them to do:

Using calculus to find the speed of a train.

Using their knowledge of the speed of light to realize that looking at stars is looking back in time a hundred, a thousand, or even a million years.

Finding the distance a ship is from shore through the use of trigonometry.

Finding the height of a tree by measuring its shadow and then using ratios.

Gifted children typically are not given the opportunity to see the wondrous side of mathematics because it is usually taught as all scales and no music. If musicians were not given the opportunity to perform or play music that stirred their hearts, it is unlikely that they would develop a passion for their field. The same holds true for children and mathematics. Children who are talented in mathematics must be exposed to material that lights a fire and nurtures their gift.

Mathematically gifted children usually pick up concepts so quickly that they are left with very little to do intellectually in a typical classroom. This situation is troubling, not only because of the obvious waste of potential, but also because there can be serious consequences if bright children are not challenged in their elementary years. The lack of opportunity to think deeply and to experience and learn from frustration, can have disastrous consequences later in life. How will these children view the inevitable challenges of high school and college if they drifted through elementary school? Young students must experience intellectual frustration in a positive way. They must learn that challenge and effort are a part of learning and a part of life.

Recognizing and Honoring Academic Brilliance

Can you imagine what it feels like for an athlete to have hundreds of parents and classmates cheering for him or her. Add to that the newspaper articles, trophies, medals, and other awards. This kind of reinforcement pushes athletes to excel. It is unlikely that this kind of motivating environment will ever become routine for those students who excel in math and science. Because there are precious few opportunities for gifted children to be formally recognized and honored, it is important that teachers make students feel that their gifts are something to be treasured.

For several years I have been recognizing and honoring my students by handing out "Einstein Awards" for problem solving brilliance. I'd like to share an experience that shows the impact this kind of recognition can have on children. During a workshop I was conducting at a neighboring district, one of the children solved a difficult problem with a very clever and insightful solution, for which she was given an Einstein Award. The next day, her teacher said that the child's parents had called and mentioned that their child felt that the Einstein Award was "the best thing that ever happened to her".

Some might say that this was a sad commentary on this child's life, but at that moment, the power and importance of recognizing and honoring academic brilliance in children became apparent. Children who have a special capacity for math must learn to treasure and value their gift.

EINSTEIN AWARD

"This award is given for brilliant insight and extraordinary problem solving"

NAME:

Astronomy and Large Numbers

People have always been fascinated by the moon, the planets, and the stars. Hundreds of stories have been written to try and explain these lights in the sky. Different cultures in different times developed varied explanations for these celestial bodies, but almost all people through the ages believed two things. One, that the moon and the sun were about the same size; and two, that the moon, the planets, and the stars were very close to the earth. Then mathematics changed everything!!

Over 2000 years ago a brilliant Greek mathematician named Eratosthenes used fairly simple mathematics to determine the circumference of the earth. This was one of the world's most valuable discoveries because once we knew the circumference of the earth, trigonometry could be used to find the distance to the moon, the sun and other heavenly bodies.

Several years after Eratosthenes's discovery, two other Greek mathematicians used trigonometry to find that the moon was approximately 250,000 miles from the earth. This provided dramatic proof that the moon, the sun and the stars weren't just miles above us as previously thought, but were hundreds of thousands, and possibly even millions of miles away. Humankind suddenly realized that everything around us was not what it appeared.

I had no idea that the moon, planets, and stars were so far away. They look so close that sometimes I think I can touch them.

We're lucky that we have mathematics to show us what our universe is really like.

Mathematics was the key to our present understanding of the earth and the universe. As we continue to try and unlock the mysteries of space, mathematics will be one of our most important tools.

The fastest traveler in our universe is light. Light travels 186,000 miles per second, which is fast enough to circle the earth over 7 times in one second.

Is light even faster than sound?

Sound is a very fast traveler, but its speed is nowhere near the speed of light. It takes sound 5 seconds to go 1 mile, while light goes 186,000 miles in 1 second!!

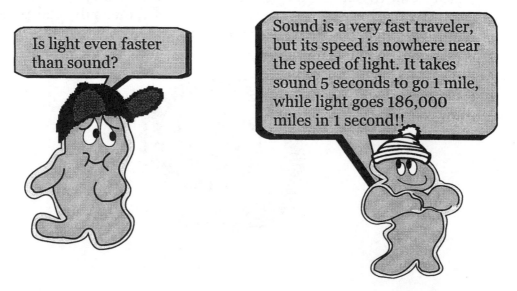

You can tell how far away a thunderstorm is by using this information about the speed of light and sound. When you see lightning, the thunder occurs at the same time, but because sound is much slower than light, it will take several seconds for the sound to reach your ears (unless the storm is directly overhead).

If I hear thunder 15 seconds after I see lightning, then the storm must be 3 miles away because I know it takes sound 15 seconds to go 3 miles.

When I want to know how far away a thunderstorm is, I count the seconds between the lightning and thunder and then divide by 5. I was on a camping trip once and counted 45 seconds between the lightning and the thunder. I felt pretty safe because I knew the storm was 9 miles away.

If thunder sounds 12.5 seconds after the lighting, can you tell how far away the storm is?

We know that light is the fastest traveler in the universe, but even with light's extraordinary speed, it still takes many years for the light from the stars to reach our eyes. The closest star to us, besides the sun, is Alpha Centauri. Astronomers once believed that Alpha Centauri was a single star, but now it is known that it is a triple star. This triple star is approximately 23,462,784,000,000 miles from the earth.

 **Distances in space are so large that astronomers find it much easier to use light-years as a measurement of distance. A light-year is the distance light travels in a year.**

Instead of saying that Alpha Centauri is 23,462,784,000,000 miles away, astronomers say that it is 4 light-years away. Another term that astronomers use to measure large distances in space is a **parsec.** Each parsec is equal to 3.26 light-years.

Is a parsec really a term to measure distances? It sounds more like the name of a vegetable.

Whether it sounds like a vegetable or not, it is still used to measure distances. For example, since Alpha Centauri is 4 light-years from earth, it could also be said that it is a little more than 1 parsec from earth.

Sometimes when we are dealing with large distances in space, our numbers become too large for a calculator. We need to learn how to multiply these large numbers on our calculator because we certainly do not want to do the math using paper and pencil!!

If I want to find the distance light travels in a week, I need to multiply 186,000 by the number of seconds in a week---which is 604,800.

If you multiply those two numbers, the answer won't fit on your calculator.

When you multiply numbers that are too large for the calculator, you must remove all the zeros at the end of the numbers, multiply, and then return the zeros to your answer.

Lets look at the example concerning the distance light travels in a week:
186,000 x 604,800 ⟶ becomes ⟶ 186 x 6048.

What are you going to do with the 5 zeros you removed?

I'll put them in this box for safe keeping.

$$186 \times 6048 = 1,124,928$$

Now I'll take the 5 zeros that were saved and return them to the answer.

$$186 \times 6048 = 112,492,8\mathbf{00,000}$$

Solve the following problems on your calculator by removing zeros:

1) $55,000 \times 96,000 =$

2) $186,000 \times 36,000 =$

3) $4005 \times 92,000,000 =$

When you are solving problems about distances in space, you will be dealing with very large numbers. The names of these numbers are shown below.

Billion......................... 9 zeros	
Trillion....................... 12 zeros	
Quadrillion.................15 zeros	
Quintillion...................18 zeros	
Sextillion..................... 21 zeros	
Septillion....................24 zeros	
Octillion...................... 27 zeros	
Nonillion..................... 30 zeros	
Decillion.....................33 zeros	
Undecillion..................36 zeros	
Duodecillion................39 zeros	
Tredecillion................. 42 zeros	
Quattuordecillion........ 45 zeros	
Quindecillion.............. 48 zeros	
Sexdecillion.................51 zeros	
Septendecillion............54 zeros	
Octodecillion.............. 57 zeros	
Novemdecillion........... 60 zeros	
Vigintillion.................. 63 zeros	
Googol.......................... 100 zeros	
Googolplex........a googol of zeros	

Mathematicians made a very interesting observation about circles that has proven to be very useful to astronomers and scientists. They found that you can find the circumference of any circle by multiplying the diameter of the circle by **pi.**

1) If the diameter of the earth is 8000 miles, what is its circumference?

2) If the diameter of the moon is 2000 miles, what is its circumference?

3) If the diameter of the sun is 800,000 miles, what is its circumference?

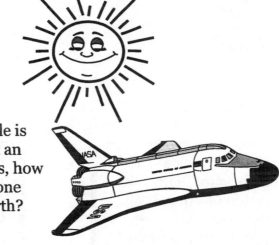

4) If the space shuttle is orbiting the earth at an altitude of 280 miles, how far does it travel in one orbit around the earth?

When we look at stars, we are looking at them as they appeared many, many years ago. If we look at a star in the year 1998 that is 100 light-years away, we are looking at that star as it appeared in 1898. This is because the light given off by that star takes 100 years to reach our eyes. We do not know how the star appears today. If a dramatic change has occurred, we wouldn't know about it for 100 years.

Astronomy
Level 1

1) How long does it take light to reach the earth from the sun? (The sun is approximately 93,000,000 miles from the earth)

2) How far does light travel in a year?

3) You are standing a distance from a rock wall. When you shout it takes 15 seconds from the time you shout until the echo reaches your ears. How far away is the rock wall?

4) During a thunderstorm, the thunder sounds 27 1/2 seconds after you see lightning. How far away is the storm?

5) If a snail moves constantly at 11 inches per hour, how long is a "snail-year" ?

6) Electric current flowing through wires is in actuality electrons flowing through wires. A 100 watt light bulb draws current equivalent to 6,000,000,000,000,000,000,000 electrons per second flowing to the bulb. How many electrons flow through this bulb during a 24 hour period?

7) Approximately how many times can light travel around the earth in one hour? (Use 25,000 miles for the circumference of the earth.)

8) How many miles does light travel in 15 years?

9) The Hubble Telescope can see quasars that are 58,656,960,000,000,000,000,000 miles away. How long does it take light to reach earth from these quasars?

10) Two friends, Luke and Rachel, are on the tops of two different mountains, but within sight of each other. They wanted to know how far apart they were, so they agreed that Luke would blow a whistle and wave a flag at exactly the same time. After Rachel saw Luke wave the flag, 36 seconds passed before she heard the whistle. How far apart are Luke and Rachel?

Astronomy
Level 2

1) The earth rotates once in a 24-hour period. What is its speed of rotation? (Speed at the equator)

2) You are watching an asteroid through your telescope. All of a sudden the asteroid explodes due to a collision with another asteroid. You glance at your watch and it is 10:30 P.M. You know the asteroid is located 1,004,400,000 miles away from earth. What time did the asteroid actually explode?

3) When the moon has orbited the earth once, approximately how many miles has it gone? (Assume a circular orbit, and use 250,000 miles as the distance between the moon and the earth.)

4) You are sitting in a tent and hear a thunderstorm. After you see lightning, you hear thunder 30 seconds later. Fifteen minutes later, the lightning and thunder occur simultaneously (at the same time). How fast is the storm moving?

5) Is a light-year a measurement of time or distance? Explain.

6) Eric and Kristin are on the tops of two different mountains. They devised a plan that would enable them to determine how far apart they were. Since they each had whistles, it was decided that Eric would blow his whistle first and when Kristin heard his whistle, she would blow her whistle. Eric blew his whistle and then looked at his watch. Thirty seconds passed before he heard Kristin's whistle. How far apart are they?

7) The moon revolves around the earth in an orbit that takes approximately 27 days and 8 hours. If you assume that its orbit is circular, at what speed is the moon traveling during its trip around the earth? (Round to the nearest hundred.)

8) If a star that is 46,925,568,000,000 miles away explodes in 1998, what year will we know about it on earth?

9) You are standing between 2 rock walls. There is a rock wall directly in front of you and one behind you. When you shout, it takes 12 1/2 seconds for the sound to echo back to you and then 67 1/2 seconds later you hear another echo as the echo bounces off the back wall and comes back to you. How far apart are the rock walls?

10) The Andromeda Nebula is 900,000 parsecs away from the earth. Approximately how many miles is that equal to?

Einstein
Level

1) Suppose an imaginary tree was planted at the time of the earth's origin and has since grown continuously at the rate of 3 inches per year. It would now just be reaching the moon. How old is the earth?

2) You see lightning flash in the North and 7.5 seconds later you hear thunder. Twelve minutes later you see lightning in the South and hear thunder 12.5 seconds after that. How fast is the storm moving?

3) Jupiter is the largest of the nine planets with a diameter of 88,000 miles. In fact, it is larger than all the other planets combined. Jupiter's rotation is so fast that it takes only 10 hours to complete one rotation. How fast is Jupiter turning? (Speed at the equator)

4) At what speed is the earth traveling as it circles the sun? (The earth orbits the sun in an elliptical orbit, but for this problem, assume that the orbit is circular).

5) Pluto is approximately 3,348,000,000 miles away from earth. Suppose there are Plutonians with advanced technology that enable them to look through a telescope and read a clock on your wall. You look at the clock and it reads exactly 1:35. At exactly the same time, a Plutonian is looking through his telescope at your clock. What time would the Plutonian be seeing?

6) A Greek mathematician named Erotosthenes used mathematics to find the circumference of the earth. He knew that the world was round and he also knew something very interesting about the placement of the sun at two cities he visited. The sun was directly overhead in the city of Syene and at the same time it was 7 1/2° away from directly overhead in the city of Alexandria. Erotosthenes also knew that Alexandria was 500 miles north of Syene. With this information, Erotosthenes determined the circumference of the earth. How did he do it?

7) In 1998 the Hubble Telescope spotted an explosion in an area that is 50 parsecs away. In what year did the explosion actually take place?

8) If the space shuttle was orbiting 250 miles above the earth and traveled 3,282,870 miles, how many orbits did it make?

 **When we look at the sun and the moon, they appear to be the same size. This is true even though the diameter of the sun is 400 times larger than the moon's diameter. The reason they appear to be the same size is because the moon is much closer to the earth than the sun. As a matter of fact, it is about 400 times closer to the earth than the sun is. Using this information, solve the following two problems.**

9) There is a meteor with a known diameter of 8 miles approaching the earth. When you look at the meteor and the moon, they appear to be the same size. How far away from earth is the meteor?

10) If the meteor is traveling at 100 times the speed of sound, how long until impact? (Sound takes 5 seconds to travel one mile)

Super Einstein Problem

A meteor that has a known diameter of 8 miles, is traveling toward the earth at 100 times the speed of sound. When you look at the meteor, it appears 4 times larger than the moon. How long until impact?

Problem Solving

1) Suppose 4 days before the day after tomorrow was Thursday. What day of the week was yesterday?

2) A group of 24 college students decided to climb Mt. McKinley. They bought enough food to last 20 days. If 16 additional students join them, how many days will their food last?

3) In a group of 22 students, 7 children like math, 12 children like science, 6 children like English, 3 like math and science, 2 like English and math, 2 like science and English, and 1 student likes all three subjects. How many students don't like any subject?

4) In the following sequence, what is the 500th term?
7   16   25   34......................?

Math problems such as the ones shown above can cause one's brain to overload and feel like it is going to explode. The brain needs additional help when solving these types of problems. It needs help organizing the information in the problem and it needs problem-solving strategies to give some direction to the brain's thinking.

There is no way I'll ever figure these problems out. Never, ever, ever!!! These problems make my brain foggy and confused.

I'm going to use my box of strategies to try and solve them.

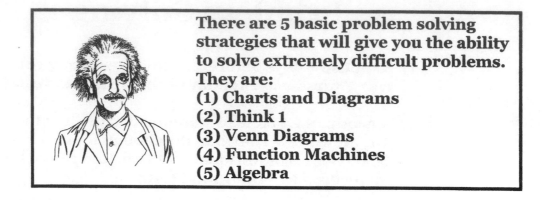

There are 5 basic problem solving strategies that will give you the ability to solve extremely difficult problems. They are:
(1) **Charts and Diagrams**
(2) **Think 1**
(3) **Venn Diagrams**
(4) **Function Machines**
(5) **Algebra**

Charts and Diagrams

Suppose 4 days before the day after tomorrow was Thursday. What day of the week was yesterday?

When you are faced with a problem such as this, the best approach is to make a chart so that your brain can process the information better.

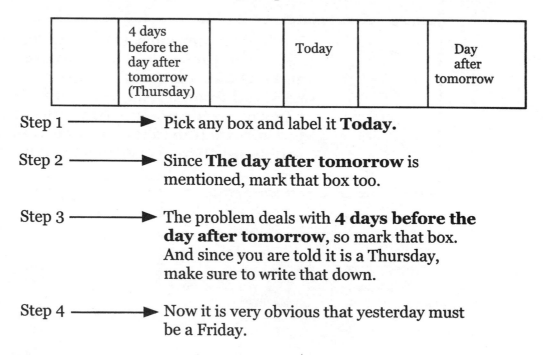

	4 days before the day after tomorrow (Thursday)		Today		Day after tomorrow

Step 1 ⟶ Pick any box and label it **Today.**

Step 2 ⟶ Since **The day after tomorrow** is mentioned, mark that box too.

Step 3 ⟶ The problem deals with **4 days before the day after tomorrow**, so mark that box. And since you are told it is a Thursday, make sure to write that down.

Step 4 ⟶ Now it is very obvious that yesterday must be a Friday.

This isn't as hard as I thought. Give me another problem.

OK, but I'm going to make it complicated. Dan worked at a camp for a week and earned some money. He spent 1/4 of his money at a computer store, then spent 1/3 of what was left on a soccer ball. He then gave 1/4 of his remaining money to his sister. If Dan ended up with $12, how much money did he earn for his week of work at camp?

The best way to approach this problem is to draw a rectangle that represents the money Dan earned.

Step 1 ——▶ Mark the amount he spent in the computer store.

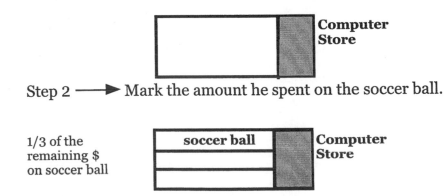

Step 2 ——▶ Mark the amount he spent on the soccer ball.

1/3 of the remaining $ on soccer ball

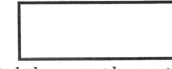

Step 3 ——▶ Show the amount he gave to his sister and then show the amount of his remaining money.

1/4 of remaining $ to his sister. $12 left over.

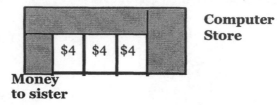

Money to sister

Computer Store

Thinking ——▶ Each little box must equal $4, so the total of the little boxes must equal $16.

So the soccer ball must be half of that or $8 .

$24	$8

It is now clear that each 1/4 of the rectangle is equal to $8. So the total amount is $32.

Charts and Diagrams

1) If 36 gallons of water are poured into an empty tank, then 3/4 of the tank is filled. How many gallons does a full tank hold?

2) Suppose 5 days before the day after tomorrow is Monday. What day of the week was yesterday?

3) Tom went to a store and spent 1/3 of his money. He then went to another store, where he spent 1/3 of what remained. He then had $12 left. How much money did he have to begin with?

4) Peter had a noon appointment 60 miles from his home. He drove from his home at an average speed of 40 miles per hour, and arrived 15 minutes late. At what time did Peter leave for the appointment?

5) The last Wednesday in a certain month is on the 26th day of that month. What day of the week is the first day of that month?

6) A group of 27 people went on a trip across a lake. Twelve people went in a motorboat, and the rest traveled by canoe (3 in each canoe). On the return trip, 4 people rode in each canoe. How many returned in the motorboat?

7) Five days after the day before yesterday is a Saturday. What day is it today?

8) Marilyn had a bag of gold coins. She gave 1/8 of them to her mother and then gave 1/2 of what was left to her brother. She then gave 2/7 of what was left to her dad. If she then had 25 coins left, how many did she have originally?

9) Suppose 3 days ago was a Wednesday. What day of the week will 365 days from today be?

10) Rachel wrote the names of her 5 fish on a piece of paper in a certain order from left to right. She put Spot before Shadow but after Einstein. She wrote Rover after Einstein, but before Spot. She wrote Buffy after Rover, but before Shadow. If Buffy was not the third one listed, in what order did Rachel write the names of her fish?

Think 1

A group of 24 college students decided to climb Mt. McKinley. They bought enough food to last 20 days. If 16 additional students join them, how many days will their food last?

When you are faced with a problem such as this, the best approach is to **Think 1**.

How does thinking about the number 1 help? It sounds boring and not very helpful.

That's not what it means. What you are supposed to do is pretend that there is only 1 person going on the trip.

If the food will last 20 days for 24 students, then for 1 student, that amount of food will last 20 x 24 or 480 days. Once you think about 1 person, the problem becomes fairly easy.

1 student..480 days
2 students..........divide by 2.................240 days
3 students..........divide by 3.................160 days
40 students........divide by 40...............12 days

Think 1 made that problem easy.

Think 1 makes very confusing problems much easier to solve. It's my favorite problem solving strategy. Use **Think 1** to try and solve this next problem.

A construction crew of 4 workers completed half of a highway in 15 days. How many days will it take a crew of 10 workers to finish the road?

4 workers would finish the remaining road in 15 days so I know that 1 worker would take 60 days.
1 worker.................................60 days
2 workers.......divide by 2.......30 days
10 workers.....divide by 10......6 days

You're so smart that it scares me sometimes.

Think 1

1) It took 6 people 8 days to build a brick wall. The construction crew needs to build an identical wall but needs it done faster. If they add 2 people to the crew, how long will the brick wall take to build now?

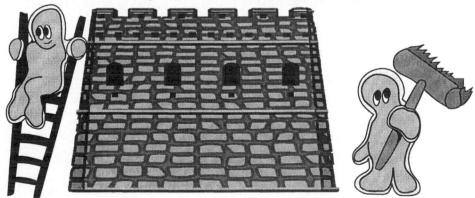

2) A class with 12 children decided to go on an 8 day canoe trip. After they bought just enough food for the trip, 2 adults decided to go on the trip. If they didn't buy any more food and an adult eats twice as much as a child, how many days will their food last?

3) Luke paints a car in 6 hours while Daniel paints the same car in 3 hours. If they work together, how long will it take them to paint the car?

4) If it takes 4 men 12 days to dig a hole, how long would it take 6 men?

5) A hose takes 15 minutes to fill a swimming pool and the drain empties the pool in 20 minutes. How long will it take to fill the pool if the drain is accidentally left open?

6) It takes Sara 2 hours to paint a fence and Daniel 4 hours to paint the same fence. How long will it take them to paint the fence if they both work together?

7) Four hoses are filling a pool. The first hose alone would fill the pool in 4 hours while the second hose takes 6 hours. The third hose and the fourth hose each take 8 hours to fill the pool. How long would it take to fill the pool if all 4 hoses are turned on?

8) Jay has 8 cats that need to be fed while he is away on a 12 day vacation. If a bag of cat food will feed 3 cats for 15 days, how many bags does he need for his vacation?

9) A crew of 8 people finished 1/4 of a tunnel through a mountain in 30 days. If they added two more workers, how long will it take them to finish the tunnel?

10) A construction firm was hired to repaint a very large bridge. Written into the contract was a 2 million dollar penalty if the bridge was not completed in 87 days. Their crew of 7 painted 1/3 of the bridge in 45 days so they knew that at that pace, they would never finish the bridge on time. How many more painters should be hired to allow the crew to paint the rest of the bridge in the 42 remaining days?

Venn Diagrams

In a group of 22 students, 7 children like math, 12 children like science, 6 children like English, 3 like math and science, 2 like English and math, 2 like science and English, and 1 student likes all three subjects. How many students don't like any subject?

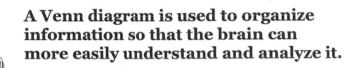

A Venn diagram is used to organize information so that the brain can more easily understand and analyze it.

Make three circles, each one representing a different subject.

Math	Science	English

Now make
the three circles
intersect.

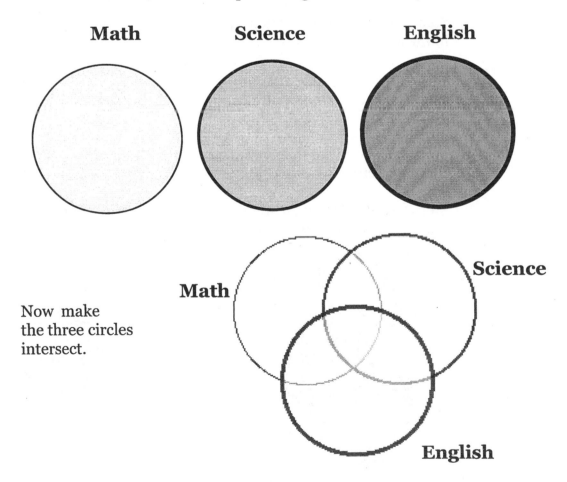

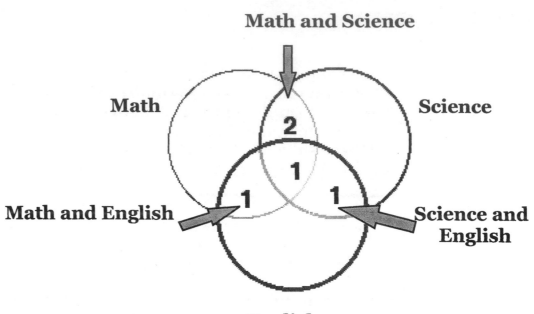

Math and Science

Math

Science

2

1

1

1

Math and English

Science and English

English

Step 1 ——► Since 1 student likes all three subjects, we put the number 1 in the area where all three circles intersect.

Step 2 ——► Since 3 children like math and science, we need a total of 3 in that area. Since there is already 1 in the center, we need to add 2 more for a total of 3.

Step 3 ——► Since 2 students like math and English, we'll put a 1 where those two circles intersect because we already have 1 in the center.

Step 4 ——► Because 2 students like science and English, we'll also put a 1 in that space so there is a total of 2 students.

I'm starting to feel crushed by all those numbers.

Don't give up yet. I think we're about to find the answer.

Step 5 ──▶ We know that the math circle should have 7 children in it, and since there are already 4 children within the math circle, the remaining space gets 3 children.

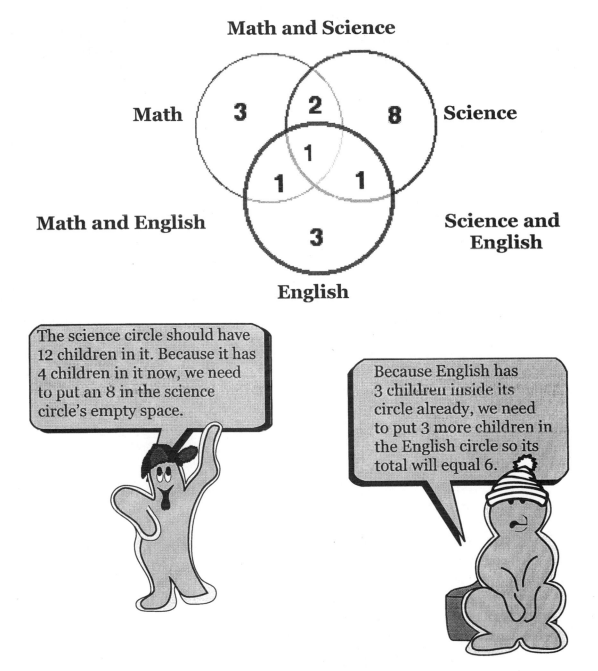

Math and Science

Math   3   **2**   **8**   **Science**

1

1   1

Math and English

3

Science and English

English

> The science circle should have 12 children in it. Because it has 4 children in it now, we need to put an 8 in the science circle's empty space.

> Because English has 3 children inside its circle already, we need to put 3 more children in the English circle so its total will equal 6.

Now we are ready to solve the problem. We have a total of 19 children in our circles. Since we started with 22 children, it is easy to see that we have 3 missing children who didn't like any subject. (22 minus 19)

In a classroom of 29 children, 7 have been to Mexico, 11 have been to Canada, and 4 children have been to both countries. How many children have not been to either country?

Mexico   **Canada**

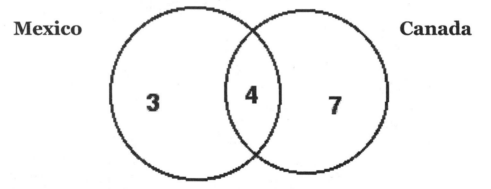

3   4   7

Step 1 ——▶ The 4 is placed in the intersection of the 2 circles because 4 children have been to both countries.

Step 2 ——▶ Since Mexico's circle must add up to 7, a 3 is placed inside the circle.

Step 3 ——▶ Because Canada's circle must add up to 11, a 7 is placed inside that circle.

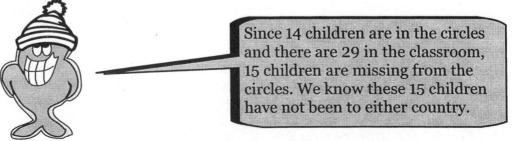

Since 14 children are in the circles and there are 29 in the classroom, 15 children are missing from the circles. We know these 15 children have not been to either country.

Venn Diagrams

1) In a 4th grade classroom there are 14 children who have a dog as a pet. There are 11 who have cats and 3 who have both. If there are 24 children in this classroom who have neither a cat or a dog, how many children are in the classroom?

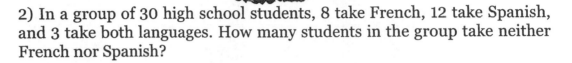

2) In a group of 30 high school students, 8 take French, 12 take Spanish, and 3 take both languages. How many students in the group take neither French nor Spanish?

3) A baseball team has 20 players. Seven players have a brother, while 6 players have a sister. If 3 players have a brother and a sister, how many members of the team have no brothers or sisters.

4) Look at the following information about the favorite colors of a group of students.

> *19 like the color green   *4 like green and red
> *11 like blue   *5 like green and blue
> *16 like red   *4 like all three colors
> *7 like red and blue   *5 don't like any color

How many students are there in the group?

5) Elementary students at a small school were asked about their favorite fruits. This is the information that was gathered:

*23 like bananas
*19 like apples
*26 like raisins
*6 like apples and bananas
*8 like bananas and raisins
*2 like all three fruits
*3 don't like any fruit

How many students are in the group?

6) In a classroom of 45 children, 20 like the Green Bay Packers, 15 like the Vikings, 19 like the Chicago Bears, 8 children like the Packers and the Bears, 9 like the Vikings and Bears, 6 like the Vikings and Packers and 5 children like all three teams. How many children don't like any of the three teams?

7) Twenty-three children in an English class had an assignment over Christmas vacation to read either *The Call of the Wild* or a book of poetry by Edgar Allen Poe. When the teacher asked about what book the children decided to read, she learned the following:

17 read *The Call of the Wild*   How many children didn't read
9 read Edgar Allen Poe   any book over Christmas vacation?
7 read both

> The following information is to be
> used to answer questions 8-10.

All people who ate at a certain restaurant were surveyed as to what they ordered on a particular Sunday morning.

40 ate eggs
42 ate sausage
32 ate pancakes
13 ate sausage and eggs
15 ate pancakes and sausage
11 ate eggs and pancakes
6 ate all three items
3 people didn't eat any of the items

8) How many people ate only pancakes?

9) How many people ate at the restaurant that morning?

10) How many people didn't eat eggs?

Patterns, Sequences and Function Machines

In the following sequence, what is the 500th term?

7	16	25	34.....................?
1st	2nd	3rd	4th 500th

It is fairly easy to see that the next number in this sequence is 43. The 500th term would be easy to find if we had an extra hour or two, but it would be a very time consuming and boring procedure to find the answer. It would be helpful if we could find a shortcut.

 **When we face problems such as this, whether we are looking for the 500th or even the 5,000,000th term of a series, a function machine can help us determine the answer in a matter of seconds.**

 What is a function machine? Does it cost a lot of money?

 A function machine isn't something you buy, its a simple machine that you draw on paper. Once you draw the function machine, you simply put the number in and the answer comes out of the machine.

7   16   25   34.....................?
1st   2nd   3rd   4th   500th

The first thing we need to do before we can solve this problem is to see what kind of function machine we used for the 1st term to change it into a 7. In this sequence, the space between the numbers is 9, so we know that the first part of the function machine is *multiply by 9*.

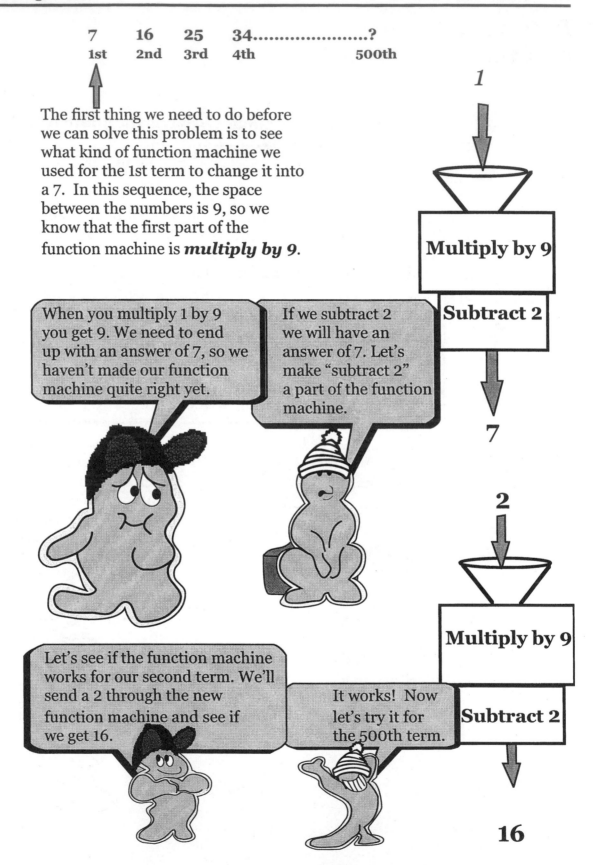

When you multiply 1 by 9 you get 9. We need to end up with an answer of 7, so we haven't made our function machine quite right yet.

If we subtract 2 we will have an answer of 7. Let's make "subtract 2" a part of the function machine.

Let's see if the function machine works for our second term. We'll send a 2 through the new function machine and see if we get 16.

It works! Now let's try it for the 500th term.

1

Multiply by 9

Subtract 2

7

2

Multiply by 9

Subtract 2

16

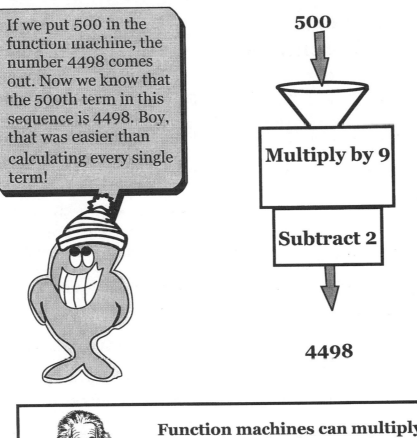

If we put 500 in the function machine, the number 4498 comes out. Now we know that the 500th term in this sequence is 4498. Boy, that was easier than calculating every single term!

500

Multiply by 9

Subtract 2

4498

Function machines can multiply or divide and they can add or subtract. Function machines can even do things like multiplying the number by itself.

Some sequence problems can be solved without function machines. All they need is some clever thinking to find the answer.

   4   16   64   256   **What is the next number?**
To get the next number, each number is multiplied by 4. The answer is 256 x 4-------which equals 1024.

   1   4   9   16   25   **What is the 100th term?**

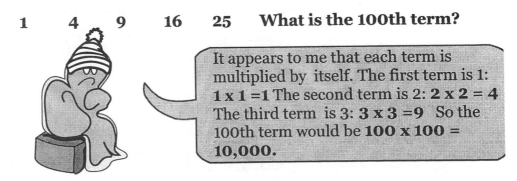

It appears to me that each term is multiplied by itself. The first term is 1: **1 x 1 =1** The second term is 2: **2 x 2 = 4** The third term is 3: **3 x 3 =9** So the 100th term would be **100 x 100 = 10,000.**

Patterns, Sequences and Function Machines

1) 3   12   21   30   Find the 1000th term of this sequence.

2) 3   5   7   9   Find the 500th term in this sequence.

3) - 5   - 3   - 1   1   Find the 200th term in this sequence.

4) 0   3   6   9   The number 12 is obviously the 5th term in this sequence. What term in the sequence is the number 747?

5) 1   8   27   64   What number would be next in this sequence?

6) 1   6   11   16   What is the millionth term in this sequence?

7) 8   11   16   23   What is the 2000th term of this sequence?

Hint for #7: The first box in the function machine is ⟶ **Multiply number by itself**

8) 10   2 1/2   5/8   5/32   What fraction is the next number in this sequence?

9) What is the total number of triangles, of any size, that point up?

10) What is the total number of squares, of any size, in this figure?

Algebra

Algebra is one of the most powerful problem-solving tools ever invented because it makes very complicated word problems much easier to solve. When you use algebra, letters are used to take the place of unknown numbers. Look at the following problem:

> Luke's weight plus 5 pounds is equal to 210 pounds

In this case, Luke's weight is not known, so we will call it **n.** Now we can write an equation ⟶ **n + 5 = 210**

This tells us that some number plus 5 is equal to 210.

It is now easy to see that Luke's weight must equal 205 pounds. I know that most algebra problems won't be this easy, but I bet I won't have to do guess and check as often when I learn algebra.

We have 9th century Arab mathematician el-Khowarizmi to thank when we solve difficult problem through the use of algebra. He invented a problem-solving system that modern algebra is based on.

He's my hero

Jill is twice as old as Jordan, who is 5 years older than Dan. Sara is 6 years older than the sum of Jordan and Jill's ages. If the sum of the ages of all four people is 78, how old is Sara?

Extremely confusing problems such as this one, usually are solved by guess and check. Algebra makes it possible to solve this problem in one minute or less.

That seems impossible!

Algebra is one of the greatest problem-solving methods ever invented. This problem is really quite simple once you know algebra.

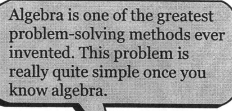

Algebra is simply a way of turning word problems into equations. These make the word problems easier to understand. An equation is a number sentence that includes letters. An example would be $7n + 9 = 23$. The letter in the equation takes the place of an unknown number.

Look at the following word problem:

Some number plus 8 is equal to 10.

This can be written as ? + 8 = 10.
Mathematicians use letters
instead of question marks.
They would write an equation
that looks like this:
n + **8** = **10**

Now it is obvious that
the number we are
looking for is 2.

Look at a more difficult problem:

**If you double a number and then add 10,
you end up with 50.**

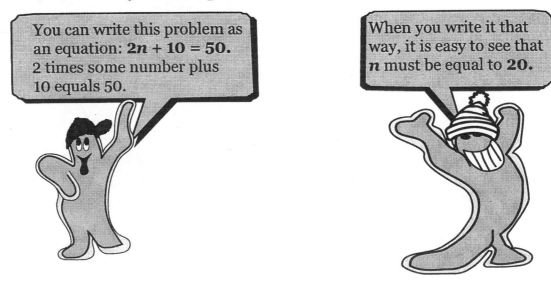

You can write this problem as
an equation: **2*n* + 10 = 50.**
2 times some number plus
10 equals 50.

When you write it that
way, it is easy to see that
n must be equal to **20.**

Let's look at an even more difficult problem:

**Larry weighs 50 pounds more than Steve.
Together they weigh 130 pounds.
What does Steve weigh?**

Since we want to know Steve's weight, we'll call that *n*.

And since Larry weighs 50 pounds more than Steve, let's call Larry's weight *n* + 50.

$$n$$ $$n + 50$$

$$+$$ $$= 130$$

Steve   **Larry**

Adding their weight together, we have:

n + (*n* + 50) = 130
Steve   Larry

or

2*n* + 50 = 130

So *n* must equal 40 pounds. Steve must weigh 40 pounds.

Those equations are fairly easy to solve in your head. What if we have one like **2n + 3n +5 + 6 = 61?** How do you solve this equation if you can't do it in your head?

To solve algebraic equations, you must go through three steps. The first step is called **collecting.**

Step 1 ⟶ $2n + 3n + 5 + 6 = 61$
(Collecting)
We collect the n's and we collect all numbers. Our equation becomes:

$5n + 11 = 61$

Step 2 ⟶ The second step in the process of solving
(Isolating)
algebra equations is called **isolating the n's**. This means we want the $5n$ all alone on one side of the equation. The 11 is preventing the $5n$ from being alone, so we will subtract it.

$5n + 11 = 61$
-11

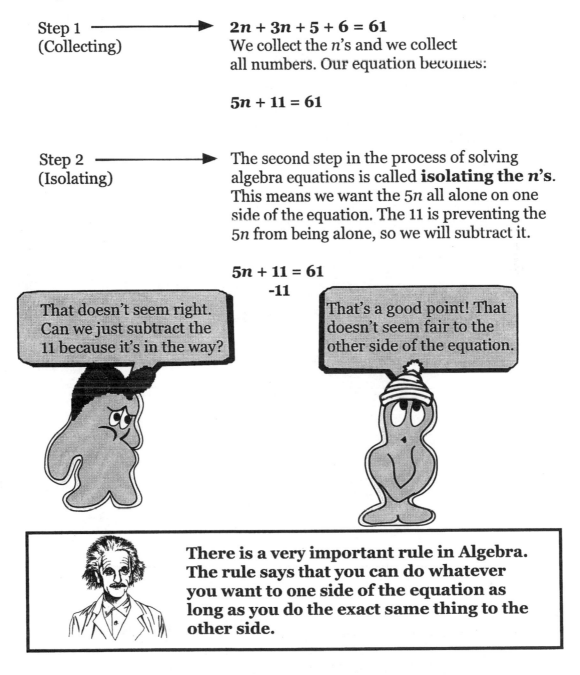

That doesn't seem right. Can we just subtract the 11 because it's in the way?

That's a good point! That doesn't seem fair to the other side of the equation.

There is a very important rule in Algebra. The rule says that you can do whatever you want to one side of the equation as long as you do the exact same thing to the other side.

So we are allowed to subtract 11 from the left side of the equation, as long as we are fair and subtract 11 from the right side of the equation.

$$5n + 11 = 61$$
$$- 11 \quad -11$$

Our new equation is ⟶ $5n = 50$

Step 3
(Just one *n*)

The third step is called **"Just one *n*"**. This means that you want just *n* on one side of the equation. You don't want 8*n*, or 5*n*, or 100*n*. You want just one *n* all alone on one side of the equation.

5*n* = 50

If we divide both sides of the equation by 5, (remember we have to be fair to both sides) we get:

$$\frac{5n}{5} = \frac{50}{5}$$

Since $\frac{5}{5} = 1$, our new equation is **_n_ = 10.**

I know the 5 caused us a problem, but why can't we just subtract it?

Anytime you have a number next to *n*, you must divide to get rid of it. You cannot just subtract it.

Let's look at another example: **7*n* + 11*n* - 7 + 15 = 62**

Step 1 (Collecting)   **18*n* + 8 = 62**

Step 2 (Isolating *n*)   **18*n* + 8 = 62**
                        - 8   - 8
                        18*n* =   54

Step 3 (Just one *n*) $\frac{18n}{18} = \frac{54}{18}$ ⟶ **_n_ = 3**

Look at the following example: **6n - 8 = 22**

Step 1
(Collecting)

No collecting needed

Step 2
(isolating n)

6n - 8 = 22

We have a different situation here. We want the - 8 to go to zero, but if we subtract 8 we will have - 16. In this type of problem, we need to add 8 to bring the -8 to zero. Of course we'll be fair to the other side of the equation and add 8 to it.

6n - 8 = 22
+8 = +8
6n + 0 = 30

Step 3
(Just one n)

$$\frac{6n}{6} = \frac{30}{6} \longrightarrow n = 5$$

When you solve equations, you must remember to go through the three steps. In addition, you must always follow the fairness rule of algebra ⟶ You can do anything you want to one side of the equation, as long as you do it to the other side.

Solve for n:

1) $2n + 9 = 23$

2) $5n - 16 = 9$

3) $5n + 4 = 49$

4) $18n - 7 = 29$

Look at this problem: $8n + 5 = 3n + 30$

Step 1   No collecting needed

Step 2

$$8n + 5 = 3n + 30$$
$$ -5 = -5$$
$$8n = 3n + 25$$

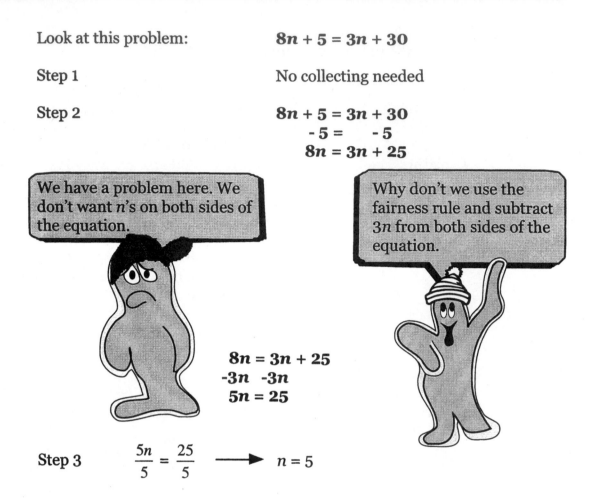

We have a problem here. We don't want n's on both sides of the equation.

Why don't we use the fairness rule and subtract $3n$ from both sides of the equation.

$$8n = 3n + 25$$
$$-3n \quad -3n$$
$$5n = 25$$

Step 3 $\dfrac{5n}{5} = \dfrac{25}{5}$ ⟶ $n = 5$

Go through all three steps and find what n is equal to in the following equations:

1) $2n + 8 = 36$

2) $3n + 9 = 24$

3) $5n - 7 = 23$

4) $2n + 5 + 7n - 8 = 15$

5) $16n + 67 + 4n + 7 - n = 112$

6) $3n + 10 + 15 = 2n + 50$

7) $3n + 85 = 91$

8) $2n - 12 = 8$

9) $9 + 3n = 42$

10) $2n - 8 = 3n + 3$

11) $16n - 75 = 85$

12) $4n - 5 = 2n + 17$

Rachel has a pile of nickels, dimes, and quarters. There are twice as many dimes as nickels and twice as many quarters as dimes. If the pile is worth $5.00, how many nickels does Rachel have?

As before, this problem could be solved using guess and check, but it would be very time-consuming. Let's try solving this problem using algebra.

Since we are looking for the number of nickels, we'll call the number of nickels in the pile n.

Since there are twice as many dimes as nickels, we'll call the number of dimes $2n$.

And since the number of quarters is twice the number of dimes, we'll call the number of quarters $4n$.

Now we know the number of each kind of coin in the pile.
Nickels--------n
Dimes---------$2n$
Quarters------$4n$

We know the number of coins, but we don't know the value of the coins.

If the number of nickels was 8, then the value of the nickels would be 5 x 8 because each nickel is worth 5 cents. Since the number of nickels is n, then the value of the nickels would be 5 x n or $5n$. The value of the dimes would be 10 x $2n$ or $20n$. The value of the quarters would be 25 x $4n$ or $100n$.

Let's make a chart to show us what we know:

	Number of coins	Value of the coins
Nickels	n	$5n$
Dimes	$2n$	$20n$
Quarters	$4n$	$100n$

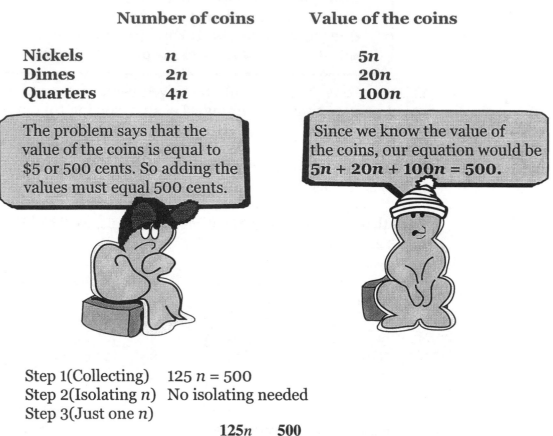

The problem says that the value of the coins is equal to $5 or 500 cents. So adding the values must equal 500 cents.

Since we know the value of the coins, our equation would be $5n + 20n + 100n = 500$.

Step 1(Collecting) $125 n = 500$
Step 2(Isolating n)   No isolating needed
Step 3(Just one n)

$$\frac{125n}{125} = \frac{500}{125}$$

$n = 4$ ⟶ **There are 4 nickels**

Try the following 3 problems. Make sure you make a chart showing the number of coins and the value of the coins.

1) Doug had a pile of quarters and nickels. He had 3 times as many nickels as quarters. If the pile of coins was worth $2.80, how many quarters does he have?

2) Cheryl has an equal number of nickels and dimes. The value of the coins is $1.65. How many dimes does she have?

3) A collector had a box of pennies, nickels, dimes and quarters. He had twice as many nickels as pennies, twice as many dimes as nickels and twice as many quarters as dimes. If the value of his money was $10.04, what was the value of his nickels?

Algebra
Level 1

1) Bill weighs 42 pounds more than Steve. Together they weigh 370 pounds. How much does Steve weigh?

2) Four consecutive numbers add up to 1850. What is the smallest number?

3) There are 4 brothers opening Christmas presents from their parents. The oldest brother received $10 more than his next younger brother who received $10 more than his next younger brother who received $10 more than the youngest brother. The total amount the 4 brothers received was $504. How much did the oldest brother receive?

4) Five sisters' ages added up to 211. The oldest sister's age was 3 times that of the youngest. The next to the oldest was 2 years younger than the oldest and the middle sister was twice as old as the youngest. The remaining sister was 3 years older than the youngest sister. What is the age of the oldest sister?

5) Jay weighs 20 pounds more than Dan, whose weight is twice what Kirsten's is. Their total weight is 320 pounds. How much does Kirsten weigh?

6) Four consecutive multiples of 5 add up to 4130. What is the largest number?

7) Kyle earned a total of $12,500 for drawing 5 pictures. The money he received for each picture was $28 more than the money he received from the previous picture. In other words, he was paid $28 more for the second picture than the first, $28 more for the third than the second, and so forth. How much was he paid for the 1st picture?

8) Eight times a number is the same as that number plus 84. What is the number?

9) Luke has $21 more than Rachel and $48 more than Daniel. All together they have $168. How much money does Luke have?

10) A horse cost $900 more than the saddle. Together they cost $1000. How much does the saddle cost?

Algebra
Level 2

1) 1/3 the weight of a bar of gold plus 30 pounds equals the weight of that bar of gold. How much does the bar of gold weigh?

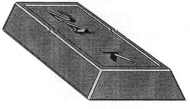

2) Cheri is $23 short of having enough money to buy a gold coin. Denzel is $28 short of having enough money to buy that same coin. If they combine their money, they will have exactly enough to buy the coin. How much does the coin cost?

3) If a 17 kilogram weight is placed on top of 2 bricks, the total weight would be the same as if 17 kilograms is removed from 3 bricks. How much does each brick weigh?

4) I have 19 coins that are worth a total of $1.10.
If they consist only of dimes and nickels, then how many nickels do I have?

5) In a pile of nickels and dimes, the number of nickels is three times the number of dimes and the pile is worth $1.75. How many nickels are there?

6) Donnie has $5.10 in nickels, dimes, and quarters. He has an equal number of dimes and nickels, with the value of the quarters being $2.40 more than the total value of the dimes and nickels. How many dimes does he have?

7) Jay's favorite book is 182 pages less than three times Mitchel's favorite book. If both books have the same number of pages, how many pages are in Jay's favorite book?

8) In the sequence 3, 8, 13, 18, what term of the series is the number 2218?

9) Blood pressure is a measure of the pressure of the blood inside the arteries. Blood pressure is expressed in the form:

$$\frac{\textbf{Systolic pressure}}{\textbf{Diastolic pressure}}$$

The systolic pressure, which is the higher number, is the pressure exerted on the arterial walls when your heart is beating. The diastolic measurement is the pressure exerted on the arterial walls when the heart is resting. To find what a normal systolic blood pressure should be, you use the following equation:

$$\textbf{Normal systolic} = \frac{\textbf{Age of person}}{2} + 110$$

What is the normal systolic blood pressure for an adult who is 56 years old?

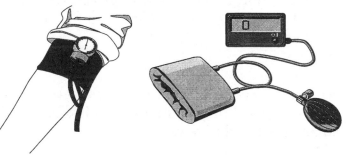

10) The number of times a cricket chirps per minute can help you determine the temperature of the air. Use the following formula to find the approximate air temperature.

$$\textbf{Temperature (in Celsius)} = \frac{\textbf{Chirps per minute + 30}}{7}$$

If a cricket chirps 159 times per minute, what is the temperature of the air expressed in Fahrenheit?

The formula for changing Celsius to Fahrenheit is: $F = \frac{9}{5}(C) + 32$

Einstein Level

1) There are 5 people standing in a room. Rick is 5 times the age of Mike who is half the age of Larry. Ed is 30 years younger than double Larry and Mike's combined ages. Daniel is 79 years younger than Rick. The sum of their ages is 271. How old is Daniel?

2) A movie theater charges $7 for adults, $5 for school-age children and $3 for babies. A group of people went to the theater. There were the same number of school-age children as babies and the number of adults was the same as school-age children and babies combined. If the group paid $1562, how many babies were in the group?

3) Dave is three times older than Jim, and Jim is half Bill's age. If their average age is 64, what is Jim's age?

4) Nick has 3 times the money Stacey has and Lindsey has 4 times the money that Stacey has. If Rick's $120 is added to the group, the average amount of money the four have is $150. How much money does each person have?

5) I have 59 coins that include pennies, nickels, dimes, and quarters. There are twice as many dimes as nickels and 3 times as many quarters as dimes. The total value of the coins is $7.23. How many of each kind of coin do I have?

6) Eric, Warren, and Mike were each given an amount of money that was determined by multiplying half their age by their grandfather's age. If the total amount of money given to the three was $1,656, and their ages total 46, what is the age of their grandfather?

7) Michelle was working as a clerk in a clothing store. She made a mistake and charged the wrong sales tax. She should have charged 5%, but she charged 6%. The total amount of money she collected for the day, including sales tax, was $620.10. How much money would she have collected if she charged the correct sales tax?

8) A rectangle has a length that is 6 times longer than its width. If the area of the rectangle is 1014 square feet, what are the length and width of the rectangle? What is the equation that you would use to solve the problem?

9) The length of a rectangle is 8 times its width. The perimeter of the rectangle is 216 inches. What is the algebraic equation you would use to solve this problem? What is the length of the rectangle?

10) I have pennies, nickels, dimes, quarters, one dollar bills, and five dollar bills. There are twice as many nickels as pennies, twice as many dimes as nickels, three fewer quarters than dimes and the same number of one dollar bills and five dollar bills as there are nickels. The total value of the money I have is $93.82. How many dimes do I have?

Super Einstein Problem

A rocket leaves earth for the sun at a speed of 28,800 mph. At the same time a photon of light leaves the sun for the earth. If we assume they are on flight paths that allow them to meet, how far will the rocket be from earth when the photon of light hits it? (Assume a distance of 93,000,000 miles to the sun and round your answer to the nearest thousand miles.) (A rocket launched from the earth will gradually build up speed. For this problem, we will assume that the rocket travels at 28,800 mph the instant it leaves the earth.)

Metric System

The American system of miles, yards, feet, and inches is very difficult to work with because there is no easy connection between each unit. Our use of these measurements arose from a long ago practice of basing measurements on the human body. The most common practice was to base measurements on a king's arm, foot, or thumb length. In addition, farmers would often measure their fields by using the length of their step. Problems arose with these types of measurements because different kings had different feet, arms, and thumbs. In addition, farmers who were tall would have long steps, while farmers who were short would have short steps.

Eventually, people realized that a worldwide standard of measurement was needed. In the 1790's, the French established a new measuring system that was based on the dimensions of the earth. One meter was equal to $\frac{1}{10,000,000}$ of the distance from the North Pole to the equator. A copy of this length was made out of platinum and placed in a safe in France. Measurements no longer changed when you visited different countries or each time a new king was crowned. This system of measurement is called the metric system and has been adopted by almost all countries. In 1983, the world was no longer dependent on the French platinum bar for determining the length of a meter. The meter was redefined as the distance light travels in $\frac{1}{299,792,458}$ of a second.

The United States is one of only a few countries that hasn't adopted the metric system. Because some industries in the United States use the metric system and some don't, problems have arisen. In 1999, a spacecraft was commanded to fire its engines as it approached Mars. The engineers at NASA wanted to put the spacecraft into orbit around the planet. The spacecraft was programmed to assume that the instructions would be in metric units. Unfortunately, the data that was sent to the spacecraft computer was not converted to metric units, so the 200 million dollar spacecraft went the wrong direction at the wrong speed and probably burned up in the Martian atmosphere.

Lengths

The relationship between kilometers, meters, decimeters, centimeters, and millimeters makes it very easy to change back and forth between each one.

Look at the following example:

17 meters is the same as 170 decimeters, or 1700 centimeters, or 17000 millimeters. Because there are 1000 meters in a kilometer, 17 meters would equal .017 kilometers.

 **If you want to work with very, very small measurements, then the metric system is the one to chose. The metric system uses the micron, which is 1/1000 of a millimeter. (A millimeter is already extremely small.) A micron is smaller than the thickness of a human hair.**

1000 Meters............ 1 kilometer
Meter....................... 10 decimeters
                          100 centimeters
                          1000 millimeters

Metric Length

1) 27 meters =_____centimeters

2) 282 millimeters=_____meters

3) 250 centimeters + 28 decimeters =_____meters

4) 8 decimeters minus 346 millimeters = _____decimeters

5) 11 kilometer =_____millimeters

6) The teeth of a Tyrannosaurus Rex were .13 meters long. How many centimeters long were its teeth?

7)) A velociraptor was 1800 millimeters long. Express this in meters.

8) The deepest known spot in the ocean is the Mariana Trench. It is 11,033 meters deep. About how many kilometers would this be?

9) The highest place on earth is the top of Mt. Everest which is 8,848 meters tall. How many centimeters is this?

10) How many microns are in a meter?

11) Viruses are shaped like rods or spheres and can be as small as .01 microns in length. If they were placed in a row, how many of these viruses would it take to make a line a meter long?

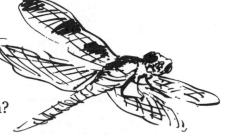

12) Among the early insects were giant dragonflies with wingspans of 7000 millimeters. How many 25 centimeter pieces of wood would you need to lay side by side to equal this length?

13) The longest elephant tusk ever found was 3500 millimeters long. What would this be in meters?

14) How many square centimeters are in a square meter?

15) How many square millimeters are in 8 square decimeters?

Metric Volume and Weights

When we deal with weight in the metric system, we use three different units of measure. Instead of tons, pounds and ounces, we use kilograms, grams, and milligrams. (Kilograms, grams, and milligrams are actually units of mass. Since they are usually compared with pounds, we will refer to them as weight.)

Milligram
(weight of a
small amount
of chalk dust)

Gram
(About the
weight of a
paper clip)

Kilogram
(Approximately the
weight of a textbook or
about 2 pounds)

1 kilogram is equal to 1000 grams and
1 gram is equal to 1000 milligrams.

When we deal with volume in the metric system, we use liters and milliliters instead of gallons, quarts, pints, or cups.

Milliliter of liquid
(eyedropper of liquid)

Liter of liquid
(A little more than a quart)

A liter equals 1000 milliliters

There are beautiful connections in the metric system between length, weight, and volume:

A liter of water weighs 1 kilogram

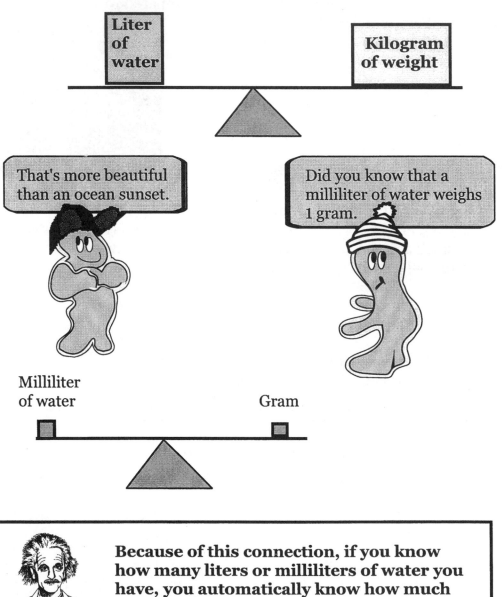

Because of this connection, if you know how many liters or milliliters of water you have, you automatically know how much they weigh.

There is also another beautiful connection between length, volumes, and weight.

A liter of something is a cubic decimeter of that substance.

and

A milliliter of something is a cubic centimeter of that substance.

Metric Volume and Weight

1) 2.45 liters =_____milliliters

2) 37 milliliters of water weighs=_____grams

3) 2.4 liters of water weight=_____kilograms

4) .85 kilograms =_____grams

5) 785 milligrams =_____grams

6) 8395 grams =_____kilograms

7) 12 grams =_____milligrams

8) 9.4 milliliters =_____liters

9) .85 kilograms =_____milligrams

10) 23 kilograms =_____grams

11) The human heart pumps approximately 310,000 milliliters of blood per hour. How many liters is that equal to?

12) The common vampire bat weighs .028 kilograms. How many grams would that be?

13) The vampire bat scoops out a small piece of a mammal's skin with his teeth and then licks blood from the wound. Each vampire bat drinks about .015 liters of blood each day. How many milliliters of blood would this be?

14) A newborn child has about 250 milliliters of blood. What fraction of a liter would this be?

15) A brontosaurus weighed approximately 27,000,000 grams. How many kilograms did a brontosaurus weigh?

16) An elephant drinks about 190 liters of water per day. What is the weight of the water an elephant drinks in a year?

17) What would be the weight of the water in a swimming pool that held 64 cubic meters of water?

18) How many milligrams are in a kilogram?

19) Some ants can lift 50 times their body weight. If an ant weighs .23 grams, how many kilograms could it lift?

20) Sara is making soap and needs to add 370 grams of rose oil to her mixture. Since her scale is a kilogram scale and not a gram scale, she will need to calculate how many kilograms there are in 370 grams. How many kilograms of rose oil should Sara add?

Temperature

Temperature is a measurement of the speed of the movement of molecules. It is commonly thought that when an item freezes, molecular movement stops ——▶ This is not true. There continues to be molecular movement until the temperature drops to absolute zero.

Most people think that temperatures have no limits on the high or low end of the scale . While temperature can go as high as a million degrees and higher, temperatures have a very strict limit on the low end. This limit is called absolute zero. Temperatures can never go lower than - 459.4 Fahrenheit. At this temperature, all molecular movement stops.

Temperatures in the United States are usually expressed in Fahrenheit. Most other countries use a different scale called Centigrade or Celsius.

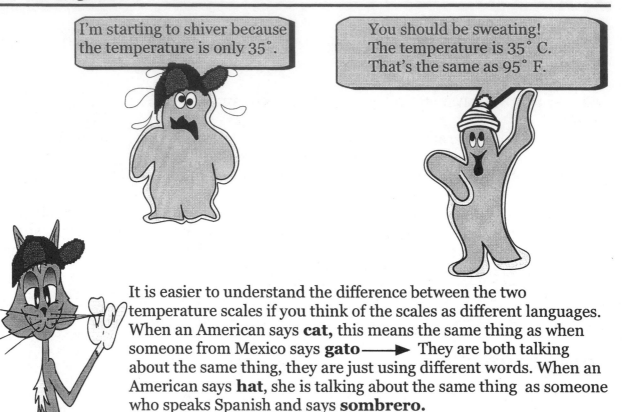

I'm starting to shiver because the temperature is only 35°.

You should be sweating! The temperature is 35° C. That's the same as 95° F.

It is easier to understand the difference between the two temperature scales if you think of the scales as different languages. When an American says **cat,** this means the same thing as when someone from Mexico says **gato** ——▶ They are both talking about the same thing, they are just using different words. When an American says **hat,** she is talking about the same thing as someone who speaks Spanish and says **sombrero.**

Just as Spanish and English words are different ways of describing the exact same thing, Fahrenheit and Celsius are different ways of describing the same temperature ——▶ They are temperature languages.

An American might say it is 95° while someone from France would say it is 35°. They are describing the same thing in different ways. Look at the chart below to see Celsius "translations" of Fahrenheit.

Fahrenheit	Celsius (or Centigrade)
95°	35°
32°	0°
212°	100°

To change Celsius to Fahrenheit, you simply put the Celsius number into the conversion machine. Example: Let's change 100° C to Fahrenheit.

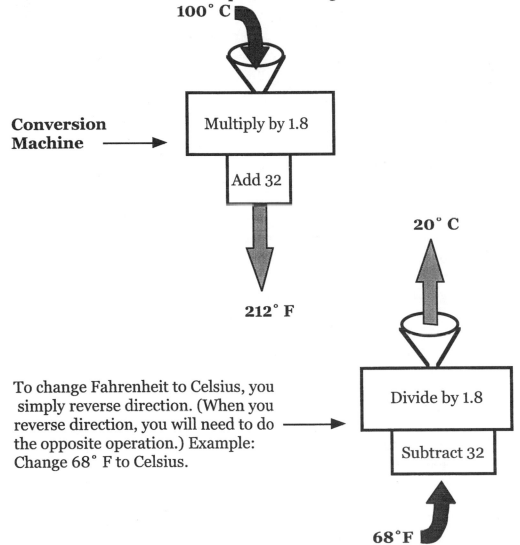

To change Fahrenheit to Celsius, you simply reverse direction. (When you reverse direction, you will need to do the opposite operation.) Example: Change 68° F to Celsius.

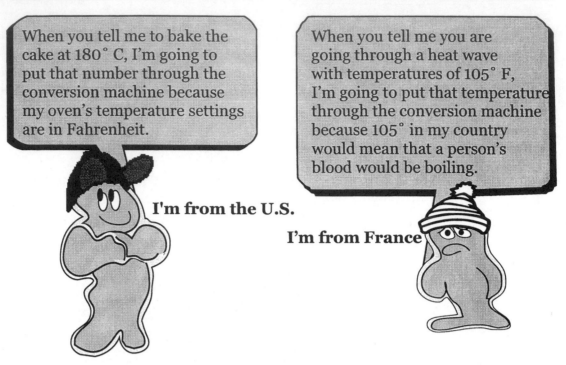

When you tell me to bake the cake at 180°C, I'm going to put that number through the conversion machine because my oven's temperature settings are in Fahrenheit.

When you tell me you are going through a heat wave with temperatures of 105°F, I'm going to put that temperature through the conversion machine because 105° in my country would mean that a person's blood would be boiling.

I'm from the U.S.

I'm from France

You will need to use the conversion machine to answer questions 1-10. Remember Celsius and Fahrenheit are like two different languages. Instead of needing a Spanish-English dictionary to find matching words, the conversion machine will change Celsius to Fahrenheit or Fahrenheit to Celsius.

1) Jake's mother said that he must wear a coat if the temperature is under 59°F. If the temperature is 14°C, should Jake wear a coat?

2) Dan is babysitting a 1 year-old child. The child's forehead seemed hot so Dan took the baby's temperature. The only thermometer that was available was a Centigrade thermometer and it said the baby's temperature was 41°C. Should Dan be concerned?

3) The world's lowest recorded temperature of -128.6°F was in Antarctica. What is this temperature in Celsius?

4) The temperature at the surface of the sun is 11,000° Fahrenheit. What would that be in Celsius?

5) Absolute zero is -273°C. What would that be in Fahrenheit?

6) The temperature inside the sun is much hotter than at the surface. If the temperature inside the sun is 13,888,871°C, what would that be in Fahrenheit?

7) Gold melts at 1064° Celsius. What is that in Fahrenheit?

8) Gold boils at 9187° Fahrenheit. What would this be on the Celsius scale?

9) The normal body temperature is 98.6° F. What would that be if you used a Celsius thermometer?

10) If it is 30° C in San Fransico and 86° F in Washington D.C., what city has the warmer temperature?

Because the United States is one of very few countries that does not use the metric system, it is very important that you know how to change from one system to the other. Instead of memorizing conversion formulas, it is much easier to change from one measuring system to another if you use conversion machines.

 **The conversion machines shown on the next page make it a simple process to change between our system of measurement and the metric system.**

Look at the following example: **Change 82 kilograms into pounds**

To solve this problem, you would send the 82 kilograms through the **kilograms to pounds** conversion machine. After going through the machine, 180.4 pounds would come out the other end.

82 Kilograms ➡️ **Multiply by 2.2** ➡️ **180.4 Pounds**

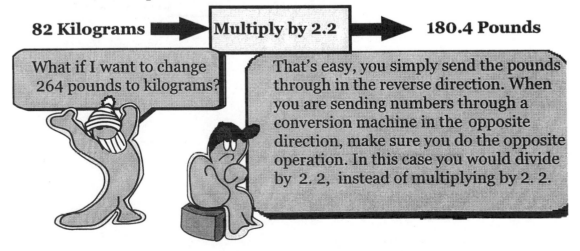

What if I want to change 264 pounds to kilograms?

That's easy, you simply send the pounds through in the reverse direction. When you are sending numbers through a conversion machine in the opposite direction, make sure you do the opposite operation. In this case you would divide by 2. 2, instead of multiplying by 2. 2.

Converting Machines

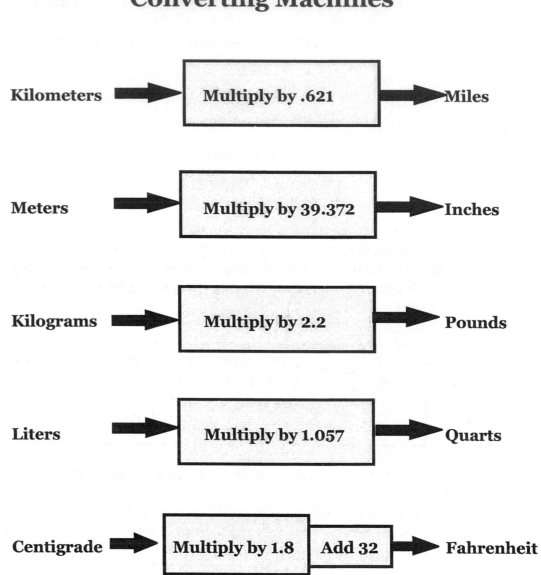

Kilometers → **Multiply by .621** → Miles

Meters → **Multiply by 39.372** → Inches

Kilograms → **Multiply by 2.2** → Pounds

Liters → **Multiply by 1.057** → Quarts

Centigrade → **Multiply by 1.8** **Add 32** → Fahrenheit

Conversions
Level 1

1) The CN Tower is the worlds tallest free-standing structure and is 553 meters tall. How many feet tall is the CN Tower?

2) Velociraptors were about 1.8 meters tall. How many feet tall were velocirators?

3) An adult heart does enough work in one hour to lift 1500 kilograms one foot off the ground. How many pounds is this?

4) A Tyrannosaurus Rex could grow to a length of 40 feet. What is this in centimeters?

5) An adult heart pumps close to 7500 liters of blood in one day. How many gallons would this heart pump in a 70-year lifetime? (Use 365 days for each year)

6) Gold is so malleable that a one ounce piece can be drawn into a wire 62 miles long. How many kilometers would this be?

7) Dan was making soap. He needed to add 5 kilograms of cottonseed oil, but the only scale he could find was one that measured in ounces. How many ounces should he use?

8) A silver-haired bat has a wing-span of about 33 centimeters. Is this more or less than a foot?

9) Elephants eat 225 kilograms of forage per day. How many pounds of forage does an elephant eat in a year?

10) The longest animal ever to fly was the Quetzalocoatus (a pterodactyl). Its wingspan of 120 decimeters was wider than some houses. What was the Quetzalocoatus's wingspan in feet?

Conversions
Level 2

1) Nik was driving a load of sand to Toronto, Canada. While on a small road in Canada, he came to a bridge with the following sign:

WEIGHT LIMIT 20,000 KILOGRAMS
DO NOT EXCEED!!!

Three hours earlier, Nik had weighed his loaded truck in the United States and found that it weighed 40,000 pounds. Can he safely cross the bridge?

2) Stacy was on a vacation in Germany. She was concerned that the rich foods there would make her gain too much weight. The scales in Europe were all in kilograms so she needed to find a way to know when her weight went above her ideal weight of 125 pounds 4 ounces. What will the kilogram scale read when she is at her correct weight?

3) Gabe needed to decide whether to fill his gas tank in Canada or wait until he returned to the United Sates. He saw a sign at a gas station in Canada that advertised gas at 38 cents per liter. He thought that was a reasonable price because he paid $1.05 per gallon in the U.S.. Should he fill his tank in Canada, or wait until he returns home?

4) How much does a cubic meter of water weigh in kilograms?

5) How much does a cubic meter of water weigh in pounds?

6) How much does it cost to fill a 100 liter gas tank if gas cost $1.20 per gallon? (Round to the nearest dollar.)

7) Adam is driving in Canada. He sees a sign that informs him that the nearest gas station is 180 kilometers away. Adam knows he has enough gas to go 110 miles. Is he going to run out of gas before he reaches the next gas station?

8) Gold is one of the most malleable and ductile of all the metals. It can easily be beaten or hammered to a thickness of .000013 centimeters. How many layers of gold that thin would you need to get the thickness of a dime? (1/16 of an inch)

9) How many square feet are in a square meter?

10) Two people are planning to climb Mt. Everest. Because the air is so thin at the upper levels of the mountain, they plan on breathing bottled oxygen once they are 8,000 feet from the summit. If Mt. Everest is 8.848 kilometers high, at what elevation (in meters), should the two climbers start breathing bottled oxygen? (Round to the nearest 100 meters)

Einstein Level

1) Grace needs to purify her swimming pool. To do so, she will need 35 grams of chlorine for each 1000 liters of water in her pool. She knows that her pool holds 30,000 gallons of water. How many grams of chlorine will she need to buy?

2) If a cubic meter of gold was selling for 80,000 dollars, what would a cubic foot of gold sell for? (Round to the nearest dollar.)

3) Christine is planning a cross-country Canadian car trip of 3000 miles. Her car can go 18 miles per gallon of gas. Since she is traveling in Canada, she will need to buy her gas in liters. If gas cost 35 cents per liter, how much money will she need to pay for gas?

4) The human brain has three main parts: The cerebrum, the cerebellum and the brain stem. The cerebrum makes up 85% of the weight of the human brain. If a typical brain weighs 3 pounds, how many grams does the cerebrum weigh?

5) A 16 1/2 ton Tyrannosaurus Rex was on one end of a scale and a 600 kilogram baby elephant was on the other end. How many 4800 kilogram adult elephants would you need to place with the baby elephant to equal the weight of the Tyrannosaurus Rex?

6) A micron equals .001 millimeters, or 1/1000 of a millimeter. What fraction of an inch is a micron?

7) The actual definition of a meter is **"The distance traveled by light, in a vacuum, during** $\dfrac{1}{299,792,458}$ **of a second"**. How long does it take light to travel 1 millimeter?

8) A tank measuring 6' x 8' x 10' is going to be filled with water. Because the tank will be sitting on a wooden deck, its weight cannot exceed 35,000 pounds. If the tank weighs 500 pounds when empty, what would it weigh if it was entirely filled with water? (Round to the nearest hundred.)

9) Since Fahrenheit and Celsius are different scales, they use different numbers to express the same temperature. For example: 100° C is equivalent to 212° F and 32° F is equivalent to 0° C. There is one temperature though that is the same in both scales. What is that temperature?

10) Jared wants to know how many kilograms of water are in his swimming pool. Using his garden hose, he filled the pool in 8 hours. When he filled a gallon jug with the same hose, it took 10 seconds to fill. How much does the water in his pool weigh? (Round to the nearest 100 kg.)

Decimals

("Related to the number 10")

For thousands of years, people have been trying to explain how the universe began. Today, most scientists believe that the universe began in a **Big Bang**. All the energy and mass that exists in the universe today always existed, but before the **Big Bang**, the universe was a lonely place. The billions upon billions of stars that make up our current universe were compressed into an extremely hot, dense fireball that was   .000,000,000,000,000,000,000,000,000,000,01 millimeters long. Since a millimeter is about the width of the period at the end of this sentence, it is very hard to imagine how all the mass in the universe could fit into an area billions upon billions of times smaller.

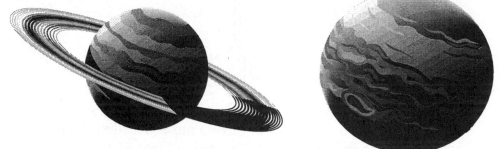

In the time since the Big Bang, the universe has continued to expand. Many scientists predict that this expansion will eventually stop, and then the universe will start collapsing. After several billion years, all matter will again be turned back into energy and the universe will again take up less space than a single atom.

In this story about the universe, we talked about a very small part of a millimeter. Imagine how small a piece we would have if we cut a period into 100,000,000,000,000,000,000,000,000,000,000 parts. Decimals are used to talk about parts of things. Decimals are not only used in science, but in hundreds of ways in our daily lives. We use decimals when we go to a restaurant and pay $5.25 for a meal, and also when we say we live 3.2 miles from our school. As a matter of fact, we use decimals hundreds of times each year, often without realizing that we are using them.

Adding and Subtracting Decimals

When you are adding or subtracting decimals, the most important rule to remember is that the decimal points must line up on top of each other.

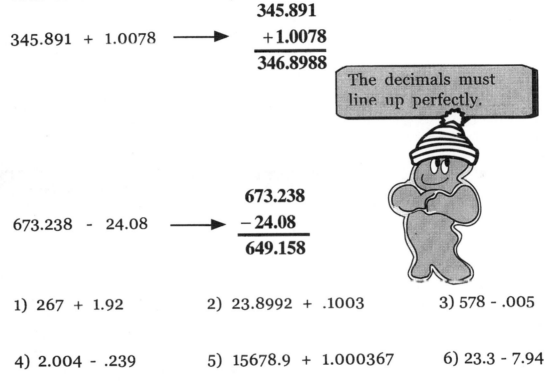

$$345.891 + 1.0078 \longrightarrow \begin{array}{r} 345.891 \\ +1.0078 \\ \hline 346.8988 \end{array}$$

The decimals must line up perfectly.

$$673.238 - 24.08 \longrightarrow \begin{array}{r} 673.238 \\ -24.08 \\ \hline 649.158 \end{array}$$

1) 267 + 1.92

2) 23.8992 + .1003

3) 578 - .005

4) 2.004 - .239

5) 15678.9 + 1.000367

6) 23.3 - 7.94

7) If the temperature went from 82.62 degrees to 71.99 degrees, how far did it drop?

8) Dave's living room is 578.67 square feet. He needed extra space so he built a 57.008 square foot addition. How many square feet is Dave's living room now?

9) Jenny bought two items at a hardware store that cost $2.87 and $0.09. If she paid for them with a $50 bill, how much change should she receive?

10) What is the perimeter of a rectangular garden that is 12.8 feet by 37.34 feet?

Multiplying Decimals

Multiplying decimals is easy if you remember one very important rule: **When you write down the problem, line up the numbers that are on the right side.** Look at the following example:

567.2 + .00035 ⟶

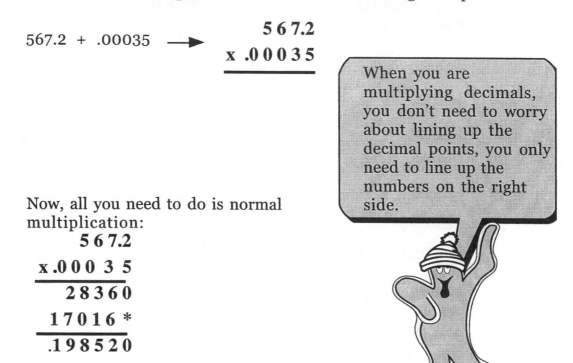

$$567.2$$
$$\text{x} .00035$$

Now, all you need to do is normal multiplication:

$$567.2$$
$$\text{x} .00035$$
$$\overline{28360}$$
$$17016*$$
$$\overline{.198520}$$

When you are multiplying decimals, you don't need to worry about lining up the decimal points, you only need to line up the numbers on the right side.

The only thing left is to put the decimal point in the right place.

There is a very important rule you must follow when determining where to place the decimal point in your answer. You need to count how many numbers there are to the right of the decimal point in each of the numbers you are multiplying. Add these, and then count off that many spaces from the right in your answer. Place the decimal point there.

567.2 ◀——— There is one number to the right of the decimal.

x.00035 ◀——— There are 5 numbers to the right of the decimal.

.198520 ◀——— The decimal point must therefore be placed after the 6th number from the right.

Multiplying Decimals

1) 23.2 x 1.89   2) .0034 x 4.33   3) 2.668 x .02

4) If Joe rides his bike at 12.7 mph, how far will he go in 3.2 hours?

5) A cup of water has 8 septillion molecules. How many molecules are there in 3.5 cups of water?

6) A project Michelle is working on at school calls for 127 pieces of wood. If each piece of wood is 2.34 inches long, what is the total length of all her wood?

7) A tree that is 17.04 feet high grows 4.88 feet per year. There is an electric wire 100 feet above the ground. How many years will it take for the tree to touch the wire?

8) If 135 people are given 87 cents, how much money do they have altogether?

9) Jay's car uses a gallon of gas for every 17.5 miles he drives. If he bought 13.5 gallons of gas, how many miles could he travel?

10) Lynn sold 86 pins for $1.37 each. How much money did she make?

Division of Decimals

When you divide with decimals, it is almost the same as normal division. One of the differences is that you must always remember to place a decimal point in your answer. The decimal point is placed directly over the decimal in the box. Look at the following example:

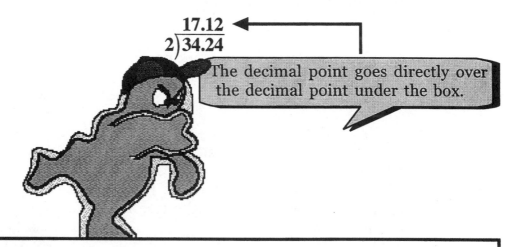

$$2\overline{)34.24} = 17.12$$

The decimal point goes directly over the decimal point under the box.

There is one other problem that you may run into when you divide decimals. If the divisor has a decimal, you must move it all the way to the right. But when you do that, you must be fair to the dividend and move its decimal point an equal number of spaces. Look at the following example:

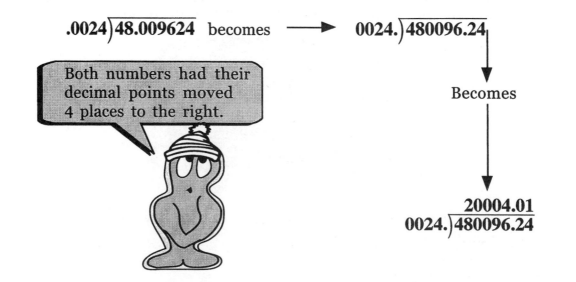

$$.0024\overline{)48.009624} \text{ becomes } \longrightarrow 0024.\overline{)480096.24}$$

Both numbers had their decimal points moved 4 places to the right.

Becomes

$$0024.\overline{)480096.24} = 20004.01$$

Dividing Decimals

1) 14.07 ÷ 7   2) 1.5300 ÷ 3   3) 1800.27 ÷ .9

4) If the area of a room is 132.98 square feet, and one side of the room is 10.9 feet, how long is the other side of the room?

5) If a rabbit hopped 16 times for a total of 125.6 feet, how far was each one of its jumps?

6) Ellen's car goes 655.5 miles on 17.25 gallons of gas. How many miles does she go on one gallon of gas?

7) A jar will hold 2.35 pounds of tomatoes. How many jars will be needed to hold 110.45 pounds of tomatoes?

8) $957.44 is going to be divided among 17 people. How much money will each person get?

9) Megan sold pumpkins and made $17.82. If she sold the pumpkins for $.22 each, how many pumpkins did she sell?

10) Nik sold a rope that was 1098 inches long. He was paid $3.40 per yard. How much money was Nik given for his rope? (Round to the nearest dollar.)

Decimals
Level 1

1) If a coin is .03" thick, how many would it take to fill a container 2.94" high? (The container is a cylinder and has the same diameter as the coin.)

2) Brianna is going on a bike trip. Her energy for the trip is going to be from specially made energy bars. She figures that 14.5 bars will provide enough energy for 264.625 miles. How many miles can Brianna go if she ate one bar?

3) Kristin's car goes 18.95 miles for every gallon of gas. If she is planning a trip of 379 miles and gas cost $1.23 per gallon, what is the cost of gas for the trip?

4) Absolute zero is -459.67° Fahrenheit. How many degrees above absolute zero is the freezing point of water?

5) The smallest living cells are .00002 inches across. The largest living cell is the yolk of an ostrich egg, which is 4" across. How many of the smaller cells would you need to line up side by side to be equal to the diameter of the ostrich yolk?

6) There were 100 students in each of three schools. School A won $1240 which was split among their 100 students. One student at School A felt badly that School B didn't win, so she gave her share to School B, which was split evenly among its 100 students. One student at School B was upset that School C received nothing, so she gave her share to School C. This was split evenly among School C's 100 students. Rounded to the nearest cent, how much money did each student at School C receive?

7) If a company charges $64.78 for 82 pens, how much would it charge for 70 pens?

8) Pluto's year is very long because it takes 90,777.6 days for it to revolve around the sun. The earth takes 365.26 days to revolve around the sun. How many earth years does it take for Pluto to revolve around the sun? (Round to the nearest hundredth.)

9) A ball that weighs one pound on Earth would have a different weight if it were being weighed on another planet. Use the information in the chart to answer the following questions.

Location	Weight of one pound ball
Sun	27 pounds
Mercury	.37 pounds
Venus	.88 pounds
Moon	.16 pounds
Mars	.38 pounds
Jupiter	2.64 pounds
Saturn	1.15 pounds
Uranus	.93 pounds
Neptune	1.22 pounds
Pluto	.06 pounds

a) What would a 160 pound man weigh on Pluto?
b) What would an 80-pound child weigh on the moon?
c) What would a car that weighs 3500 pounds on earth, weigh on the sun?

10) Four-tenths of some number equals 32. What is 1/10 of that number?

Decimals
Level 2

1) A room that is 20.8 feet by 14.6 feet has a 2.4 foot-wide slate walkway around the edge of the room. The interior of the room is carpeted. What is the perimeter of the carpeted part of the room?

2) Chantelle is going on an 8-day hike of 82.5 miles. She plans to hike 8.25 hours every day for each of those 8 days. How many miles will she cover each hour of her trip?

3) What is a better buy, a 2" wide roll of tape that is 55 yards long and sells for $5.75, or a 1.75" wide roll that is 48 yards long and sells for $5.25?

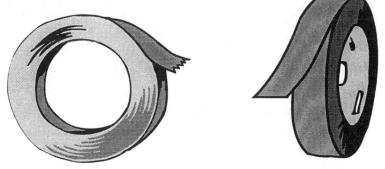

4) If a 50-gallon water heater leaks .4 gallons of water every 17 minutes, how long until it is completely empty?

5) Red blood cells do not reproduce. They are created in bone marrow at the rate of approximately 150,000 per minute. How many red blood cells would be created in .125 seconds?

6) We measure time based on the rotation of the earth ———▶ One rotation of the earth is equal to one day. The spin of the earth is slowing down, so the length of our day is gradually getting longer. Each century, the length of the day increases by .0015 of a second. If the length of a day in 1998 is equal to 23 hours and 56 minutes, how long will a day be in the year 16,001,998?

Use the following information to answer questions 7-9

A microsecond is a millionth of a second ———▶ *.000001*
A nanosecond is a billionth of a second ———▶ *.000,000,001*
A picosecond is a trillionth of a second ———▶ *.000,000,000,001*
A femosecond is a quadrillionth.
         of a second. ———▶*.000,000,000,000,001*

7) Light travels approximately one foot in a nanosecond. How far does light travel in a microsecond?

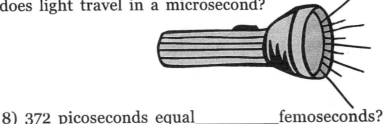

8) 372 picoseconds equal_____femoseconds?

9) How many picoseconds does it take for light to travel a mile?

10) If one inch of rain is the equivalent of 10.65 inches of snow, how many inches of rain would 8.75 inches of snow be equal to?

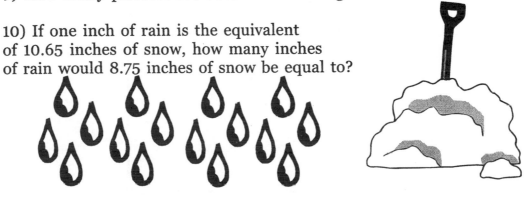

Einstein Level

1) Emily wanted her average salary for five weeks of work to be $248.95. She has already been paid the following amounts:

Week 1.............$182.40
Week 2.............$621.00
Week 3.............$52.10
Week 4.............$18.20

How much money should Emily earn during her 5th week of work to average $248.95 for her five weeks of work?

2) If a circle has a radius of 4.5 inches, what is the length of 1° of its circumference? (Round to the nearest hundredth.)

3) How many quarters would it take to equal the the volume of a piece of paper? (Round your answer to the nearest quarter.)

A quarter has a diameter of .9375 inches and a thickness of .0625 inches

The piece of paper is 10.5 inches by 8 inches and is .0025 inches thick.

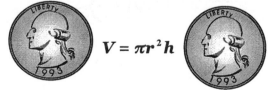

$$V = \pi r^2 h$$

4) A square piece of paper has a perimeter of 38.25 after it is folded in half. What was the length of each side of the square before it was folded?

5) Ten 100-watt light bulbs use 1 kilowatt of electricity per hour. If electricity cost 8.4 cents per kilowatt, how much does it cost when a 40-watt, a 75-watt, and a 100-watt bulb are on for 8 hours?

6) An Isosceles triangle with a height of 9.375 inches is folded along its only line of symmetry. The perimeter of the folded triangle is 23.75 inches. What is the perimeter of the original triangle?

7) Nancy has a choice between two cars. The first car cost $16,000 and gets 19.6 miles to a gallon of gas. Car B cost $18,600 and gets 27.3 miles to a gallon of gas. If gas costs $1.35 per gallon, how far must Nancy drive in the more expensive car before she saves enough money to offset the higher cost of the car? (Round to the nearest thousand miles.)

8) Travis's car can go 19.21 miles on .85 gallons of gas. If gas cost $1.16 per gallon, how much will a 3000 mile trip cost Travis?

9) A year is thought of as having 365 days. Actually the time it takes the earth to revolve around the sun is 365.242 days. This is why we have a February 29th every 4 years. If we didn't have a leap year, eventually we would have the beginning of winter on June 21st instead of December 21st. If the practice of having leap years was discontinued, how many years would it take before winter started on June 21st?

10) If a kilometer is equal to .621 miles, how many kilometers is one mile equal to?

Chapter Six

Fractions
(Latin for break)

A fraction is a part of something. The word fraction comes from a Latin word that means to break. If you fracture your leg, it means you broke your leg. Fractions are needed to measure these "fractured" parts of a whole. It would be nice if everything in the world could be measured and come out a whole number. Unfortunately for children who have to learn fractions, the world doesn't work that way. When you weigh yourself, your weight is usually between two different weights, say 95 and 96 pounds. Because it is not important to have an exact weight, you could always round the measurement. But you cannot round all the time. What would happen to a cake if the recipe said **1/8** cup of baking soda and you rounded to **0** cups, or even worse, **1** full cup. Your taste buds would be sorry you didn't learn fractions.

A fraction has two parts ⟶ $\dfrac{\textbf{numerator}}{\textbf{denominator}}$

The line in a fraction means two different things. The first meaning is **"divided by"**. Look at the fraction below:

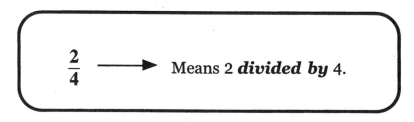

$\dfrac{2}{4}$ ⟶ Means 2 *divided by* 4.

The line in a fraction also means **"compare"**.

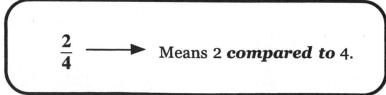

$\dfrac{2}{4}$ ⟶ Means 2 *compared to* 4.

Adding Fractions

I have $\frac{1}{4}$ of a pie and $\frac{1}{2}$ of a pie. How much pie do I have?

It is much easier to add fractions if you make the denominators the same. Change $\frac{1}{2}$ to $\frac{2}{4}$. Now the problem is easy. You have $\frac{3}{4}$ of a pie.

I can see how to add $\frac{1}{2}$ and $\frac{1}{4}$, but how would I add $\frac{1}{3} + \frac{1}{4}$?

Adding fractions is easy if you remember two rules:
(1) Before you can add, you must change the denominators of the fractions so they are the same.
(2) To change the denominator of a fraction, you can multiply the denominator by any number you want———▶ As long as you are fair and multiply the numerator by that same number.

Look at the following example: $\frac{1}{3} + \frac{1}{4}$

Since the denominators are not the same, we have to change them so they are the same. In this case, we will change both of the denominators to 12.

$$\frac{1 \times 3}{4 \times 3} = \frac{3}{12}$$

$$+ \frac{1 \times 4}{3 \times 4} = \frac{4}{12}$$

$$\frac{7}{12}$$

To get the first fraction's denominator to 12, we multiplied by 3. Then to be fair, we multiplied the numerator by 3.

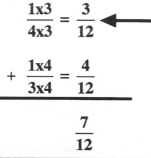

To get the second fraction's denominator to 12, we multiplied by 4. Then to be fair to the numerator, we also multiplied it by 4. Now the fractions are easy to add: $\frac{3}{12} + \frac{4}{12} = \frac{7}{12}$

Try adding the fractions shown below. The hints after each problem give a number that the denominators should be changed to. Remember, you can multiply the denominator by any number, but you must be fair and multiply the numerator by the same number.

1) $\frac{2}{3} + \frac{1}{6}$ Hint: 6

2) $\frac{1}{2} + \frac{1}{3}$ Hint: 6

3) $\frac{1}{10} + \frac{2}{5}$ Hint: 10

4) $\frac{2}{3} + \frac{3}{4}$ Hint: 12

5) $\frac{3}{5} + \frac{2}{12}$ Hint: 60

6) $\frac{2}{5} + \frac{1}{4}$ Hint: 20

7) Kirsten saved half the money she needed for a new bike in the month of March. In April, she saved another 1/8 of the money. What fraction of the money that she needs for the bike does she have saved?

8) Dan ate 1/2 of an apple pie. He then ate 3/8 of a pumpkin pie. How much pie did Dan eat altogether?

9) Mark had $2\frac{1}{3}$ pounds of gold and Michelle had $3\frac{2}{5}$ pounds of gold. How much gold did they have altogether?

10) Mark ran $\frac{1}{2}$ of a mile on Monday. On Tuesday he ran $\frac{3}{4}$ of a mile. On Wednesday and Thursday, he ran $\frac{1}{2}$ mile each day. What was the total distance Mark ran?

Subtracting Fractions

When you are subtracting fractions, just like in addition, you must make the denominators the same.

$$\frac{3}{4} = \frac{3}{4}$$

$$- \frac{1 \times 2}{2 \times 2} = \frac{2}{4}$$

$$\frac{1}{4}$$

Make sure you are fair to the numerator and multiply it by the same number you multiplied the denominator by.

There is a very difficult kind of subtraction problem where you need to borrow. When you borrow, you borrow a **1**, but how do you write **1** as a fraction?

You can write the number **1** as a fraction in many different ways: $\frac{4}{4}$ or $\frac{2}{2}$ or $\frac{9}{9}$. As a matter of fact, any fraction with an equal numerator and denominator is equal to **1.**

Look at this subtraction problem:

$$12\frac{1}{7}$$
$$-6\frac{3}{7}$$

You cannot subtract $\frac{3}{7}$ from $\frac{1}{7}$ so you need to borrow 1 from the 12. We will write 1 as $\frac{7}{7}$ because our fractions have a 7 as a denominator.

$$11\frac{1}{7} + \frac{7}{7}$$
$$-6\frac{3}{7}$$

Notice that the 12 is reduced to 11 because we borrowed 1 from the 12. Now we can add $\frac{1}{7} + \frac{7}{7}$ and get $\frac{8}{7}$

$$11\frac{8}{7}$$
$$-6\frac{3}{7}$$
$$\overline{5\frac{5}{7}}$$

The answer is $5\frac{5}{7}$. That was a little confusing, so I think I'll practice a few subtraction problems. Who took my hat?

Try the following subtraction problems. The first two are done for you.

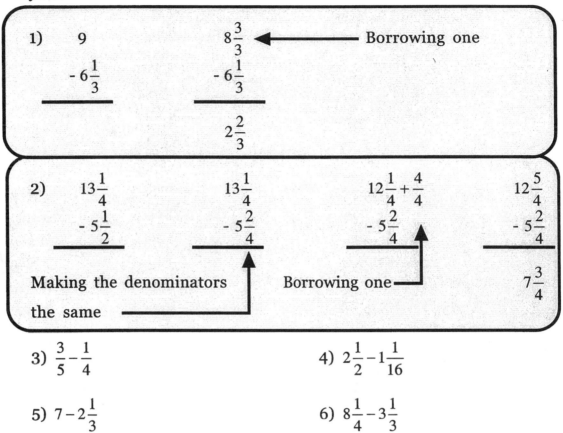

1)   9 $8\frac{3}{3}$ ←———————— Borrowing one

   $-6\frac{1}{3}$ $-6\frac{1}{3}$

                              $2\frac{2}{3}$

2) $13\frac{1}{4}$ $13\frac{1}{4}$ $12\frac{1}{4}+\frac{4}{4}$ $12\frac{5}{4}$

   $-5\frac{1}{2}$ $-5\frac{2}{4}$ $-5\frac{2}{4}$ $-5\frac{2}{4}$

Making the denominators   Borrowing one $7\frac{3}{4}$

the same

3) $\frac{3}{5}-\frac{1}{4}$

4) $2\frac{1}{2}-1\frac{1}{16}$

5) $7-2\frac{1}{3}$

6) $8\frac{1}{4}-3\frac{1}{3}$

7) Larry bought 10 candy bars. He gave $2\frac{2}{3}$ bars to his sister and $3\frac{2}{5}$ bars to his brother. How many candy bars does Larry have left?

8) If Anna's hair is $12\frac{1}{2}$ inches long and she gets $5\frac{1}{8}$ inches cut off during a haircut, how long will Anna's hair be after her haircut?

9) A carpenter bought a 10 foot board. He used three $2\frac{1}{5}$ foot long pieces for shelves. How much wood does he have left?

10) When Rick walks along the road, the distance to school is $3\frac{2}{3}$ miles. If he takes a path through the woods, the distance is $1\frac{7}{8}$ miles. How much shorter is the path through the woods?

Improper Fractions

When a fraction's numerator is larger than its denominator, we call it an improper fraction because it needs changing. If you had nine halves of something------say pies-----you wouldn't say you had nine half pieces of pie, you would say you had $4\frac{1}{2}$ pies. If you had 22 quarter pieces of pie, you wouldn't say you had $\frac{22}{4}$ pies, you would say you had $5\frac{1}{2}$ pies.

> To change improper fractions to mixed numbers, you simply divide the numerator by the denominator.

> A good thing to remember about fractions is that the line in a fraction means divide.

Change the following improper fractions to whole numbers and proper fractions. (These are called mixed numbers.) The first one is done for you.

1) $\frac{7}{2} = 3\frac{1}{2}$　　2) $\frac{8}{3}$　　3) $\frac{10}{2}$　　4) $\frac{15}{1}$　　5) $\frac{24}{6}$

 **One of the most important things to remember about fractions is that the line in a fraction means divide. If you wanted to turn a fraction such as 1/8 into a decimal, all you would need to do is the division problem: 1 ÷ 8 = .125.**

Mixed Numbers

When you divide or multiply fractions, sometimes you have to temporarily change mixed numbers into improper fractions. To change a mixed number into an improper fraction, say $5\frac{2}{3}$, you will need to multiply the whole number by the denominator of the fraction.

$$5\frac{2}{3} \qquad\qquad 5 \times 3 = 15$$

Now add the numerator ⟶ $15 + 2 = 17$

17 is your improper fraction numerator.

The denominator stays the same. ⟶ $\dfrac{17}{3}$

Change the following mixed numbers into improper fractions. The first one is done for you.

1) $5\frac{2}{7} = \frac{37}{7}$ 2) $8\frac{1}{3}$ 3) $6\frac{3}{4}$ 4) $21\frac{1}{2}$ 5) $12\frac{2}{9}$

Reducing Fractions

If you had 2/4 of a pie, you would probably say you had 1/2 of a pie. You have just reduced a fraction. When we reduce fractions, we don't change the amount of the fraction, we just say the fraction in a different way. When you reduce fractions, you need to see if there is any number by which you can evenly divide both the numerator and the denominator. For example: $\dfrac{9}{12}$

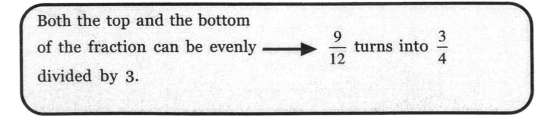

Both the top and the bottom of the fraction can be evenly ⟶ $\dfrac{9}{12}$ turns into $\dfrac{3}{4}$

divided by 3.

Reduce the following fractions to their lowest terms. The first two are done for you.

1) $\dfrac{12}{15}$ The top and bottom can be evenly divided by 3 $\longrightarrow$ $\dfrac{4}{5}$

2) $\dfrac{25}{100}$ Divided by 5 $\longrightarrow$ $\dfrac{5}{20}$ Can still be divided by 5 $\longrightarrow$ $\dfrac{1}{4}$

3) $\dfrac{12}{14}$ 4) $\dfrac{6}{9}$ 5) $\dfrac{15}{20}$

6) $\dfrac{10}{45}$ 7) $\dfrac{21}{24}$ 8) $\dfrac{24}{48}$

Multiplying Fractions

Multiplying fractions is much easier than addition or subtraction of fractions. When you multiply fractions, you simply multiply the numerators and then multiply the denominators:

$$\frac{1}{7} \times \frac{2}{5} = \frac{2}{35}$$

When you are multiplying mixed numbers such as $2\frac{1}{5} \times 3\frac{1}{4}$, you need to change them into improper fractions and then multiply. Let's see how this works in the mixed numbers given above:

$$2\frac{1}{5} \times 3\frac{1}{4} \longrightarrow \frac{11}{5} \times \frac{13}{4} = \frac{143}{20} \longrightarrow 7\frac{3}{20}$$

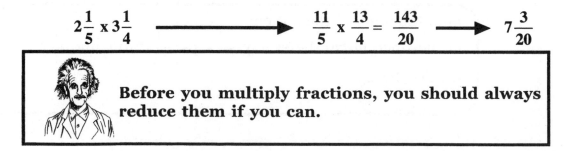

Before you multiply fractions, you should always reduce them if you can.

Try the following multiplication problems. The first one is done for you.

1) $35 \times 2\frac{1}{8}$ ⟶ $\frac{35}{1} \times \frac{17}{8}$ ⟶ $\frac{595}{8}$ ⟶ $74\frac{3}{8}$

2) $\frac{1}{2} \times \frac{1}{8}$

3) $\frac{1}{3} \times \frac{2}{3}$

4) $2\frac{2}{3} \times 4\frac{1}{2}$

5) $3\frac{2}{5} \times 2\frac{1}{3}$

6) $9\frac{1}{2} \times \frac{1}{2}$

7) $5\frac{1}{3} \times 3$

8) Bonnie bought $8\frac{1}{5}$ pounds of shrimp at $9\frac{1}{2}$ dollars per pound. How much did Bonnie spend on shrimp?

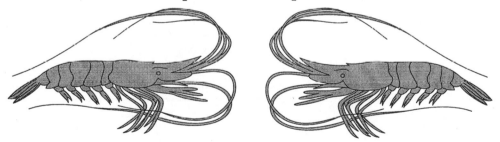

9) If 18 people ate $\frac{2}{3}$ of a pie each, how many pies did they eat?

10) Ashley walks $\frac{1}{3}$ of a mile to school each day and $\frac{1}{3}$ of a mile home. How far does she walk in a school year that has 180 days?

Cross Reducing

Sometimes you can avoid multiplying large fractions by cross reducing before you multiply. When you reduce a normal fraction, you are using a number that can be evenly divided into the numerator and the denominator. Look at the fraction multiplication problem below:

$$\frac{10}{21} \times \frac{7}{24} \times \frac{12}{25}$$

If we went ahead and multiplied, not only would we have a lot of multiplying to do, but we would end up with a very large fraction. In cross reducing, we match up top and bottom numbers and reduce them. Look at how the matching numbers reduce.

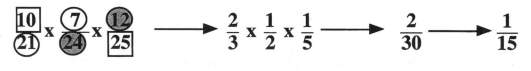

Try cross reducing the following fractions before you multiply.

1) $\frac{25}{6} \times \frac{18}{3} \times \frac{9}{5}$ 2) $\frac{100}{7} \times \frac{3}{600} \times \frac{28}{9}$ 3) $\frac{95}{4} \times \frac{24}{125}$

Dividing Fractions

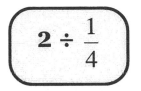

$$2 \div \frac{1}{4}$$

The division problem $2 \div \frac{1}{4}$ can be said another way: How many times will $\frac{1}{4}$ of a pie fit into 2 pies?

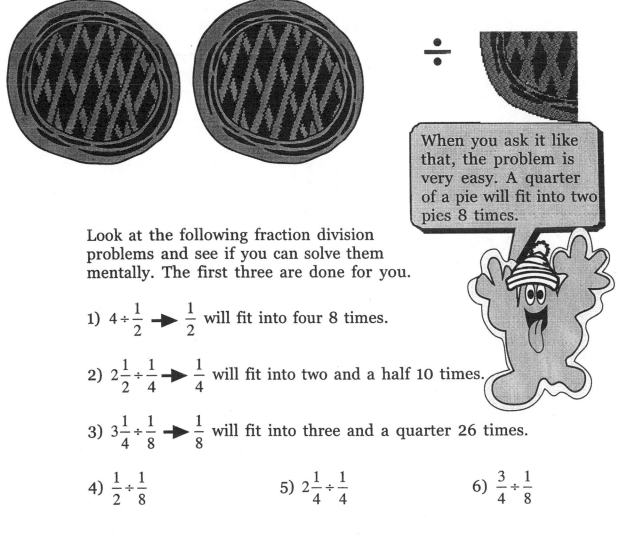

When you ask it like that, the problem is very easy. A quarter of a pie will fit into two pies 8 times.

Look at the following fraction division problems and see if you can solve them mentally. The first three are done for you.

1) $4 \div \frac{1}{2}$ ➤ $\frac{1}{2}$ will fit into four 8 times.

2) $2\frac{1}{2} \div \frac{1}{4}$ ➤ $\frac{1}{4}$ will fit into two and a half 10 times.

3) $3\frac{1}{4} \div \frac{1}{8}$ ➤ $\frac{1}{8}$ will fit into three and a quarter 26 times.

4) $\frac{1}{2} \div \frac{1}{8}$ 　　　　5) $2\frac{1}{4} \div \frac{1}{4}$ 　　　　6) $\frac{3}{4} \div \frac{1}{8}$

7) $5 \div \frac{1}{5}$ 　　　　8) $20\frac{1}{2} \div \frac{1}{4}$ 　　　　9) $\frac{1}{2} \div \frac{1}{16}$

Sometimes it is impossible to mentally solve fraction division problems. When you are faced with this type of problem, you can solve it by using the method described below:

Problem: $\frac{6}{9} \div \frac{1}{18}$

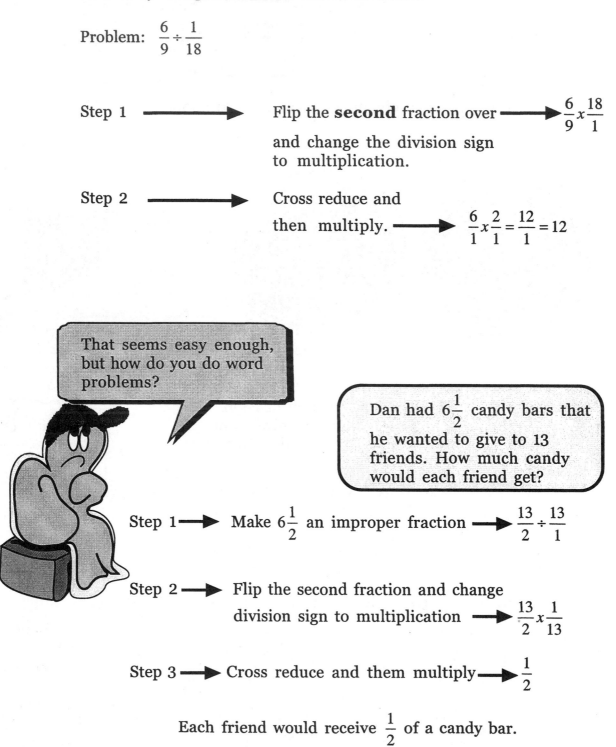

Step 1 ⟶ Flip the **second** fraction over ⟶ $\frac{6}{9} x \frac{18}{1}$

and change the division sign
to multiplication.

Step 2 ⟶ Cross reduce and
then multiply. ⟶ $\frac{6}{1} x \frac{2}{1} = \frac{12}{1} = 12$

That seems easy enough, but how do you do word problems?

Dan had $6\frac{1}{2}$ candy bars that he wanted to give to 13 friends. How much candy would each friend get?

Step 1 ⟶ Make $6\frac{1}{2}$ an improper fraction ⟶ $\frac{13}{2} \div \frac{13}{1}$

Step 2 ⟶ Flip the second fraction and change division sign to multiplication ⟶ $\frac{13}{2} x \frac{1}{13}$

Step 3 ⟶ Cross reduce and them multiply ⟶ $\frac{1}{2}$

Each friend would receive $\frac{1}{2}$ of a candy bar.

When you are doing fraction division problems, it is very important to make sure that the fractions are in the proper order. The fraction that you are splitting up (dividend) always goes first:

$$\text{This fraction goes second}\overline{)\text{This fraction goes first}}$$

Let's try another example:

A board that is $15\frac{3}{4}$ feet long is going to be cut into shelves that will be $2\frac{1}{4}$ feet long. How many shelves will there be?

Since $15\frac{3}{4}$ is what is being split up, it will be the first fraction.

Step 1   (Write problem) $15\frac{3}{4} \div 2\frac{1}{4}$

Step 2   (Improper fractions) $\frac{63}{4} \div \frac{9}{4}$

Step 3   (Flip and change to multiplication) $\frac{63}{4} x \frac{4}{9}$

Step 4   (Cross reduce and multiply) $\frac{7x1}{1x1} = 7$

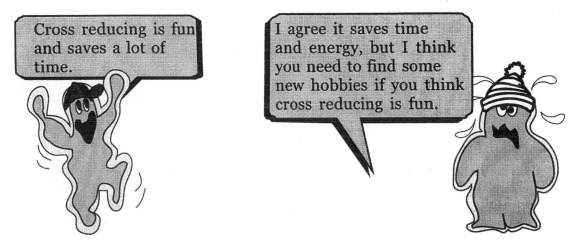

Cross reducing is fun and saves a lot of time.

I agree it saves time and energy, but I think you need to find some new hobbies if you think cross reducing is fun.

1) $2\dfrac{1}{2} \div \dfrac{1}{5}$

2) $9\dfrac{3}{5} \div \dfrac{5}{8}$

3) $\dfrac{1}{8} \div 25$

4) $20\dfrac{2}{5} \div 1\dfrac{1}{5}$

5) $12 \div \dfrac{1}{12}$

6) $\dfrac{1}{12} \div 12$

7) There were 48 people attending a picnic. If $3\dfrac{3}{7}$ pies were to be split evenly among the people at the picnic, how much pie would each person get?

8) Grace drove 159 miles and used $5\dfrac{3}{10}$ gallons of gas. How far could she go with one gallon of gas?

9) Claire had to cut a board that was $9\dfrac{1}{5}$ feet long into 6 equal pieces. How long would each piece be?

10) Heather worked for $15\dfrac{3}{4}$ hours. She was paid a total of $102\dfrac{3}{8}$ dollars. What is Heather's hourly wage?

Fractions
Level 1

1) Emily needs to read 85 pages from her history book. If she can read $1\frac{1}{16}$ pages per minute, how long will it take her to finish her assignment?

2) Gordan worked for $7\frac{5}{8}$ hours and was paid $13\frac{3}{4}$ dollars per hour. How much did Gordan earn?

3) Jay can paint a car in 6 hours. Mike can paint the same car in 3 hours. If they work together, how long will it take them to paint the car?

4) Zach bought $8\frac{1}{8}$ pies and ate $5\frac{2}{5}$ of them over a week's time. How many pies does he have left?

5) Jayme had 7 pizzas for a birthday party of 42 people. How much pizza should each person get?

6) If thunder travels at $\frac{1}{5}$ of a mile per second, how far will thunder travel in $12\frac{1}{5}$ seconds?

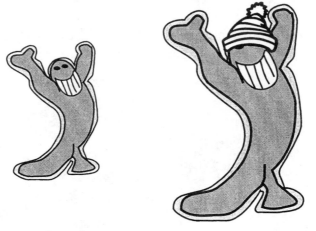

7) A store spends $\frac{1}{5}$ of its income on salaries and $\frac{1}{6}$ of its income on advertising. If the store pays \$180,000 for salaries, how much does it spend on advertising?

8) Nik is $\frac{7}{12}$ of his dad's weight. If Nik weighs 140 pounds, what does his dad weigh?

9) Half the weight of a brick plus 20 pounds is equal to $\frac{1}{3}$ the weight of the brick plus 30 pounds. How much does the brick weigh?

10) If it takes 5 hours to paint $\frac{5}{6}$ of a truck, how long will it take to paint the whole truck?

Fractions
Level 2

1) A meter is defined as the distance light travels in $\dfrac{1}{299,792,458}$ of a second. How many meters does light travel in $\dfrac{1}{4}$ of a second?

2) Find the average height of these five children.

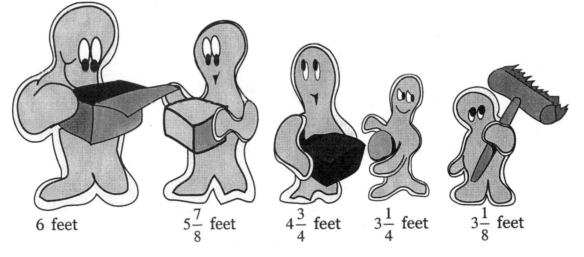

6 feet $5\dfrac{7}{8}$ feet $4\dfrac{3}{4}$ feet $3\dfrac{1}{4}$ feet $3\dfrac{1}{8}$ feet

3) Jay gave away $\dfrac{1}{2}$ of his money on Monday. He then gave away $\dfrac{1}{3}$ of what was left on Tuesday. On Wednesday he spent $\dfrac{1}{4}$ of his remaining money. What fraction of his original money does he have left?

4) Eight workers took $2\dfrac{1}{4}$ days to dig half of a tunnel. If only two workers are going to finish the tunnel, how long will it take them?

5) What is $\dfrac{1}{8}$ of $\dfrac{3}{11}$ of 66 ?

6) Use a fraction to compare a white blood cell's life span to a nerve cell's life span.

> White blood cell.............14 days
> Red blood cell................120 days
> Liver cell......................18 months
> Nerve cell.....................100 years

7) Sara's weight is $\frac{1}{2}$ of Luke's weight, whose weight is $\frac{3}{4}$ of Dan's weight, whose weight is $\frac{7}{8}$ of Ed's weight. If Sara weighs 105 pounds, how much does Ed weigh?

8) Claire said to Anna "I will give you half of my remaining money after I give $\frac{7}{8}$ of it to my favorite charity. If Claire gave $43,750 to her favorite charity, how much money will Anna receive?

9) Christine has two boxes of crackers that she will share evenly with six friends during a 7-day canoe trip. (Seven people altogether) What fraction of a box will each person eat per day?

10) Ben, who owns a music company, decided that he wanted his four best friends to be part owners in the business. He gave shares to his friends in the following way:

Friend 1.................$\frac{1}{3}$ of the company

Friend 2.................$\frac{1}{4}$ of the company

Friend 3.................$\frac{1}{5}$ of the company

Friend 4.................$\frac{1}{6}$ of the company

What fraction of the company does Ben still own?

Einstein Level

1) Shannon bought a piece of plywood that was $4\frac{1}{2}$ feet wide and $8\frac{1}{4}$ feet long. She cut out a three foot diameter circle for a table she was making. Shannon then sold the leftover plywood to a friend for $1.75 per square foot. How much did Shannon's friend pay for the leftover plywood?

2) A jet is traveling at 720 mph towards a thunderstorm. At the instant the pilot sees a bolt of lightning, the jet is $8\frac{1}{2}$ miles away from the storm. How long until the pilot hears the thunder from that lightning bolt? (Assume that sound takes 5 seconds to travel a mile.)

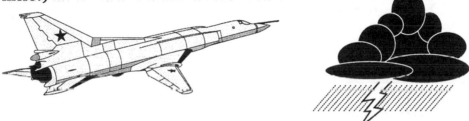

3) A father left all his money to his three children. Child A received $\frac{1}{6}$ of his father's money while child B received $\frac{1}{7}$. Child C, who received the remainder of the money was given $23,490. How much money did child A receive?

4) Luke hiked up a $4\frac{1}{2}$ mile trail to the top of Mt. Washington at an average speed of $2\frac{1}{7}$ mph. His dad hiked the same trail at an average speed of $2\frac{1}{4}$ mph. If Luke's dad reaches the top of the mountain at noon, what time will Luke arrive?

5) When his dad reaches the top, what fraction of a mile does Luke have remaining?

6) Wendy spent $\frac{3}{8}$ of her money at the first store she visited. She then spent $\frac{3}{4}$ of her remaining money at the second store. If Wendy had $20 left, how much money did she start with?

7) Kyle can paint a fence in 4 hours while Gabe takes 6 hours to paint the same fence. If they work together, how long will it take them to paint the fence?

8) Three hoses are filling a swimming pool. If only hose A was used, it would take six hours to fill the pool, while using only hose B would take two hours. Hose C is identical to hose A. How long will it take to fill the pool if all three hoses are used?

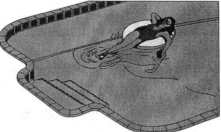

9) When her mother won a lottery ticket, Kayla was given $\frac{1}{3}$ of the prize money. Each of her four brothers received $\frac{1}{4}$ of the remaining money. When Kayla and one of her brothers put their money together, they had $75,000. What was the total amount of the lottery winnings?

10) A business is planning to provide sandwiches at their company picnic. Adults eat 1 3/4 times the amount that school-aged children eat, and babies eat half of what school-age children eat. 56 adults, 14 school-age children and 28 babies are attending the picnic. If adults eat 5/8 of a sandwich, how many sandwiches should be ordered?

Perimeters and Circumferences

It is often assumed that when Columbus sailed to North America in 1492, people of the time thought the earth was flat. This is not true. By 1492, it was very clear to most educated people that the earth was round. Even though Columbus is usually given credit for proving that the earth was round, that honor really belongs to a Greek mathematician named Eratosthenes. Eratosthenes, who was born 2000 years before Columbus, used mathematics in a very clever way to not only prove that the earth was round, but also to show that the circumference of the earth was equal to approximately 24,000 miles.

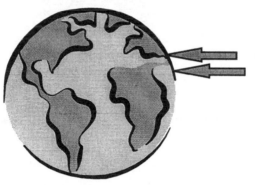

Alexandria
Syene

Eratosthenes knew that the distance between Alexandria and Syene was 500 miles. He also knew that when the sun was directly overhead in Syene, it was not directly overhead in Alexandria ⟶ It was off by 7 1/2° degrees. Eratosthenes knew that a circle had 360 degrees, so he divided 360 by 7 1/2 and ended up with 48. This meant that there were 48 pieces to the circumference of the earth, each of which was equal to 500 miles (the distance from Syene to Alexandria). From this information it was an easy calculation to show that the circumference of the earth was approximately 24,000 miles.

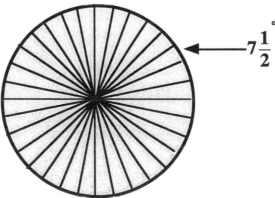

Rectangles and Squares

Finding the perimeter of a rectangle or a square is a very easy procedure:
You simply add all four sides. For example: What is the perimeter of the
square shown below?

3 feet

That's easy. Since each
side is 3 feet, the perimeter
must be 3 x 4 or 12 feet.

What is the perimeter of the rectangle shown below?

That's seems easy also.
The perimeter must be
8 + 8 + 5 + 5, which
equals 26 feet.

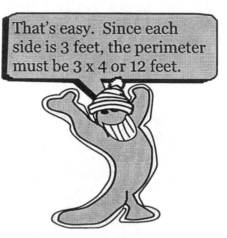

5 feet

8 feet

Find the perimeters of the three objects shown below.

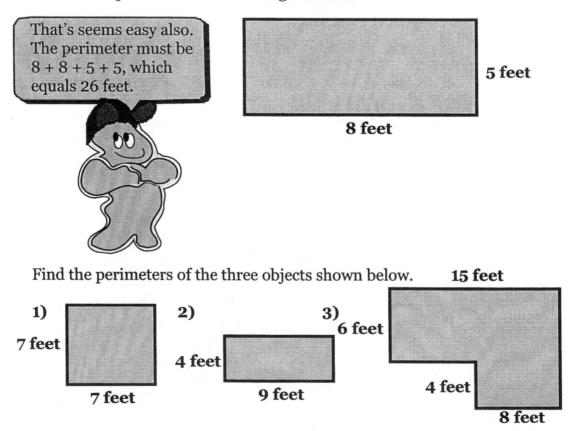

1)

7 feet

7 feet

2)

4 feet

9 feet

3)

15 feet

6 feet

4 feet

8 feet

Circles

There is a special name for the perimeter of a circle ——▶ It is called the circumference. You can find the circumference of any circle by multiplying the diameter of the circle by **pi.**

There is a symbol that mathematicians use instead of writing the word **pi.** It looks like two t's put together..................π

Look at the following example:
What is the circumference of a circle with a diameter of 25 inches?
Diameter x π = Circumference
25 x 3.14 = 78.5 feet

Find the circumference of each circle shown below.

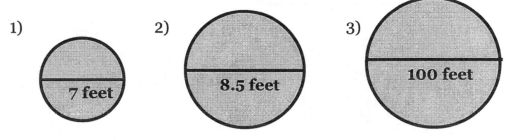

1)   **7 feet**

2)   **8.5 feet**

3)   **100 feet**

4) What is the diameter of a circle that has a circumference of 122.46 inches?

Pythagorean Theorem

The perimeter of a right triangle can be found if you use the Pythagorean Theorem. Before you learn how to use the Pythagorean Theorem, you need to know the different parts of a right triangle.

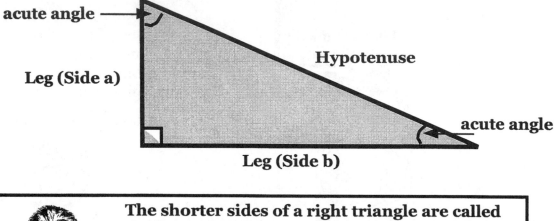

acute angle →

Hypotenuse

Leg (Side a)

acute angle

Leg (Side b)

The shorter sides of a right triangle are called the legs. The shorter leg is usually referred to as side a, while the other leg is referred to as side b. The longer diagonal side is called the hypotenuse or side c. In addition, the two angles in a right triangle that are under 90° are called the acute angles.

The Pythagorean Theorem says that if you square the measurement of each leg of a right triangle and then add them together, that number will be equal to the square of the hypotenuse of the triangle.

$$a^2 + b^2 = c^2$$

I am very, very confused.

I know how to square the measurement of each leg of the triangle, you simply multiply each number by itself. Maybe it would help if we looked at a problem.

What is the length of the hypotenuse of a right triangle whose legs are 3 feet and 4 feet?

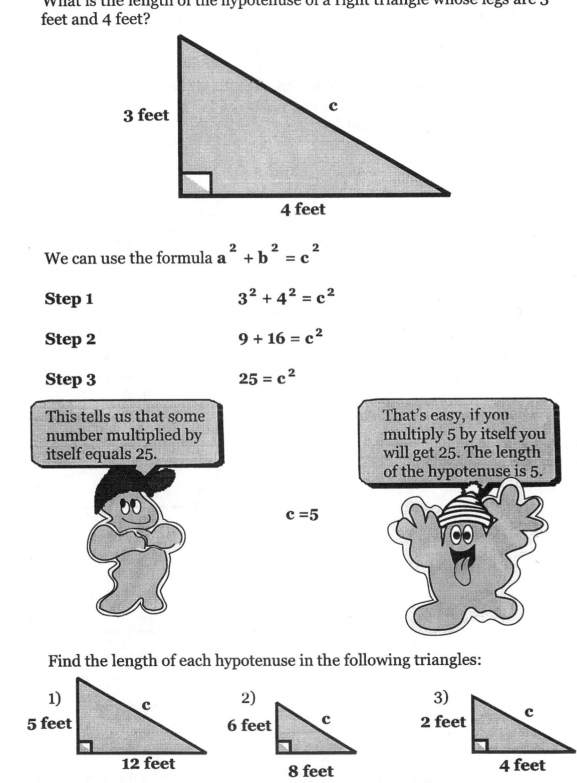

We can use the formula $a^2 + b^2 = c^2$

Step 1 $3^2 + 4^2 = c^2$

Step 2 $9 + 16 = c^2$

Step 3 $25 = c^2$

This tells us that some number multiplied by itself equals 25.

That's easy, if you multiply 5 by itself you will get 25. The length of the hypotenuse is 5.

$c = 5$

Find the length of each hypotenuse in the following triangles:

1)
5 feet
c
12 feet

2)
6 feet
c
8 feet

3)
2 feet
c
4 feet

Perimeter and Circumference Level 1

1) Mack needs to buy fencing to surround his circular garden. If his garden is 30 feet across and fencing cost $4.50 per foot, how much will it cost to fence in Mack's garden?

2) Perimeter_____

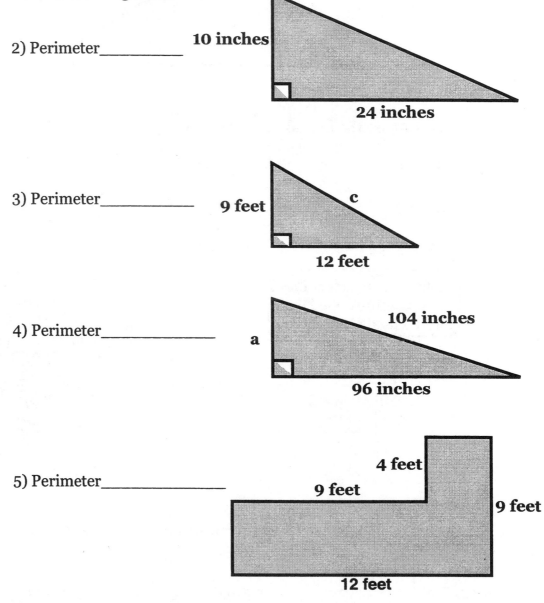

10 inches

24 inches

3) Perimeter_____

9 feet

c

12 feet

4) Perimeter_____

104 inches

a

96 inches

5) Perimeter_____

4 feet

9 feet

9 feet

12 feet

6) If the circumference of a circle is 219.8 feet, what is its diameter?

7) If the radius of a circle is 4 feet, what is its circumference?

8) What is the perimeter of this figure?

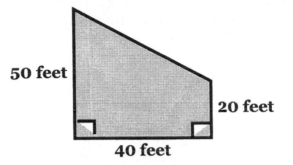

50 feet

20 feet

40 feet

9) Kyle needs to walk through a circular farm field. Because he is worried about the possibility of bulls being in the field, he is thinking about going around the field. How much further will Kyle's walk be if he decides to walk around the field instead of through it?

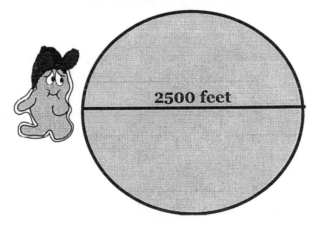

2500 feet

10) What is the perimeter of this figure?

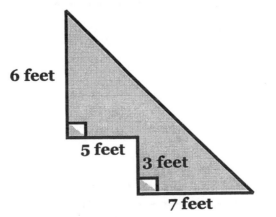

6 feet

5 feet

3 feet

7 feet

Perimeter and Circumferences Level 2

1) The space shuttle orbited the earth 20 times at an altitude of 280 miles. If the diameter of the earth is 8000 miles, how many miles did the space shuttle travel?

2) Jayme has to travel from his home on one side of a circular lake to a store on the other side. He has his choice of canoeing across the lake at a speed of 4 mph or running on a path along the shore of the lake at a speed of 7 mph. If the lake is 2 miles across, what method would be faster? Why?

3) Two runners are racing 4 times around a circular track with a circumference of 1000 feet. The first runner will run on the line, while the second runner will run 3 feet outside the line. How much more distance will the second runner cover than the first runner?

4) If a greyhound dog needs a training run of 3 miles, how many times will it need to run around the track. Round your answer to the nearest whole number. (The ends of the track are semicircles.)

200 feet

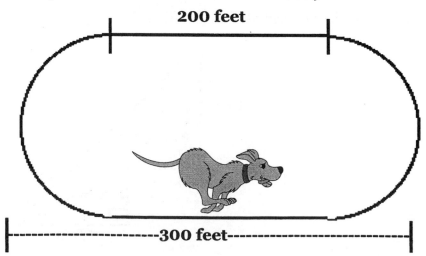

300 feet

5) How far does the tip of a 4" long hour hand travel in a 24-hour period?

6) A clock has an 8-inch minute hand and a 6-inch hour hand. How much further does the tip of the minute hand travel in a 24-hour period than the tip of the hour hand?

7) A circle has a radius of 8 feet. If you travel from point A to B to C and then back to A along the circle, how far will you have traveled? **AB is the radius of the circle.**

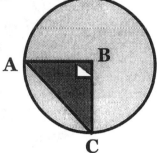

8) Two runners are racing around a circular track with a diameter of 400 feet. Runner A runs on the line and runner B runs 5 feet outside the line to ensure safety for the runners. If the race is for 4 laps, how much of a head start should runner B get to make the race fair?

9) How many revolutions will a bike tire make during a 15-mile trip if the diameter of the wheels is 3 feet? (Round to the nearest whole number.)

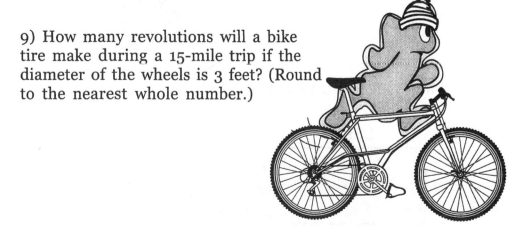

10) A clock has a minute hand that is 10" long and an hour hand that is 4" long. The distance that the minute hand travels during a 3-hour period is how many times farther than the distance traveled by the hour hand?

Einstein
Level

1) Ben ran 10 times around a circular track. If the total distance he ran was 8 miles, what was the diameter of the track?

2) A wheel on a bike turns 1320 times during a 1-mile trip. What is the diameter of the wheel?

3) A clock has a 12" minute hand and a 9" hour hand. At 3:00, how far apart are the tips of the hands?

4) The radius of this circle is 8". What is the length of arc AB?

A
20°
B

5) What is the perimeter of this figure?

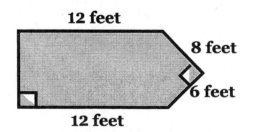

12 feet

8 feet

6 feet

12 feet

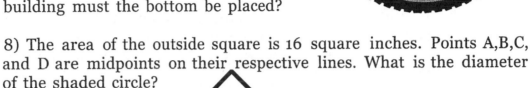

6) If a bug held on to a 16" diameter exercise bike tire midway between the center and the outside of the tire, how many miles would the bug travel when the bike has "traveled" 10 miles?

7) If a 52 foot ladder needs to reach the top of a 48 foot building, how far out from the bottom of the building must the bottom be placed?

8) The area of the outside square is 16 square inches. Points A,B,C, and D are midpoints on their respective lines. What is the diameter of the shaded circle?

9) A tire with an 8 decimeter diameter has a 2 centimeter thick rubber edge which loses .00001 millimeters of rubber every time it rotates. If you want to replace the tire when half the rubber is gone, how many kilometers could you go before you need to replace the tire?

2 cm. thick

10) An odometer registers the number of miles traveled by counting the number of times a tire turns. Adam's odometer is set for 18" diameter tires, but he decided to put 16" diameter tires on his bike. After a long ride, Adam's odometer said that he traveled about 47 miles. How far did Adam really travel?

Chapter Eight

Area

When a planet is close to the sun, the sun's gravity pulls more strongly than when the planet is far away. Because the pull of gravity is more powerful, the planet moves faster. When the planet is far away, the pull of the sun's gravity is weaker, and therefore the planet moves more slowly.

In the early 1600's, Johannes Kepler made a dramatic discovery about the speed and orbits of planets. This discovery, called Kepler's second law, had to do with the areas planets sweep out as they orbit the sun.

"Planets sweep out equal areas
in equal times"

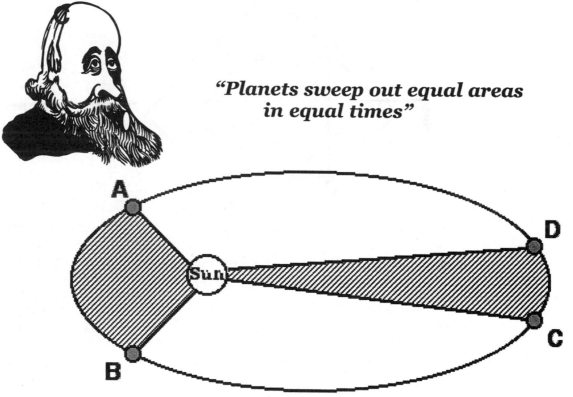

What this law says is that there is something very special about a planet as it moves in its orbit. If the time it takes to travel from point A to B is the same as the amount of time it takes the planet to travel from C to D, then the swept out areas made by extending an imaginary line from the planet to the sun are equal. (Shaded part)

Area of Rectangles

The area of a rectangle is found by multiplying the length times the width. Look at the rectangle shown below.

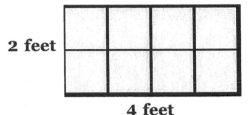

2 feet

4 feet

The area of this rectangle is 2 x 4 or 8 square feet.

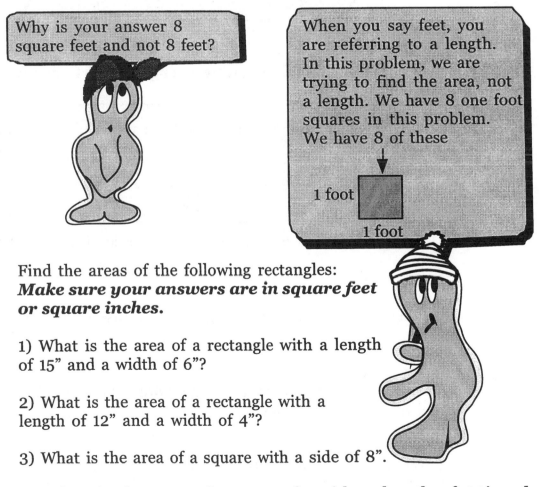

Why is your answer 8 square feet and not 8 feet?

When you say feet, you are referring to a length. In this problem, we are trying to find the area, not a length. We have 8 one foot squares in this problem. We have 8 of these

1 foot

1 foot

Find the areas of the following rectangles:
Make sure your answers are in square feet or square inches.

1) What is the area of a rectangle with a length of 15" and a width of 6"?

2) What is the area of a rectangle with a length of 12" and a width of 4"?

3) What is the area of a square with a side of 8".

4) What is the area of a rectangle with a length of 20' and a perimeter of 44'?

Area of Triangles

The area of a triangle is found by multiplying the base times the height, and then dividing the answer by two. The height (or altitude) of a triangle is found by drawing a perpendicular line (90°) from the base to the highest point of the triangle. Various ways of finding heights of triangles are shown below:

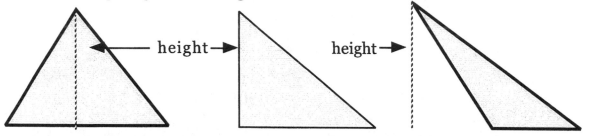

Find the areas of the following triangles. The first one is done for you.

1) What is the area of a triangle with a base of 15 feet and a height of 8 feet?

Solution: 8 x 15 = 120   120 ÷ 2 = 60 square feet

2) What is the area of a triangle with a base of 100" and a height of 15"?

3) What is the area of a triangle with a base of 14" and a height of 4"?

4) What is the height of a triangle with a base of 20 inches and an area of 50 square inches?

5) What is the base of a triangle with a height of 8' and an area of 16 square feet?

Area of Circles

The area of a circle is found by multiplying π by the radius of the circle squared. $A = \pi r^2$

I know that the radius of a circle is the distance from the center of the circle to the outside. I'm having a lot of trouble remembering what π is.

π or pi is simply the ratio of the circumference of a circle to its diameter. When solving problems, most people use the number 3.14 for pi. If you'd like, you can also use the fraction $\frac{22}{7}$.

Try answering the following questions. The first one is done for you.

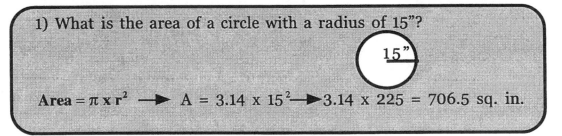

1) What is the area of a circle with a radius of 15"?

15"

$\text{Area} = \pi \times r^2 \longrightarrow A = 3.14 \times 15^2 \longrightarrow 3.14 \times 225 = 706.5 \text{ sq. in.}$

2) What is the area of a circle with a radius of 7 feet?

3) What is the area of a circle with a diameter of 16 feet?

4) What is the radius of a circle with an area of 28.26 sq. in.?

5) What is the radius of a circle with an area of 78.5 sq. in.?

Area
Level 1

1) If carpet cost $5 per square yard, what would it cost to carpet a room that is 5 yards wide and 22 yards long?

2) If you wanted to carpet a circular room that is 20 feet across and carpet cost $3.50 per square foot, how much money would you need?

3) Area=_____

4) Area=_____

5) Area=_____

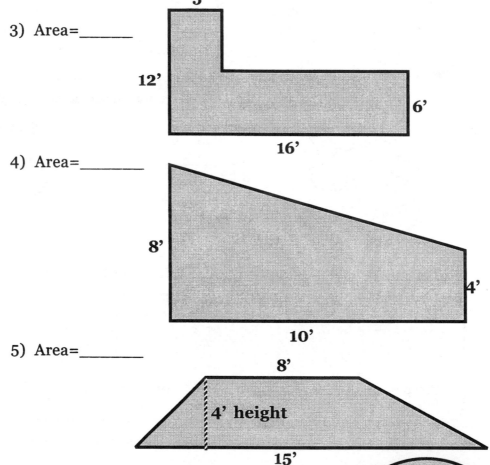

6) Dan has a dog that is tied up in the center of his lawn with a 30' chain. The dog has killed the grass everywhere it can reach, so Dan is buying grass seed to replant the grass. If each package of grass seed is enough for 200 square feet, how many packages will Dan need?

7) Area=_____

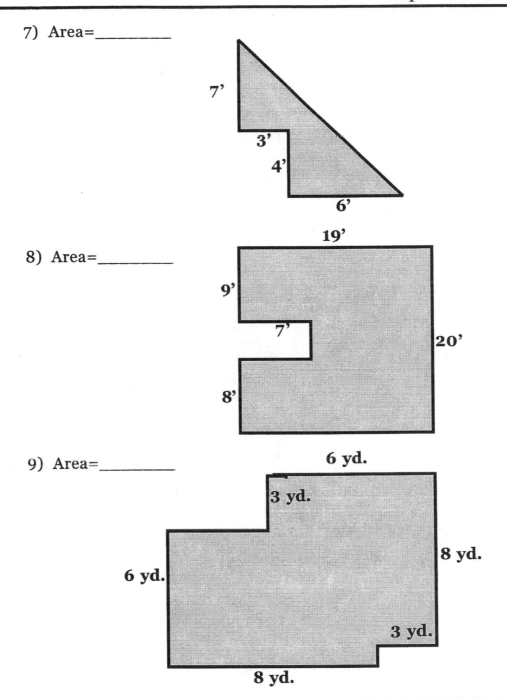

8) Area=_____

9) Area=_____

10) Rick wants to carpet his room with a 5 foot wide strip of carpet that goes around the outside of his room. If he leaves the inside bare wood, what is the area of the carpet he will need? **28'**

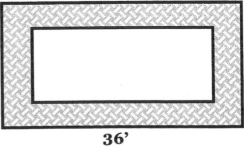

36'

Area
Level 2

1) Kristin needed to paint the floor of her circular room. She started working from the outside and gradually moved towards the center of the room. She has used a gallon of paint and has painted only a 2 foot wide strip around the outside of her room. If the diameter of the entire room is 20 feet, how many more gallons of paint will she need to buy? (Paint can only be purchased in full gallons.)

2) A rotating lawn sprinkler, that is in the middle of a square lawn, shoots water to a distance of 20 feet. What is the area of those parts of the lawn that the sprinkler cannot reach?

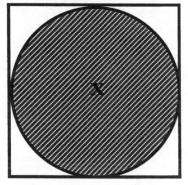

3) What is the area of the shaded part if the radius of the circle is 8 feet?

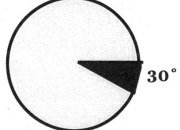

4) What is the area of the shaded part if the diameter of the circle is 10 feet?

5) The area of the outside square is 64 square inches. What is the area of the inside square?

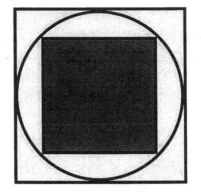

6) Red blood cells are so small that 50,000 can fit into a circle with a $\frac{1}{4}$ inch diameter. How many red blood cells would fit into a circle with a one inch diameter?

7) What is the area of the shaded part if the diameter of the circle is 8 feet?

8) A dark circle is drawn in the middle of a larger circle. The small dark circle has a diameter of 2 inches and the diameter of the larger circle is 10 inches. If 25.12 square inches of the light circle are removed each day, how long will it take before only the dark circle remains?

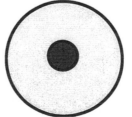

9) What is the area of the shaded part if the rectangle has a length of 8 inches?

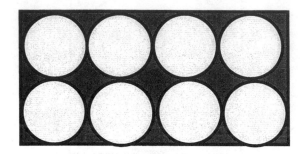

10) The amount of light a telescope receives depends on the area of the mirror. The same is true for the human eye. If a telescope mirror has a diameter of 200 inches and the pupil of the human eye has a diameter of .2 inches, how many times more light does the telescope receive than the human eye?

Einstein Level

1) A dog is tied to the middle of one side of a barn. The dog ruins the grass wherever it can reach. The dog is on a 26 foot leash and the side of the barn where he is tied is 26 feet long. (The farthest out the dog can reach is 26 feet.) What is the area of the grass that the dog will ruin.

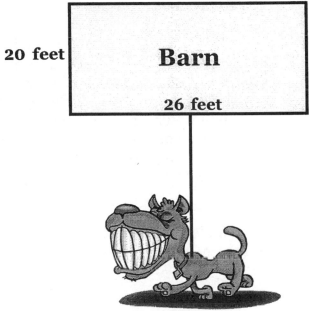

20 feet

Barn

26 feet

2) The area of the outside square is 81 square feet. What is the area of the shaded Isosceles triangle that is inside the small square?

3) A recipe will make 10 pancakes that are each 8 inches in diameter. If you decided to make 2 inch diameter pancakes, how many of the smaller pancakes would this recipe make?

4) Find the area of the shaded region. The diameter of the circle is 10 feet.

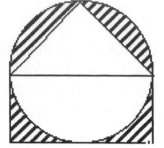

5) Wendy is growing corn in a 100' by 100' farm field. Some friends decided to play a trick on Wendy to make it appear as though aliens visited her farm. They fastened one end of a 20 foot board to the ground and rotated it in a complete circle. In the process they destroyed all the corn plants within that circle. Wendy was going to make $1500 profit from her corn, but because some of the field was damaged, she will make less money. How much money should Wendy expect to make now?

6) The radius of the cylinder shown below is 4" and the height is 6". What is the surface area of the cylinder?

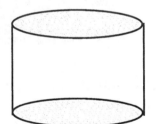

7) This hexagon is made up of six equilateral triangles. The length of each side of the hexagon is 8 feet. What is the area of the hexagon?

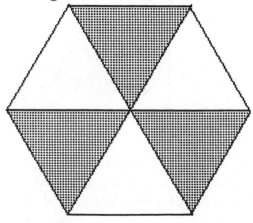

8) What is the area of the shaded part inside the 10 foot square?

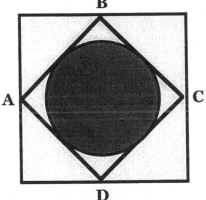

9) The area of the outside square is 64 square inches. Points A,B,C,and D are midpoints on their respective lines. What is the area of the shaded circle?

10) The circle is perfectly centered on top of a rectangle that is 20 inches long. Lines AC and BD are both diameters of the circle and are equal to $\sqrt{50}$. What is the area of the shaded part?
(Worth three Einsteins)

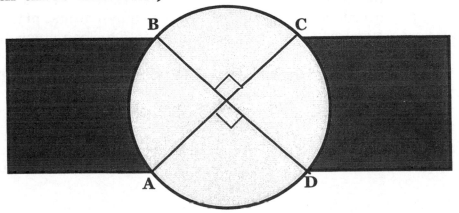

Volume

Archimedes was a famous Greek mathematician who lived over 2000 years ago. He is most famous for using mathematics to determine whether a king's crown was solid gold. The story of Archimedes and the gold crown is one of the most interesting stories from the history of mathematics. The ruler of the Greek city of Syracuse, who was named Hiero, gave a goldsmith some gold to make a crown. After the crown was completed, Hiero heard rumors that this goldsmith had a habit of stealing some of his customers' gold and replacing it with silver, a much cheaper metal. The King's finished crown was clearly gold on the outside and it weighed exactly the same amount as the gold that Heiro gave to the goldsmith. Still, Heiro worried that the goldsmith substituted silver for some of the gold. He asked Archimedes to try and determine whether any of his gold was stolen.

Archimedes was given this task with one very difficult condition. The crown was not to be damaged in any way. This meant that Archimedes had to test what was on the inside of the crown without being able to drill or scrape the crown. Archimedes pondered day and night on how to accomplish this seemingly impossible feat.

One night as Archimedes sat down in his bathtub, he watched water spill over the side. His eyes grew wide as he leapt from the tub. "Eureka, I have found it". Archimedes had discovered that he could use what he knew about volumes to determine whether the crown was solid gold. The first thing that Archimedes did was fill a container with water and then drop the crown into the water. He determined the volume of the water that overflowed. He then refilled the container and placed an amount of gold equal to the weight of the crown into the container. If the crown was pure gold, the amount of spilled water must be exactly the same for both items. It wasn't. The goldsmith did steal some of the king's gold.

Archimedes was so passionate about mathematics, that as the city of Syracuse was captured by Roman soldiers, he continued to work on math problems by drawing in the sand. Unwilling to abandon the problems he was working on and flee, Archimedes was killed by the invading soldiers.

We have talked in previous chapters about perimeters and areas. We are now going to study an area of mathematics that deals with the amount of space an object takes up ——► **Volume.** All objects have volume because they take up space. The air in a room, water, and paper are all examples of items that have volume. A solid wood cube that is one foot long, one foot wide and one foot high is said to have a volume of 1 **cubic** foot.

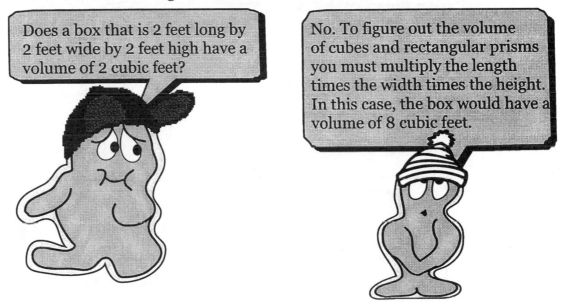

Does a box that is 2 feet long by 2 feet wide by 2 feet high have a volume of 2 cubic feet?

No. To figure out the volume of cubes and rectangular prisms you must multiply the length times the width times the height. In this case, the box would have a volume of 8 cubic feet.

Rectangular Boxes

 **To find the volume of a rectangular or square box, you simply multiply the length by the width by the height.**

The volume of this rectangular box is 20' x 22' x 32' = 14,080 cubic feet.

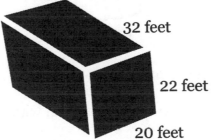

32 feet

22 feet

20 feet

1) What is the volume of a cube that is 7 feet on each side?
2) What is the volume of a rectangular box that is 1 foot high, 6 inches wide and 18 inches long?
3) What is the volume of a die that is 3 centimeters long?

Cylinders

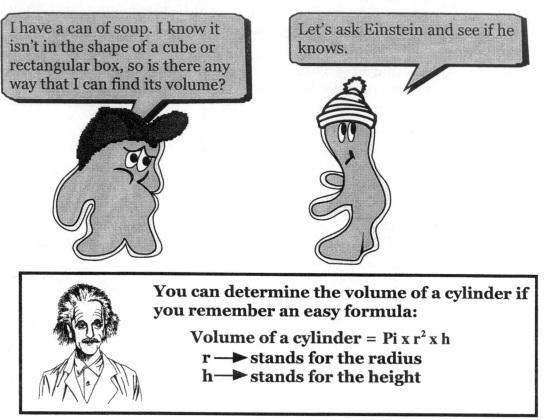

You can determine the volume of a cylinder if you remember an easy formula:

Volume of a cylinder = Pi x r² x h

r ➤ stands for the radius

h ➤ stands for the height

Example: What is the volume of the cylinder shown below?

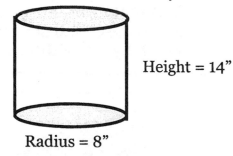

Height = 14"

Radius = 8"

Using the formula ──➤ **3.14 x 8² x 14 = 2813.44 cubic inches**

1) What is the volume of a can with a radius of 4" and a height of 15" ?

2) What is the volume of a wooden dowel that is 3 feet long and has a diameter of 1 inch?

3) What is the volume of a tuna can that is 2" high and has a radius of 3 inches?

Spheres

It is also possible to find volumes of other shapes besides boxes and cylinders. The volume of a sphere is found by using the formula:

$$V = \frac{4}{3} \times pi \times r^3$$

For example: What is the volume of a ball that has a radius of 4"?

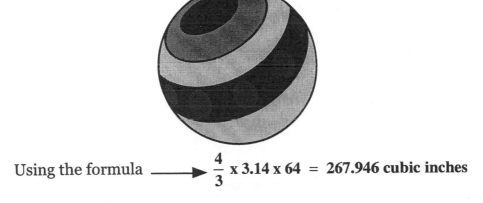

Using the formula ⟶ $\frac{4}{3}$ x 3.14 x 64 = **267.946 cubic inches**

1) What is the volume of a baseball that has a radius of 2"?

2) What is the volume of a basketball that has a diameter of 12"?

3) What is the volume of the moon if it is assumed that it is a perfect sphere and its radius is 1000 miles?

Can we find the volume of objects that are oddly shaped? Is there a formula for every different shape?

There are other formulas, but finding the volume of things like chairs and rocks seems almost impossible.

It is possible to find the volume of odd-shaped objects as long as you are able to put them into a tank of water. If you slowly drop a rock into a full tank of water, water will overflow the tank. The amount of water that overflows the tank is equal to the volume of the object that was dropped into the tank. This is because the rock takes up a certain amount of space. Since the tank of water was full, some water must leave to make way for the rock. To find the volume of the rock you would simply pour the spilled water into a measuring container.

Volumes
Level 1

1) What is the volume of the water in a swimming pool that is 10' deep by 25' long by 20' wide?

2) What is the volume of a cylinder that is 10 feet high and has a diameter of 8 feet?

3) If the diameter of the earth is 8000 miles, and we assume it is a perfect sphere, what is its volume?

4) If the weight of a cubic decimeter of water is 1 kilogram, what is the weight of a cubic meter of water?

5) A cubic decimeter of water is called a liter of water. How many liters of water would fit into a cylinder that is 4 meters in diameter and is 10 meters high?

6) What is the weight, in kilograms, of the water in a tank that is 4 meters wide, 5 meters long, and 4 meters high?

7) A room is 20 meters wide by 30 meters long by 3 meters high. All the air in this room is compressed and placed in a one foot metal cube that weighs 10 kilograms when it is empty. What is the weight of the metal cube now? (Air weighs 1.29 kilograms per cubic meter.)

8) A cubic foot of limestone from a particular site has 60,000 fossils in it. How many fossils would there be in a cubic yard of limestone from this site?

9) If you put a metal sphere with a 6' diameter into a tank that is 12' x 12' x 14', what is the volume of the water that would overflow?

10) How many cubic inches are in a cubic foot?

Volume
Level 2

1) What is the volume of the water in a full 50' garden hose that has a 2 inch inside diameter?

2) If a cylinder of height 8' and a diameter of 4' is dropped slowly into a full tank of water measuring 10' x 10' x 10', what is the volume of the water that overflows?

3) If a cubic meter is dropped into a full tank of water, what is the weight (in kilograms) of the water that overflows?

4) Concrete is ordered by the cubic yard. If a contractor says that he needs 10 yards, that means he wants 10 cubic yards of concrete. Kathy is going to make a cement driveway 12' wide, 81' long, and 6 inches thick. How many yards of concrete will she need?

5) A contractor has been asked to pave 15 miles of new road. Before he can set his price, he needs to know how much the cement will cost. If the road is 45 feet wide and 9 inches thick and the cost of cement is $35 per cubic yard, what will be the cost of the cement needed for the road?

6) The moon and the earth are almost perfect spheres. The moon is 2000 miles in diameter compared to the earth's 8000 mile diameter. The diameter of the earth is 4 times that of the moon. The volume of the earth is how many times larger than the moon's volume?

7) How many cubic yards are in a cubic mile?

8) Three cubes are dropped into a container of water that is filled to the top. They are a 1 inch cube, a 1 foot cube, and a 1 yard cube. What is the volume of water that spills out?

9) A waterfall has a flow rate of 2700 cubic feet of water per second. How many cubic yards of water go over the waterfall in a year?

10) Heather is building a parking area that will be 36 feet long and 21 feet wide. She is trying to decide whether to make the concrete 5 inches or 6 inches thick. If concrete costs $35 per cubic yard, how much extra money would it cost to build the parking area 6 inches deep?

Einstein Level

1) What is the volume of water in a full 100 foot hose that has an outside diameter of one inch and a wall thickness of 1/8 inch?

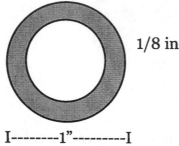

1/8 inch wall thickness

I--------1"---------I

2) A truck that weighs 6500 pounds when it is empty, must travel over a bridge that has a weight limit of 40 tons. The truck has a rectangular box for hauling that is 25' x 12' x 8' tall. The truck will be hauling salt that weighs 35 pounds per cubic foot. To what depth can the salt be loaded in the box and still ensure that the weight limit of the bridge will not be exceeded?

Weight Limit
40 tons

3) How many cubic centimeters are in a cubic yard? (Round to the nearest 1/4 million.)

4) Gold can be pounded into very thin sheets. If a 1 cm. cube is pounded into a sheet exactly 1.25 cm. wide and 20 cm. long, how thick is the sheet?

5) A paint can holds 3 liters of paint. When the paint is brushed on a wall, the paint is .05 mm thick. How many cans of paint would be needed to paint a wall that is 10 meters high and 24 meters long?

PAINT

6) The electricity to Jason's electric water heater is shut off because he needed to drain the tank to clean out mineral deposits. Jason now needs to refill his water heater. He has to be very sure that it is completely full of water before the electricity is turned back on because there are two heating elements in the heater that must be completely covered with water, or they will burn out and cause an expensive repair. The inside of the tank, which is a cylinder, measures 5 decimeters in diameter and is 1 1/2 meters high. When Jason runs water, it fills a liter container in 6 seconds. It is now 6:35 P.M. and Jason has just turned on the water to fill the tank. At what time will the tank be full so Jason can turn the electricity to the water heater back on. (Round to the nearest minute.)

7) What is the weight, in pounds, of a gallon of water? (Round to the nearest whole number.)

> 1 quart = .946 liters
> 1 liter weighs 1 kilogram
> 1 kilogram = 2.2 pounds

8) What is the volume of 40 washers that are each 1/8 inch thick with 4 inch outside diameters and 2 inch inside diameters?

9) Don's water heater is a cylinder that is 4 feet high and 1.5 feet in diameter. Don desperately wants to take a shower, but his water heater is broken. Don decided to try and heat water by placing garden hoses that are full of water out in the sun. The garden hoses have 3/4 inch inside diameters and Don wants to heat the same amount of water that he normally uses for a shower. During a typical shower, Don will use 1/10 the volume of the amount of water in his water heater. How many feet of hose should Don lay out in the sun? (Round your answer to the nearest ten.)

10) A rectangular box measuring 8'x4'x4' weighs 4 pounds when it is empty. If it is placed on a board that has a weight limit of 708 pounds, and if sand weighs 22 pounds per cubic foot, what fraction of the box can you safely fill with sand?

Percents

Credit card companies will often send credit cards to students when they turn 18. These cards allow the holder of the card to make purchases without immediately paying for them, but these cards also have interest rates that can run as high as 22.9%. What does it mean when companies charge interest? Let's take a look at what would happen to a student who makes one purchase with his new credit card, and then chooses not to pay his bill for 50 years.

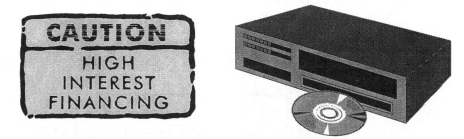

Gabe received a credit card on his 18th birthday that had an interest rate of 22.9%. The next day he bought a CD player for $100 and paid for it with his credit card. Gabe never used his card again, but he also never paid the money he owed to the credit card company. Look at how Gabe's debt grew over the next 50 years.

Time	Money Gabe owes
1 year	$122.90
2 years	$151.04
5 years	$280.39
10 years	$786.17
20 years	$6180.70
30 years	$48591.07
40 years	$382,010.49
50 years	$3,003,268.21

Gabe's $100 debt grew to over 3 million dollars because of the 22.9% interest that he was charged. After you've studied the chapter on percents, you will understand how and why this can happen.

 Students are often confused about the meaning of percents. Percents are fairly easy to understand if you remember that percent means *"out of 100"*. If you had 50 worms and were going to sell 20% of them, how many would you be selling? Since percent means "out of 100", you have to ask yourself the following question: How many worms would I be selling if I had 100 worms? Your answer of course would be 20% of 100 or 20 worms. Because you started with only 50 worms, 20% of 50 would be 10.

Before you can work with percents, you need to know how to change percents into decimals and fractions. You also need to be able to change fractions and decimals into percents.

Changing a Percent to a Decimal

To change a percent to a decimal, you need to move the decimal point **two** places to the **left,** and then take away the percent sign. For example: **50% becomes .50**

I can never remember which way to move the decimal point.

Just remember that if you want the % sign to disappear, you must move the decimal point to the **left**.

Change the following percents to decimals

1) 65%   4) 24%
2) 150%   5) 5%
3) 2%   6) 54.2%

Changing a Decimal
To a Percent

To change from a decimal to a percent, you move the decimal point **two** places to the **right** and then add the percent sign.

Change the following decimals to percents.

Think to yourself that if I want the percent sign to appear, I move the decimal point to the **right**.

1) .78
2) 1.15
3) .05
4) .23
5) .005
6) 5

Notice that even though there are no decimal points in numbers such as 8, the decimal is still there, it just isn't written. The same applies to 50%, the decimal isn't written, but it is still there. If you wanted to show the decimal point, 50% could be written as 50.%

Changing Fractions
to Percents

Changing fractions to percents is easy if you remember that the line in a fraction means divide.

$\frac{2}{5}$ means 2 divided by 5 ⟶ which equals .4

$$\frac{2}{5} = .4 = 40\%$$

Change the following fractions to percents:

1) $\frac{1}{2}$ 2) $\frac{4}{5}$ 3) $\frac{1}{10}$ 4) $\frac{3}{8}$ 5) $\frac{1}{20}$

6) $2\frac{1}{2}$ 7) $\frac{2}{3}$ 8) $\frac{1}{100}$ 9) $\frac{1}{40}$ 10) $3\frac{1}{5}$

Changing Percents to Fractions

Changing percents to fractions is easy if you remember that % means hundredths. 8% means 8 hundredths or 8/100. 28% means 28 hundredths, or 28/100.

Example: Change 5% and 30% to fractions.

$$5\% \longrightarrow \frac{5}{100} = \frac{1}{20} \qquad 30\% \longrightarrow \frac{30}{100} = \frac{3}{10}$$

Change the following percents into fractions. Reduce if you can.

1) 20%   4) 1%
2) 56%   5) 110%
3) 3%   6) 400%

Find the missing numbers

Percent	Decimal	Fraction
50%	.5	1/2
15%	___	___
___	.35	___
___	___	3/16
___	.05	___
6%	___	___
1/2%	___	___
___	2.5	___
480%	___	___
.0006%	___	___

Finding a Percent of a Number

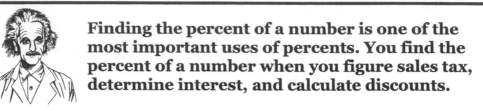

Finding the percent of a number is one of the most important uses of percents. You find the percent of a number when you figure sales tax, determine interest, and calculate discounts.

How do you find the percent of a number?

Finding the percent of a number is easy. All you do is change the percent to a decimal and then multiply.

Example 1: Find 45% of 900

Step 1 (Change the percent to a decimal.)   **.45**
Step 2 (Multiply the decimal by the number.) **.45 x 900 = 405**

Example 2: What is the sales tax on a $85 item in a state that charges 6% sales tax?

Step 1 ⟶   **6% changes to .06**
Step 2 ⟶   **.06 x 85 = 5.1**
Step 3 ⟶   **5.1   equals $5.10**

Example 3: Ben has a savings account in a bank that pays 3% interest. If Ben leaves $68 in his account for a year, how much interest will he earn?

Step 1 ⟶   **3% changes to .03**
Step 2 ⟶   **.03 x 68 = $2.04**

Try the following problems:

1) 50% of 84=   4) 150% of 46=
2) 35% of 80=   5) .5% of 200=
3) 5% of 300=

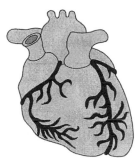

6) The survival rate of heart transplant patients in the first year is about 80%. If 400 people received heart transplants in January of 1990, how many would you expect to be alive in January 1991 ?

7) Tyler bought a bowling ball for $80. Sales tax is 7%. What is the total cost of the bowling ball?

8) A dress is on sale for 15% off. If the regular price is $60, what is the sale price?

9) If a company is offering raises of 24%, what would the new salary be for someone making $10,000?

10) Michelle put $84 in a savings account that paid 5% interest per year. How much money will she have at the end of one year?

Sometimes the Problem is Backward

Sometimes the problem is backward. Look at the following problem: Zach bought a new bike in a state with a sales tax of 6%. The amount of tax he paid was $2.70. How much did his bike cost?

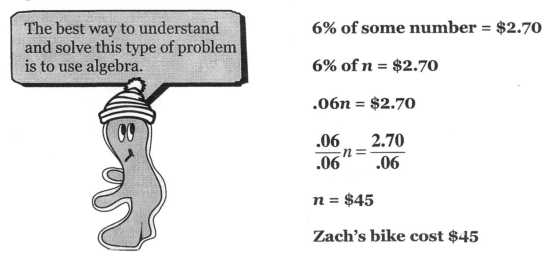

The best way to understand and solve this type of problem is to use algebra.

6% of some number = $2.70

6% of n = $2.70

$.06n = \$2.70$

$$\frac{.06}{.06}n = \frac{2.70}{.06}$$

$n = \$45$

Zach's bike cost $45

Try the following "backwards" problems:

1) 8 is 25% of what number?

2) 150 is 300% of what number?

3) 40% of some number equals 36. What is that number?

4) 85 is 5% of what number?

5) The sales tax in a state is 5%. If the sales tax for a certain item is $4.20, what is the cost of the item?

6) Approximately 30% of the earth's surface is land. There are about 57,250,000 square miles of land. What is the total surface area of earth?

Comparing Numbers using Percents

Comparing numbers using percents is easy if you remember two things:

(1)The line in a fraction means "compared to". Say you wanted to compare 20 to 400; all you need to do is make a fraction: $\dfrac{20}{400}$

(2) The line in a fraction also tells you to divide. 20 ÷ 400 = .05 = 5%.

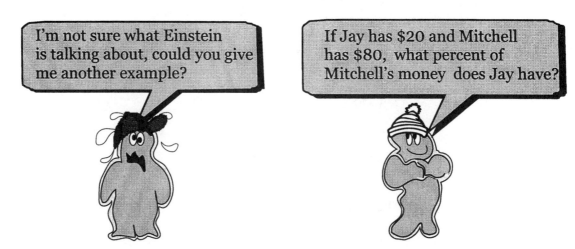

I'm not sure what Einstein is talking about, could you give me another example?

If Jay has $20 and Mitchell has $80, what percent of Mitchell's money does Jay have?

In this problem we are comparing Jay's money to Mitchell's money, or 20 to 80.

Step 1 ⟶ $\dfrac{20}{80}$

Step 2 ⟶ $20 \div 80 = .25$

Step 3 ⟶ $.25 = 25\%$

The amount of money Jay has is equal to 25% of Mitchell's money.

Another Example:

A 6th grade class is made up of 21 girls and 4 boys. Boys make up what percent of the class? Here we are not comparing boys to girls, we are comparing boys to the total class ⟶ 25 students.

Step 1 ⟶ $\dfrac{4}{25}$

Step 2 ⟶ $4 \div 25 = .16$

Step 3 ⟶ $.16 = 16\%$

Boys make up 16% of the class

Elephants, people, and hummingbirds have very different heart rates. An elephant's heart beats 25 times per minute while a hummingbird's heart beats 1000 times per minute. The average heart rate for a person is 72 beats per minute.

Compare the following heart rates using percents:
1) Elephant to hummingbird
2) Hummingbird to elephant
3) Elephant to human
4) Human to elephant
5) Hummingbird to human

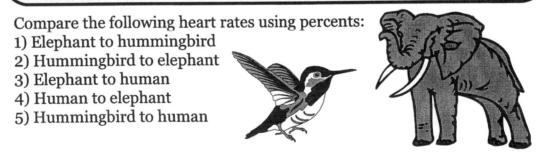

6) The amount of blood in your body depends on your size and the altitude at which you live. An adult who weighs 160 pounds has about 5 quarts of blood. A 160 lb. person who lives at high altitudes, where air contains less oxygen, may have 7 quarts of blood. The low altitude person has what percent of the blood volume of a person living at a high altitude?

7) What percent of 200 is 14?

8) What percent of a foot is a yard?

9) What percent of a yard is a foot?

10) If Carlos makes $480 a month and spends $120 a month for rent, what percent of his income does he spend on rent?

Percent of Increase or Decrease

To find the percent of increase or decrease, you start by making a fraction: $\dfrac{\textbf{Amount of increase or decrease}}{\textbf{Original}}$.

Could you give me an example? I'm not quite sure what this kind of percent is.

What if the price of a TV went from $250 in 1980 to $300 in 1990. What was the percent of increase?

Step 1 (Make a fraction) ⟶ $\dfrac{\$50}{\$250}$ $\dfrac{\text{(amount of increase)}}{\text{(original price)}}$

Step 2 (Divide) ⟶ **50 ÷ 250 = .2**
Step 3 (Change to percent) ⟶ **.2 = 20%**

The television went up by 20%

Remember that the top of the fraction is the *amount* of increase or decrease, not the new price. The most common mistake in this type of percent is to put the new price for the numerator of the fraction.

Find the percent of increase or decrease in problems 1-5.

1) 10 to 15_____ %
2) 80 to 120 _____ %
3) 80 to 88 _____ %
4) 120 to 78 _____ %
5) 200 to 40 _____ %

6) If a truck increased its load from 2000 pounds to 2500 pounds, by what percent did its load increase?

7) If Josh decreased his weight from 160 to 120 pounds, by what percent did his weight go down?

8) A newborn baby's heart weighs approximately 20 grams. An adult's heart weighs about 300 grams. As a baby grows to an adult, by what percent does his heart increase in weight?

9) Anna's allowance went from $5 to $6. What percent increase did she receive?

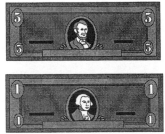

10) Claire's salary went from $20,000 to $30,000. What percent raise did she receive?

Percents
Level 1

1) Mark wanted to buy a new road bike that cost $120. Mark's dad told him that if he saved 20% of the money he needed, his dad would pay the rest. How much money does Mark need to save?

2) In a class of 40 children, there are 12 who have a dog, 15 who have a pet cat, and 13 children who have no pet. What percentage of the children in this class have a dog as a pet?

3) Mark's $120 bike cost only $80 two years ago. The price of $120 is what percent increase over the previous price of $80?

4) Kristin put $150 in a saving account that pays 5% annual interest (per year). At the end of one year, how much money would Kristin have in her savings account?

5) Emily gets an allowance of $8 per week. Her mom said that she is going to give her a raise of 10%. What is Emily's new allowance?

6) Michelle has $60. If her friend Kristin has $300, what percent of Kristin's money does Michelle have?

7) To pass a test, Kirsten had to get 75% of the answers correct. If there were 84 questions on the test, how many questions would Kirsten need to answer correctly to pass the test?

8) Thirty years ago, calculators sold for $200. Today they sell for $10. By what percent did they decrease in price?

9) The best bike in a small bike shop sells for $400. The cheapest bike sells for $50. The best bike's price is what percent of the price of the cheapest bike.

10) Carla has 22% of her paycheck taken for taxes. If the amount taken for taxes is $136.40, what is the amount of Carla's paycheck **before** taxes are taken out?

Percents
Level 2

1) 48,000 people voted in the last election in the town of Southboro. If only 55% of the registered voters voted in the last election, how many people are registered to vote?

2) 10% of the students in a school like the color purple. 162 students don't like the color purple. How many students are in the school?

3) Nik put $264 in a savings account that pays 3% annual interest. How much will he have in his account in 6 months?

4) Ellen has 40% of the amount of money Megan has. Megan has 80% of what Kristin has. Kristin has $200. How much money does Ellen have?

5) Maria wanted to buy a coat that regularly sells for $120. It is on sale for 35% off and the sales tax is 6%. What is the total cost of the coat?

6) Noah received a credit card on his 18th birthday that charges a 22.9% annual rate of interest. If he spent $3000 the day he received his credit card and never made any payments, how much money will he owe on his 38th birthday?

7) A car that cost $2000 in 1967 cost $15,000 today. What is the percent of increase for that car?

8) Daniel earns 32% of Luke's salary. If Daniel makes $12,000 per year, what is Luke's salary?

9) Zach went into store A and spent 40% of his money. He then spent 25% of his remaining money at store B. He then spent all but 20% of what was left. He ended up with $27 left over. How much money did Zach start with?

10) The largest bird ever to fly weighed approximately 150 pounds. A typical bird today might weigh 1/2 pound. The weight of a bird today is what percent of the weight of the Pterodactyl?

Einstein Level

1) A 5" x 7" picture is enlarged to 8" x 10". By what percent did it's area increase?

2) If Karen put $4000 in a bank that pays 4% annual interest, how much money will she have at the end of 4 years?

3) If Tim charges $4000 on a credit card that charges 22% interest, how much will he owe in 4 years?

4) A store is going out of business and having a sale where the price of all merchandise drops by a certain percentage every day. Their ad in the newspaper reads:

Sunday	Monday	Tuesday	Wednesday	Thursday	Friday	Saturday
Regular price	15% off Sunday's price	25% off Monday's price	35% off Tuesday's price	45% off Wednesday's price	55% off Thursday's price	75% off Friday's price

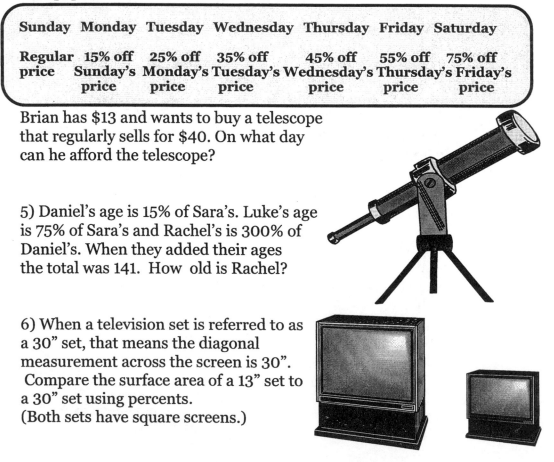

Brian has $13 and wants to buy a telescope that regularly sells for $40. On what day can he afford the telescope?

5) Daniel's age is 15% of Sara's. Luke's age is 75% of Sara's and Rachel's is 300% of Daniel's. When they added their ages the total was 141. How old is Rachel?

6) When a television set is referred to as a 30" set, that means the diagonal measurement across the screen is 30". Compare the surface area of a 13" set to a 30" set using percents. (Both sets have square screens.)

7) A cubic foot is what percent of a cubic yard?
A cubic inch is what percent of a cubic foot?

8) On Jessica's first day of work at a
hardware store, she charged the wrong
tax all day. She thought the sales tax rate
was 5% when it was really 6%. The total
amount of money Jessica collected was
$1202.25. How much money would
she have collected if she charged the
correct tax?

9) If the side of a square is doubled in size to 8", by what percent did its
area increase?

10) If the radius of a circle is cut in half, by what percent does the area of
the circle decrease?

Super Einstein Problem

Selena has a 1 meter cube box filled with 1 centimeter cubes. 2.7% of
these cubes are solid gold. Selena wants to build a cube that will hold
these gold cubes. What size cube does she need to build?

Ratio and Proportion

Brianna stepped from the school bus and slowly walked up the driveway to her home. From the back yard she heard the roar of her dad's chainsaw. He was just about to cut into the large dead elm tree that dominated the back yard when he spotted Brianna and shut off the saw. "How do you know the tree won't hit the house when you cut it down?" Brianna asked. "Well, its shadow isn't touching the house, so I think that means the tree won't hit the house when it falls," her dad replied.

Brianna had just finished studying ratios and proportions at school, so she knew how to determine the height of a tree by using its shadow. She was especially concerned about the tree hitting the house because her room was directly in the path of where the tree would fall. "Give me five minutes before you cut the tree," Brianna yelled to her dad as she ran into the house to get her tape measure.

Brianna knew she was 5 feet tall, and when she measured her shadow, she found it was 4.25 feet long. The distance from the base of the tree to her house was 72 feet, and the tree's shadow was 68 feet. Brianna set up two ratios and then did some calculations. When she was finished, the color drained from her face. She ran to the backyard just as her dad was about to start up the chainsaw again. "You can't cut the tree down, the top 8 feet of the tree will crash into my room!!!"

Ratio

A ratio compares two numbers. You can write a ratio in three different ways:

You can write a ratio as a fraction ⟶ 3/4

You can write a ratio with a colon ⟶ 3 : 4

You can write a ratio using the word "to" ⟶ 3 to 4

> I think I can compare the amount of money we each have by using a ratio. I have $50 and you have $100. Would the ratio be 50 to 100 or 50 : 100 or 50/100?

> Each of those says exactly the same thing. As a matter of fact, you could even call our money ratio 1/2 because ratios are like fractions and can be reduced.

The parents in a family with four children have decided to give their children an allowance equal to half their age. We can easily make a chart that will show ages and allowances for the four children in this family. If they adopt a ten year old child, what would her allowance be?

Age	3	5	7	16
Allowance	$1.50	$2.50	$3.50	$8.00

Let's see how to solve ratio problems that are a little more difficult.

> **A mother gives her 3 year old a $4 allowance, her 6 year old an $8 allowance, and her 9 year old a $12 allowance. This family also has a 4 year old child. What allowance should the 4 year old receive and still have the same ratio as the other children?**

The three children have $\dfrac{\text{age}}{\text{allowance}}$ ratios of: $\dfrac{3}{4}$ and $\dfrac{6}{8}$ and $\dfrac{9}{12}$.

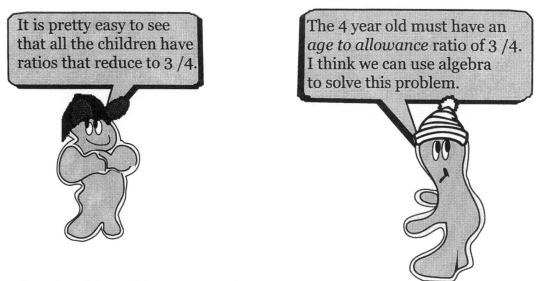

It is pretty easy to see that all the children have ratios that reduce to 3 /4.

The 4 year old must have an *age to allowance* ratio of 3 /4. I think we can use algebra to solve this problem.

To solve this problem, we need to set up an equation.

$$\frac{\text{age}}{\text{allowance}} = \frac{3}{4} \quad \text{so} \quad \frac{3}{4} = \frac{4 \,(\text{age of child})}{n \,(\text{allowance})}$$

Cross multiplying $3n = 16$ or $n = 5\dfrac{1}{3}$ or \$5.33

Let's look at another example: Some children are trying to find the height of a tree in their schoolyard. They know that a ten-foot stick casts a shadow of 8 feet. The tree has a shadow of 56 feet, how tall is the tree?

The ratio of the stick to its shadow is $\dfrac{10(\text{stick})}{8(\text{shadow})}$, so the ratio of the tree to its shadow must be $\dfrac{n(\text{tree})}{56(\text{shadow})}$.

$\dfrac{10}{8} = \dfrac{n}{56}$ or $8n = 560$ $n = 70$ The tree is 70 feet tall.

Ratio and Scale

The last type of ratio problem we will look at is scale. Scales are used to show the relationship between things such as maps and real distances.

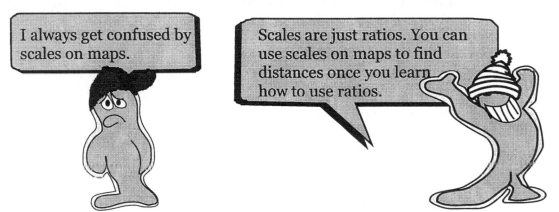

A map has a scale of 1.5 inches : 8 miles. This means that every 1.5 inches on the map stands for 8 miles in real distance. For example: If two towns are 3 inches apart on the map, how far apart are they in real distance? It's pretty easy to see that they would be 16 miles apart.

1) $\dfrac{3}{5} = \dfrac{n}{40}$ $n=$

2) $\dfrac{3}{8} = \dfrac{n}{30}$ $n=$

3) $\dfrac{5}{9} = \dfrac{12}{n}$ $n=$

4) $\dfrac{9}{9.1} = \dfrac{n}{14.8}$ $n=$

5) $\dfrac{25}{6} = \dfrac{n}{93}$ $n=$

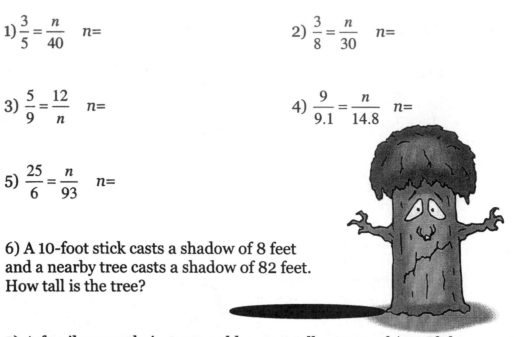

6) A 10-foot stick casts a shadow of 8 feet and a nearby tree casts a shadow of 82 feet. How tall is the tree?

7) A family pays their 9 year old son an allowance of $5. If they want to keep the same age to allowance ratio, what allowance should they give their 8 year old son?

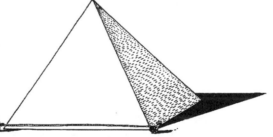

8) A model of an Egyptian pyramid has a scale of 1.2 " : 38 feet. If the height of the model is 3", what is the height of the real pyramid?

9) Kristin is trying to guess Dan's height. He gave Kristin one clue: The ratio of my height to my fathers height is 5 to 6 and my father is 68" tall. How tall is Dan?

10) Ellen is going to drive from New York City to Los Angeles. She looks at a map and finds the two cities are 6.5 " apart. If the scale on the map is 1" = 460 miles, how many miles will Ellen's trip be?

Proportion

This problem can easily be solved if you look at the 3:2 ratio and notice that there are 5 parts to the drink. (3 parts soda and 2 parts milk) Since the special mixture has 5 parts, we must make 5 parts out of the 8-cup container. To do this we must divide 8 by 5. 8 ÷ 5 = 1.6

Now we know that each part is equal to 1.6 cups. So the amount of soda is equal to 3 x 1.6 or 4.8 cups. The amount of milk is equal to 2 x 1.6 or 3.2 cups.

Let's look at another problem:

> **A statue is made up of copper and nickel. The ratio of their weights is 5 : 7. If the statue weighs 1,344 pounds, how many pounds of copper are in the statue?**

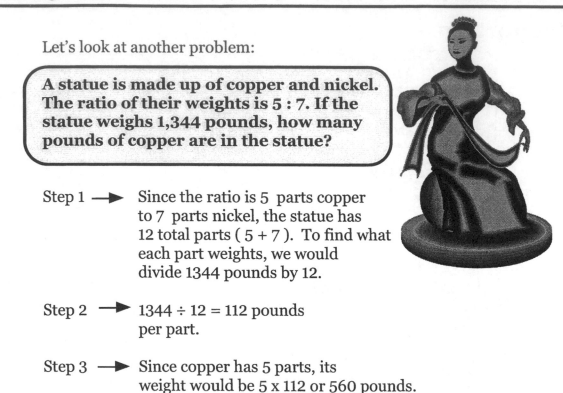

Step 1 ➞ Since the ratio is 5 parts copper to 7 parts nickel, the statue has 12 total parts (5 + 7). To find what each part weights, we would divide 1344 pounds by 12.

Step 2 ➞ 1344 ÷ 12 = 112 pounds per part.

Step 3 ➞ Since copper has 5 parts, its weight would be 5 x 112 or 560 pounds.

Let's look at a slightly more difficult problem:

> **A statue is made of gold and silver. The ratio of the weights of the metals is 3 to 16 (gold to silver). If the weight of the gold is 570 pounds, what is the weight of the statue?**

Step 1 ➞ Since there are three parts gold, each part would equal 570 ÷ 3 or 190 pounds.

Step 2 ➞ We know there are 19 parts to the statue (3 + 16), so the weight of the statue would be the weight of each part, 190 pounds, times the number of parts, which is 19.

Step 3 ➞ 190 x 19 = 3610 pounds

1) Jody has a favorite drink she makes that is 3 parts lemonade and 5 parts cranberry juice. If she is making the drink for a party and wants to fill a 60 cup bowl, how much lemonade would she put in the bowl?

2) A statue is made up of iron and nickel in a ratio of 2:7. If the statue weighs 81 pounds, what is the weight of the nickel in the statue?

3) A box is filled with pennies, nickels, and dimes in a ratio of 2:3:4. If the total number of coins in the box is 1620, how many pennies are in the box?

4) A strange bowling ball is made up of plastic and wood. The weights of the two materials are in a ratio of 5 to 9 (plastic to wood). If the bowling ball weighs 238 ounces, what is the weight of the plastic?

5) A trophy is made up of copper and nickel. The ratio of their weights is 6:11. If the amount of copper in the trophy is 48 pounds, how much does the trophy weigh?

Ratio and Proportion
Level 1

1) Mark, who is 5 feet tall, told his dad that he could tell his dad's height just by measuring his dad's shadow. Mark knew that his own shadow was 8 feet and his dad's shadow measured 10 feet. How tall is his dad?

2) If a person walks 32 feet in 10 seconds, how far will he go in 72 seconds?

3) If there are 65 boys in a classroom and the ratio of boys to girls is 13:15, how many students are in the class?

4) The population of the United States is 280 million. If 2 out of 3 Americans know who the vice-president is, how many Americans know who the vice-president is?

5) The perimeter of the triangle is 40 inches. If you wanted to construct a similar triangle with a perimeter of 50 inches, what would be the length of the shortest side of the triangle?

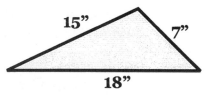

6) A star football player has written into his contract that the ratio of his salary to the next highest paid player in the league will be 4:3. If the next highest player makes $3,900,000, how much is the star player's salary?

7) A statue is made of a mixture of copper and zinc in a ratio of 11:4 (copper to zinc). If the weight of the statue is 3165 pounds, what is the weight of the copper?

8) A famous baseball player has a home run/strike out ratio of 2:13. This means that for every two home runs he hits, he strikes out 13 times. How many home runs would he hit in a season in which he strikes out 234 times?

9) The scale on a map is 1 cm = 14.7 miles. Jessie wanted to ride his bike for 100 miles, how many centimeters would 100 miles be on the map? (Round to the nearest tenth.)

10) Lindsey wanted to find out how tall a tree was at her school. Lindsey knew that she is 5 feet tall and at 3:00 her shadow is 6 feet. The tree's shadow at 3:00 is 38 feet. How tall is the tree?

Ratio and Proportion
Level 2

1) Statistics tell us that 85 out of 100 lung cancer victims are smokers. If there are 3150 lung cancer patients in a particular state who are not smokers, how many lung cancer patients who are smokers are there in that state?

2) The scale of a map is 1/8 inch = 260 miles. How far apart are two cities that are 1 1/16 inches apart on the map?

3) The largest carnivore that lives on land is the Alaskan brown bear. It can weigh 1500 pounds. A newborn Alaskan brown bear cub weighs about 1 pound. A typical person weighs 150 pounds and human newborns weigh about 7 pounds. If human babies were proportionally the same as Alaskan brown bear cubs are to their mothers, how much would a newborn weigh?

4) A flea 1/16 of an inch tall can jump 9 3/8 inches high. If a person 6 feet tall had the ability to jump like a flea, how high could he jump?

5) The scale on a globe is 1/8 inch equals 125 miles. How many inches is the circumference of that globe? (Use 25,000 miles for the circumference of the earth.)

6) In a particular year the fatality rate for airline travel is 1 fatality per 200 million miles and the rate for auto travel is 1 fatality per 50 million miles. Is a vacationer more likely to be killed on a trip to Chicago by car (200 miles), or on a trip by plane to London, England (3200 miles)? Why?

7) If driving a car under the influence of alcohol quadruples the fatality rate, how would this affect his chances if the vacationer in the previous problem drives to Chicago while under the influence of alcohol?

8) Nancy has a tree in her yard that is 83 feet from her house. She is trying to find out if the tree will hit her house in the event it blows down in a storm. Nancy is 5' 2" and casts a shadow of 2' 11". At the same time the tree casts a shadow of 52.5'. How tall is the tree?

9) Diane is making a large batch of soap. The recipe is as follows:

> 200 pounds of lye
> 25 pounds of fragrance
> 125 pounds of olive oil
> 287.5 pounds of coconut oil

Diane has to reduce the recipe because she only has 138 pounds of lye. What should she reduce the coconut oil to?

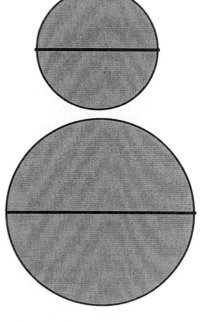

10) Compare the ratio of circumference to diameter for a circle with a circumference of 81.64?

$$\frac{\textbf{circumference}}{\textbf{diameter}} = \underline{\hspace{2cm}}$$

What is the ratio of circumference to diameter for a circle with a circumference of 276.32?

$$\frac{\textbf{circumference}}{\textbf{diameter}} = \underline{\hspace{2cm}}$$

What can you say about the ratio of circumference to diameter in all circles?

Einstein Level

1) Mark's family bought 4 pounds of ice cream (64 ounces). Mark suggested that the fair way to split it was to give people their share based on their weights. If Mark weighs 80 pounds and there are three other people in his family who weigh 120, 150, and 162 pounds, how many ounces of ice cream should Mark get?

2) The ratio of the area of a circle to the area of a square that fits perfectly around that circle is 78.5 : 100. What is the ratio of the area of a circle to the area of a square that fits perfectly inside the circle?

3) A glass container is 3/4 full with blue and red dye that are in a ratio of 7 : 8 (blue to red). If enough blue dye is then poured into the container to fill it, what is the new ratio of blue to red dye?

4) A glass container is 3/4 full with blue dye and red dye that are in a ratio of 5 : 3 (blue to red). Green dye is poured in until the container is full. What is the ratio of blue to red to green dye?

5) If the container is now (after thorough mixing) half emptied and then filled again with only red dye, what is the ratio of blue to red to green dye?

6) There are three times as many cars as trucks in a parking lot. The number of motorcycles is twice the number of bikes and there are four times as many trucks as bikes. If the total number of vehicles is 285, how many cars are there?

7) Meagan needs to find out how tall a tree is in her yard. She doesn't know how tall she is, but she knows her shadow is 10' 7 1/2". She also knows that she is 5" shorter than Mark, and his shadow is 11' 8". If the tree's shadow is 110', how tall is the tree?

8) If a statue is made of copper, brass, gold, and nickel in a ratio of 6:8:1:4, what is the weight of the gold if the total weight of the statue is 10,679 pounds and 3 ounces?

9) The ratio of cats to dogs is 2:1 and the ratio of dogs to parrots is 15:2. In addition, the ratio of parrots to snakes is 3:1 and the ratio of snakes to turtles is 6:7. What is the ratio of cats to turtles?

10) A bathtub is filled with 100 gallons of water. A cup of milk is then poured in and mixed thoroughly with the 100 gallons of water. A cup of liquid is then taken out and placed in a bowl. What **fraction** of the liquid in the bowl is milk? What is the ratio of milk to water?

Trigonometry

(Greek for "to measure a triangle")

Trigonometry is one of the most interesting areas of mathematics. The problems that can be solved when one uses trigonometry are so amazing that it seems like magic instead of mathematics.

Suppose you were on a 200-foot cliff that overlooks the ocean. As you scan the horizon, you spot a ship sailing toward you. Trigonometry would give you the ability to find the exact distance the ship is from shore.

An interesting use of trigonometry occurred approximately 2000 years ago when a Greek mathematician used trigonometry to find the distance between the moon and the earth. Before this was done, people thought that the moon, sun, and stars were a short distance overhead. Trigonometry showed them the truth.

During that same time period, a famous Greek mathematician named Heron was able to use trigonometry to aid in the digging of tunnels. Imagine how difficult it would be to start digging on opposite ends of a mountain and then trying to meet in the middle. How could the workers on each end of the mountain possibly know which direction to dig so that they would meet in the middle? If they used trigonometry, they could meet exactly in the middle!!

What is trigonometry and how can we use it?

Do you remember when we studied the Pythagorean Theorem? We learned that if we know the measurements of two sides of a right triangle, we could easily find the third side. I think Trigonometry has to do with this type of triangle. I think we should ask Einstein.

Trigonometry does involve finding the unknown measurements of triangles. But unlike the Pythagorean Theorem, trigonometry allows us to find the length of any side of a right triangle as long as we know the length of one side of the right triangle and one of the acute angle measurements.

Why is that such a big deal?

Trigonometry allows us to do all kinds of things. We can use trigonometry to find the height of buildings, the distance to the moon, the distance ships are from shore, and even the correct direction two work crews need to dig, on opposite sides of a mountain, so they will meet in the middle. The problems that you can solve using trigonometry are so amazing that it seems like magic instead of mathematics.

Let's look at an example to see how trigonometry works.

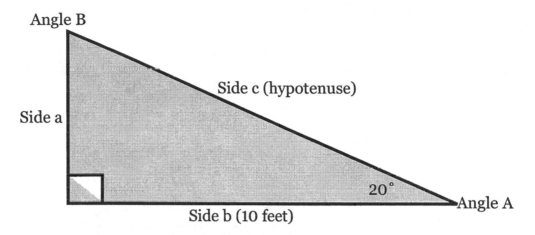

Look at the triangle. Angle A is 20° and the base is 10 feet. Since we know the measurement of one acute angle and the length of one side, we can find the other angle and we can also find the lengths of the other 2 sides.

Angle B = 70°
Side a = 3.64 feet
Side c = 10.64 feet

Before you learn trigonometry, you will need to know three special definitions:

1) The leg of the triangle across from an angle is named for the angle. It is also said to be the opposite side. You can see that side a is across from angle A and that side b is across from angle B.

Side **a** is the side opposite of angle A

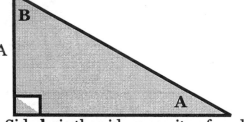

Side **b** is the side opposite of angle B

2) The leg of the triangle next to the angle is called the adjacent side. (Adjacent means next to.) The hypotenuse is never an adjacent side.

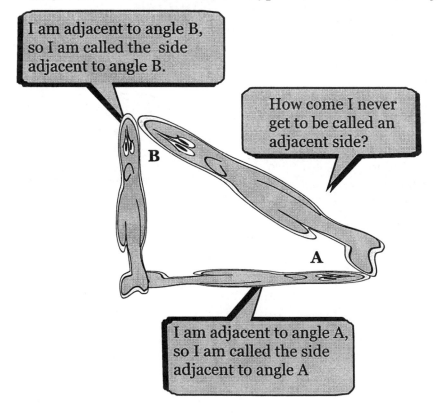

I am adjacent to angle B, so I am called the side adjacent to angle B.

How come I never get to be called an adjacent side?

I am adjacent to angle A, so I am called the side adjacent to angle A

3) The longest side of a triangle is called side c, or the hypotenuse.

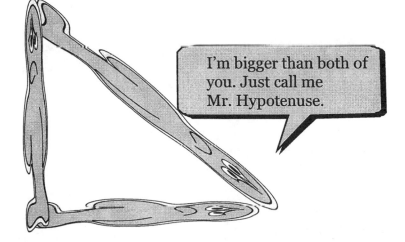

I'm bigger than both of you. Just call me Mr. Hypotenuse.

To be able to do trigonometry, you must learn and remember three definitions.
1) The side across from angle A is called side a and is said to be the side opposite of angle A. The side across from angle B is called side b and is said to be the side opposite of angle B.
2) The side next to angle A is referred to as the side adjacent to angle A. The side next to angle B is referred to as the side adjacent to angle B.
3) The longest side of a right triangle is called side c, or the hypotenuse.

Now you are ready for the first part of trigonometry.

I'm so excited!!

Look at the triangles on the next page. As you can see, angle A is equal to 45° in all three triangles. If you look carefully, you'll notice something very interesting about all three triangles. Even though their sizes are very different, the ratio of $\dfrac{\text{opposite side}}{\text{adjacent side}}$ is the same in all three triangles and is equal to 1/1 or 1.

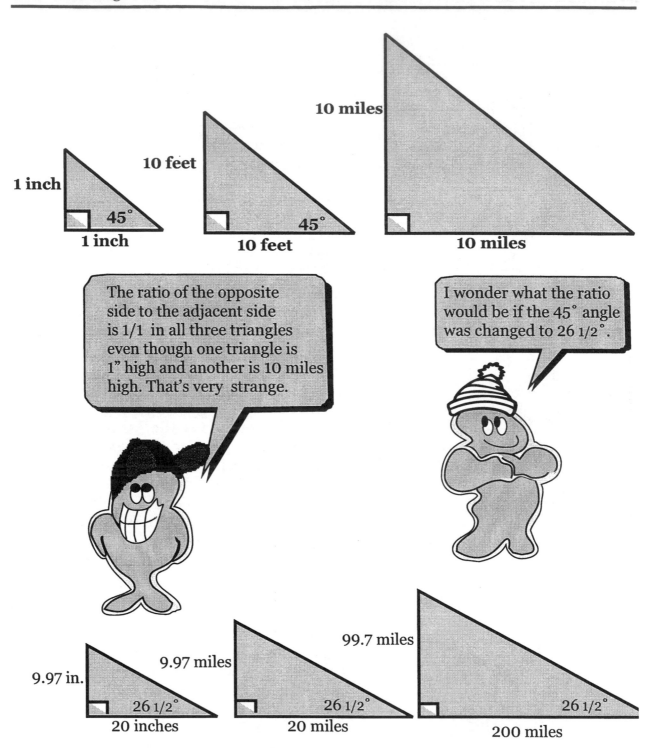

As before, angle A is the same for all three triangles. Something very interesting also happens with these triangles. The ratio of opposite side to adjacent side is again the same for all three triangles, but is equal to a ratio that is very close to 1/2.

These two examples illustrate a basic rule of similar right triangles. If the angles are the same, then the ratios of the opposite side to the adjacent side are the same, no matter how large the triangles are. It doesn't matter if the triangles are 1" high or a million miles high ——► If the angles are the same, then the ratios of opposite side to adjacent side will always be the same.

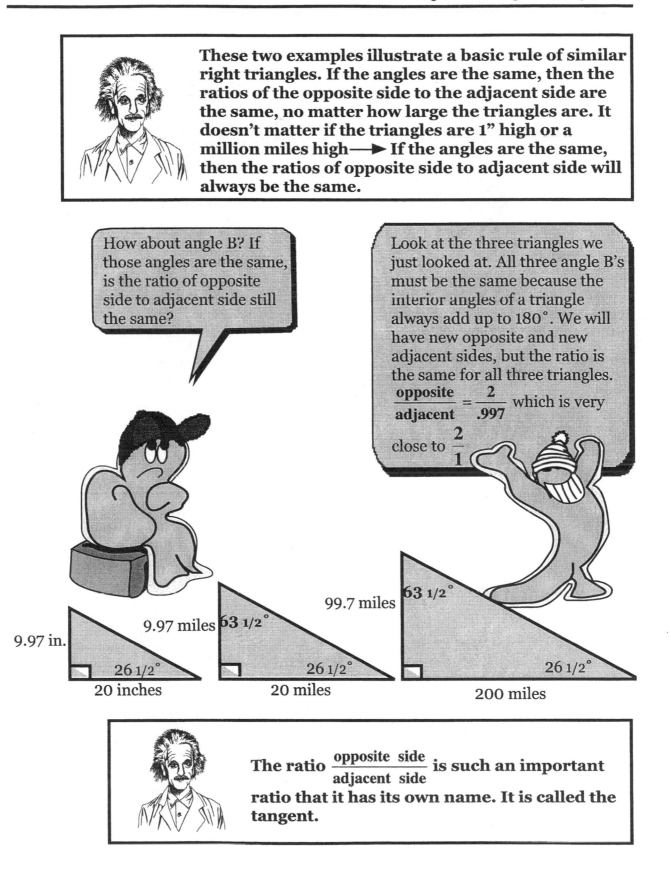

How about angle B? If those angles are the same, is the ratio of opposite side to adjacent side still the same?

Look at the three triangles we just looked at. All three angle B's must be the same because the interior angles of a triangle always add up to 180°. We will have new opposite and new adjacent sides, but the ratio is the same for all three triangles. $\dfrac{\text{opposite}}{\text{adjacent}} = \dfrac{2}{.997}$ which is very close to $\dfrac{2}{1}$

9.97 in.

9.97 miles 63 1/2°

99.7 miles

63 1/2°

26 1/2°
20 inches

26 1/2°
20 miles

26 1/2°
200 miles

The ratio $\dfrac{\text{opposite side}}{\text{adjacent side}}$ is such an important ratio that it has its own name. It is called the tangent.

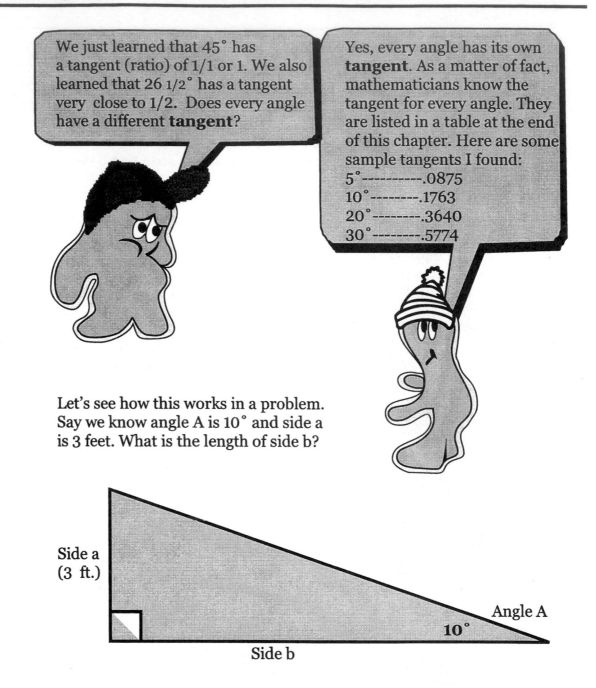

We just learned that 45° has a tangent (ratio) of 1/1 or 1. We also learned that 26 1/2° has a tangent very close to 1/2. Does every angle have a different **tangent**?

Yes, every angle has its own **tangent**. As a matter of fact, mathematicians know the tangent for every angle. They are listed in a table at the end of this chapter. Here are some sample tangents I found:
5°-----------.0875
10°--------.1763
20°--------.3640
30°--------.5774

Let's see how this works in a problem. Say we know angle A is 10° and side a is 3 feet. What is the length of side b?

We know from the chart that the tangent of 10° is equal to .1763, so the ratio of $\dfrac{\textbf{opposite side}}{\textbf{adjacent side}}$ or $\dfrac{\textbf{side a}}{\textbf{side b}}$ must equal .1763. Remember that a ratio compares two numbers. When you have a ratio written as a decimal, you are comparing the decimal to the number 1. So .1763 is actually written as $\dfrac{.1763}{1}$.

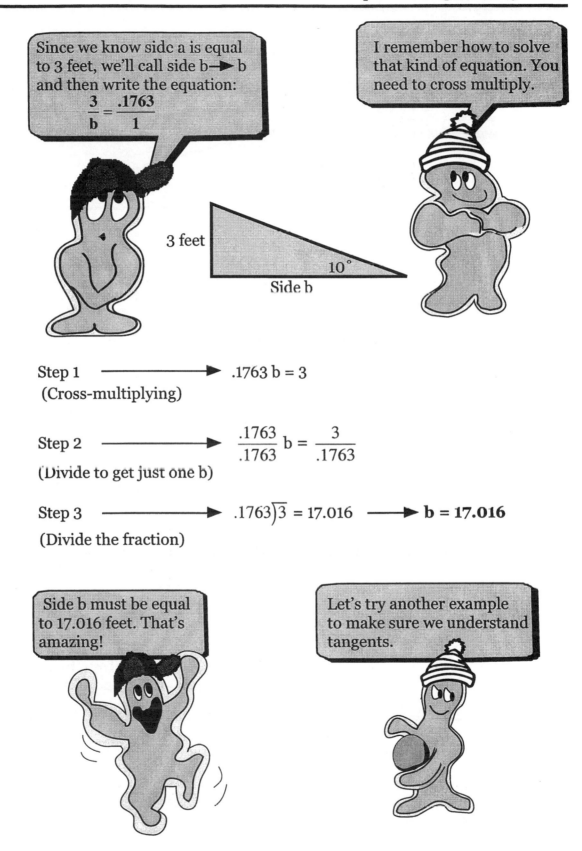

Since we know side a is equal to 3 feet, we'll call side b ➤ b and then write the equation:
$$\frac{3}{b} = \frac{.1763}{1}$$

I remember how to solve that kind of equation. You need to cross multiply.

3 feet

10°

Side b

Step 1 ⟶ .1763 b = 3
(Cross-multiplying)

Step 2 ⟶ $\frac{.1763}{.1763} b = \frac{3}{.1763}$
(Divide to get just one b)

Step 3 ⟶ .1763$\overline{)3}$ = 17.016 ⟶ **b = 17.016**
(Divide the fraction)

Side b must be equal to 17.016 feet. That's amazing!

Let's try another example to make sure we understand tangents.

Angle A is 30° and the length of side b is 8 feet. What is the length of side a?

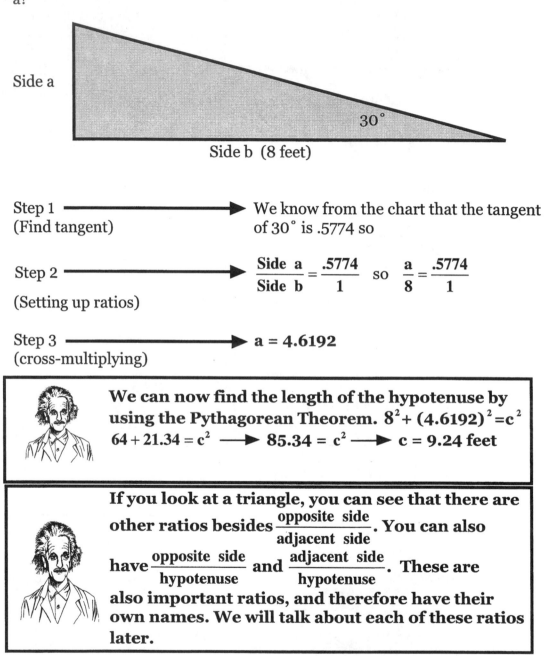

Step 1 ————————————➤ We know from the chart that the tangent
(Find tangent)   of 30° is .5774 so

Step 2 ————————————➤ $\dfrac{\text{Side a}}{\text{Side b}} = \dfrac{.5774}{1}$ so $\dfrac{a}{8} = \dfrac{.5774}{1}$
(Setting up ratios)

Step 3 ————————————➤ **a = 4.6192**
(cross-multiplying)

> **We can now find the length of the hypotenuse by using the Pythagorean Theorem.** $8^2 + (4.6192)^2 = c^2$
> $64 + 21.34 = c^2$ ——➤ $85.34 = c^2$ ——➤ **c = 9.24 feet**

> **If you look at a triangle, you can see that there are other ratios besides $\dfrac{\text{opposite side}}{\text{adjacent side}}$. You can also have $\dfrac{\text{opposite side}}{\text{hypotenuse}}$ and $\dfrac{\text{adjacent side}}{\text{hypotenuse}}$. These are also important ratios, and therefore have their own names. We will talk about each of these ratios later.**

Remember that the tangent of an angle is the ratio of $\dfrac{\text{opposite side}}{\text{adjacent side}}$. The tangents for every angle are found in the trigonometry table at the end of the chapter. Use the table and your knowledge of tangents to find the missing sides or angles in the following problems. The first two are done for you.

Tangents: Find the missing sides or angles. The first two are done for you.

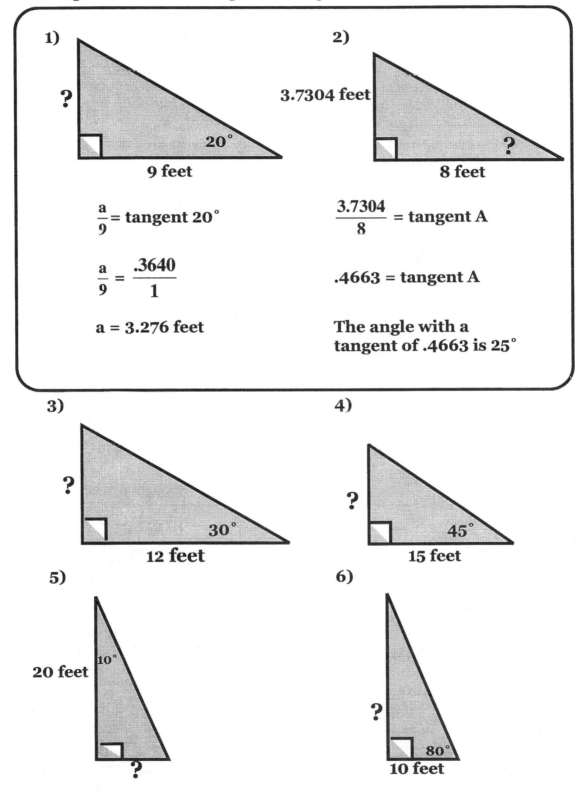

1)

?

20°

9 feet

$$\frac{a}{9} = \text{tangent } 20°$$

$$\frac{a}{9} = \frac{.3640}{1}$$

$$a = 3.276 \text{ feet}$$

2)

3.7304 feet

?

8 feet

$$\frac{3.7304}{8} = \text{tangent } A$$

$$.4663 = \text{tangent } A$$

The angle with a tangent of .4663 is 25°

3)

?

30°

12 feet

4)

?

45°

15 feet

5)

20 feet

10°

?

6)

?

80°

10 feet

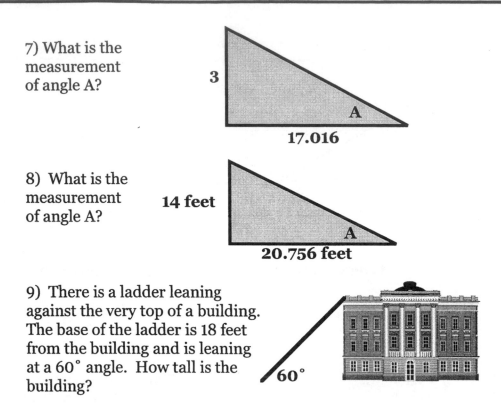

7) What is the measurement of angle A?

3

17.016

8) What is the measurement of angle A?

14 feet

20.756 feet

9) There is a ladder leaning against the very top of a building. The base of the ladder is 18 feet from the building and is leaning at a 60° angle. How tall is the building?

60°

10) A carpenter needs to build a ramp to make a school accessible to the handicapped. The doorway is 6 feet off the ground and the ramp must be at a 6° angle to allow for easy use. How far from the doorway should the carpenter start the ramp?

11) A ship's captain needs to find out how far she is from shore. She knows a certain lighthouse is 150 feet high and the angle of sight when she looks at the top of the lighthouse from her ship is 14 degrees. Approximately how far away is the captain from shore?

Sine

We have talked about the ratio of opposite side to adjacent side of an angle ——▶ Which is called the **tangent** of the angle. There are other important ratios that we use in trigonometry. One is the ratio of $\frac{\textbf{opposite side}}{\textbf{hypotenuse}}$. Because this ratio is very important, it also has its own name. This ratio is called the **sine** of an angle.

Just like tangents, every angle has its own **sine** ratio. For example:
1° has a sine of .0175
10° has a sine of .1736
20° has a sine of .3420
35° has a sine of .5736

Let's see how this works in a problem. Say we know that angle A is 10° and side c is 500 feet. What is the length of side a?

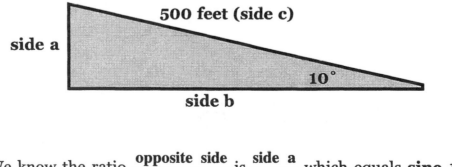

We know the ratio $\frac{\textbf{opposite side}}{\textbf{hypotenuse}}$ is $\frac{\textbf{side a}}{\textbf{side c}}$ which equals **sine 10°**.

That seems pretty easy. We could look up the the sine of 10° and then write the equation:

$$\frac{a}{500} = \frac{.1736}{1}$$

That's easy to solve by cross-multiplying. a = 86.8

Let's try a little more difficult example. Say angle A is 1° and the length of side a is 10,000 feet. What is the length of side c?

I always draw a picture to help me visualize the problem.

$$\frac{\text{Side a}}{\text{Side c}} = \text{sine } 1° \quad \text{or} \quad \frac{10,000}{c} = \frac{.0175}{1}$$

$$.0175 \, c = 10,000 \quad \text{or} \quad c = 571,428.57 \text{ ft.}$$

(Rounding, c = 571,429 feet)

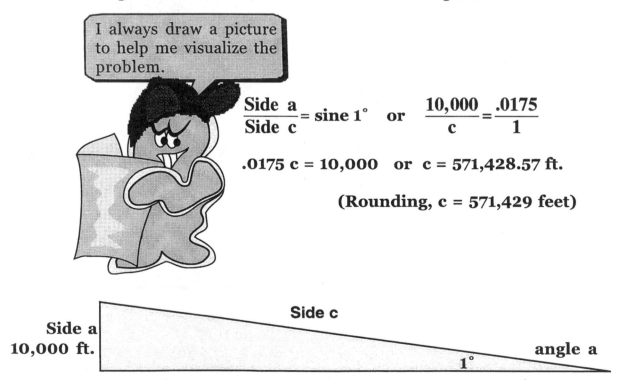

Side a 10,000 ft. | Side c | angle a | 1°

Side c is 571,428.57 feet. I guess we can use trigonometry even when we are working with huge numbers. I really like trigonometry!!

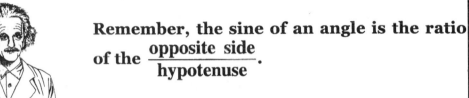

Remember, the sine of an angle is the ratio of the $\dfrac{\text{opposite side}}{\text{hypotenuse}}$.

The sines for every angle are found in the trigonometry table at the end of the chapter. Use the table and your knowledge of sines to find the missing sides or angles. The first two problems are done for you.

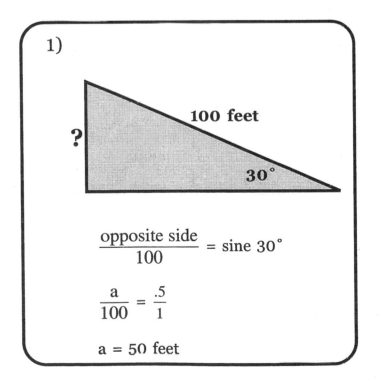

1)

100 feet

?

30°

$$\frac{\text{opposite side}}{100} = \text{sine } 30°$$

$$\frac{a}{100} = \frac{.5}{1}$$

a = 50 feet

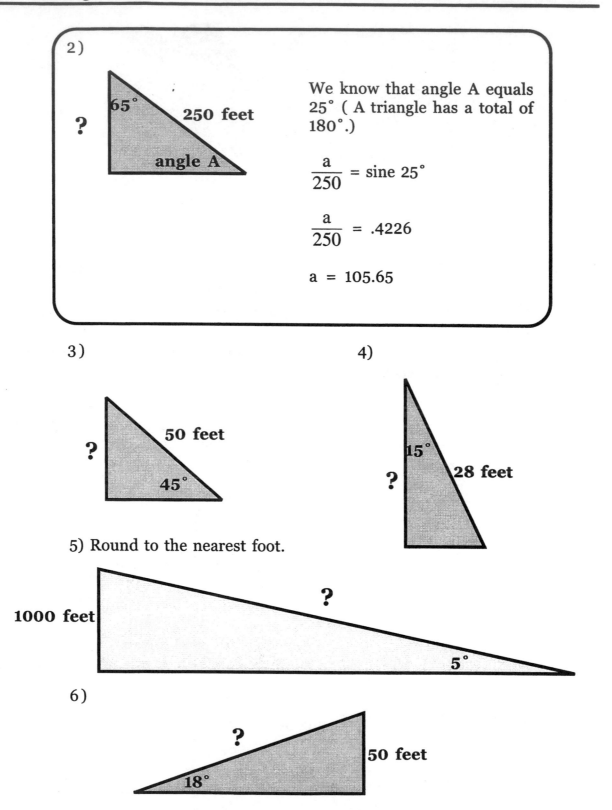

2)

65°

?

250 feet

angle A

We know that angle A equals 25° (A triangle has a total of 180°.)

$$\frac{a}{250} = \text{sine } 25°$$

$$\frac{a}{250} = .4226$$

$$a = 105.65$$

3)

?

50 feet

45°

4)

15°

?

28 feet

5) Round to the nearest foot.

1000 feet

?

5°

6)

?

50 feet

18°

7) The height of an Isosceles triangle is 25 feet. The angle at the top of the triangle is 40°. What is the length of each leg of the triangle?

40°

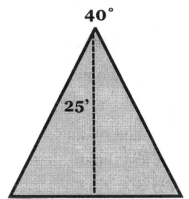

25'

8) What is the length of the base of this triangle?

9) An 80 foot ladder must be set at a 65° angle when it is leaned against a building. What is the maximum building height that this ladder will reach?

10) A large truck is not permitted to travel on any streets with an incline of more than 6°. Route 95 is a straight road that starts at the ocean and continues uphill for 4.5 miles until it reaches an elevation of 1800 feet above sea level. Would this truck be allowed to travel on Route 95?

11) An airplane's altimeter reads 8000 feet. If its angle of flight with the ground is 5°, how many miles will the plane need to travel before it reaches the ground? (Round to the nearest tenth of a mile.)

Cosine

We have talked about the tangent of an angle, which is the ratio of **opposite side / adjacent side**.

We have also learned that the sine of an angle is the ratio of the **opposite side / hypotenuse**.

I wonder if there are any other ratios.

The last ratio we are going to talk about is the ratio of the **adjacent side / hypotenuse**. This ratio is also very important and has its own name. It is called the **cosine.**

Just like the tangent and the sine, each different angle has its own **cosine** value. For example:

1°.................has a cosine of .9998
15°..............has a cosine of .9659
25°..............has a cosine of .9063
50°..............has a cosine of .6428

It looks like cosines are just like tangents and sines. The only difference appears to be that the ratio is the adjacent side of the angle over the hypotenuse. Since I already know tangents and sines, this is going to be easy.

Let's see how cosines work in problems. Look at the triangle below. If angle A is 25° and the hypotenuse is 48 feet, what is the length of side b?

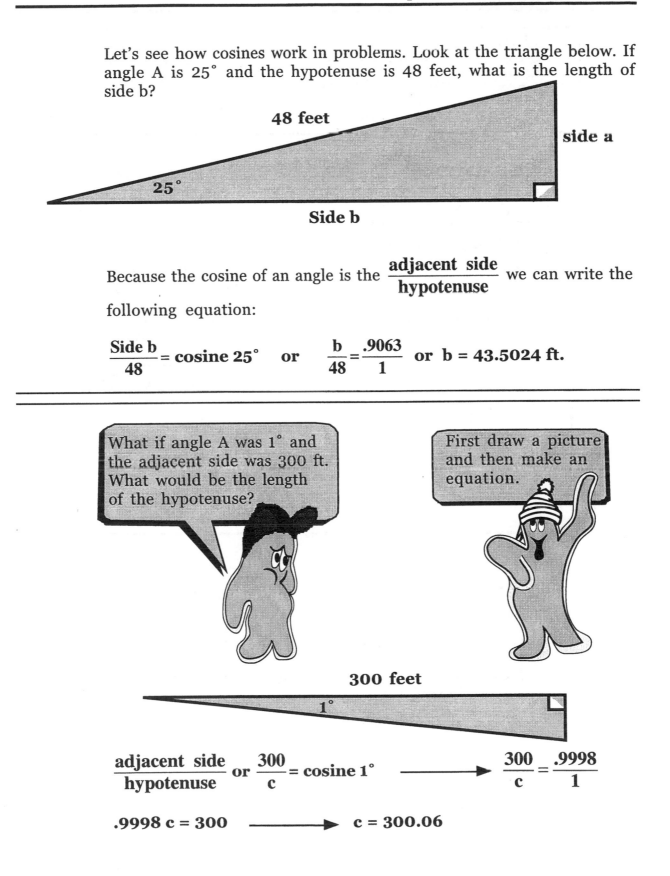

Because the cosine of an angle is the $\dfrac{\textbf{adjacent side}}{\textbf{hypotenuse}}$ we can write the following equation:

$$\frac{\textbf{Side b}}{\textbf{48}} = \textbf{cosine } 25° \quad \textbf{or} \quad \frac{\textbf{b}}{\textbf{48}} = \frac{\textbf{.9063}}{\textbf{1}} \quad \textbf{or } \textbf{b} = \textbf{43.5024 ft.}$$

What if angle A was 1° and the adjacent side was 300 ft. What would be the length of the hypotenuse?

First draw a picture and then make an equation.

300 feet

1°

$$\frac{\textbf{adjacent side}}{\textbf{hypotenuse}} \quad \textbf{or} \quad \frac{\textbf{300}}{\textbf{c}} = \textbf{cosine } 1° \quad \longrightarrow \quad \frac{\textbf{300}}{\textbf{c}} = \frac{\textbf{.9998}}{\textbf{1}}$$

$$\textbf{.9998 c} = \textbf{300} \quad \longrightarrow \quad \textbf{c} = \textbf{300.06}$$

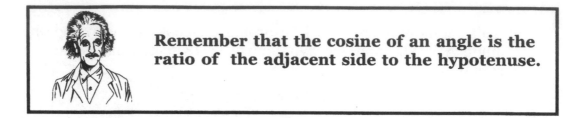

Remember that the cosine of an angle is the ratio of the adjacent side to the hypotenuse.

The cosines for every angle are found in the trigonometry table at the end of the chapter. Use that table and your knowledge of cosines to find the missing sides or angles. The first two are done for you.

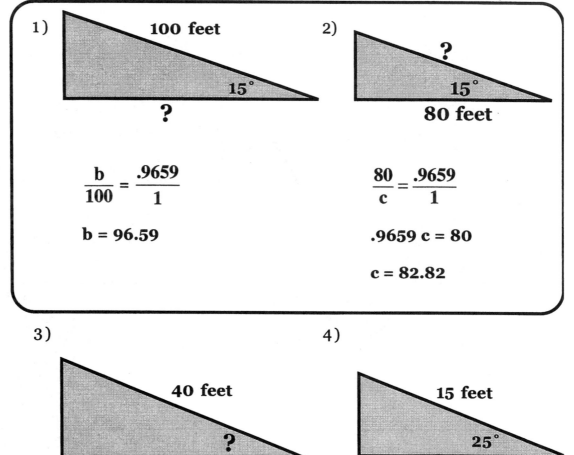

1)

100 feet

15°

?

$$\frac{b}{100} = \frac{.9659}{1}$$

$$b = 96.59$$

2)

?

15°

80 feet

$$\frac{80}{c} = \frac{.9659}{1}$$

$$.9659\ c = 80$$

$$c = 82.82$$

3)

40 feet

?

36.252 feet

4)

15 feet

25°

?

5)

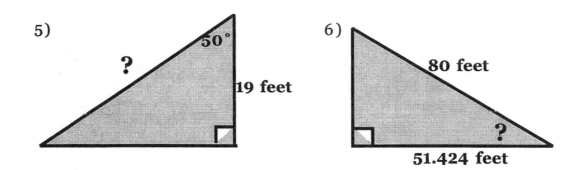

6)

7) An equilateral triangle has a height of 18.186 feet. What is the length of each side?

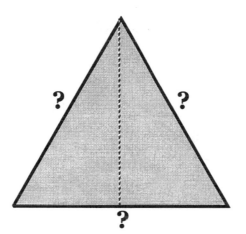

8) A 150 foot ladder is going to lean against a 200 foot building. For safety reasons, it must lean at a 65° angle. How far out from the base of the building should the ladder be set?

9) A carpenter is planning to build a house in a part of the country where the snowfall is very heavy. He wants to make sure that the angle of his roof is steep enough so the snow will slide off. He has determined that the angle of pitch must be at least 40° or his roof will collect too much snow and probably collapse. Look at the plan for his roof below. Is the angle of pitch 40° or steeper? What is the approximate pitch of his roof?

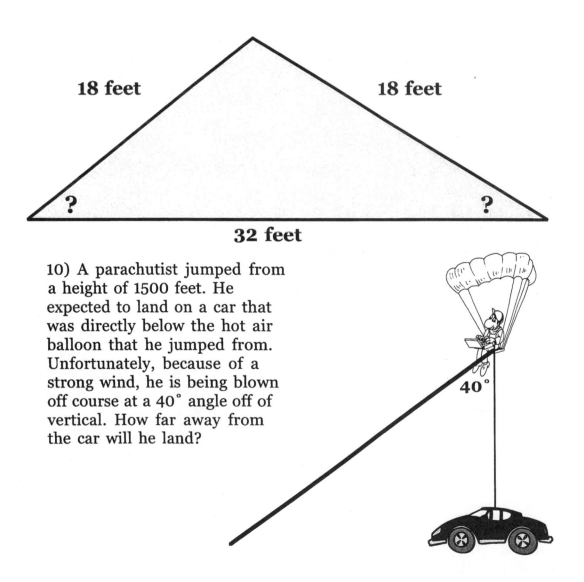

18 feet   **18 feet**

?   **?**

32 feet

10) A parachutist jumped from a height of 1500 feet. He expected to land on a car that was directly below the hot air balloon that he jumped from. Unfortunately, because of a strong wind, he is being blown off course at a 40° angle off of vertical. How far away from the car will he land?

40°

Einstein Level

1) A fire department needs to order a ladder that will reach to the top of the tallest building in the community, a 180-foot hotel. For safety reasons, the angle to the ground must be 65°. What is the shortest ladder the fire department can order and still reach the top of the building? (Round to the nearest foot.)

2) A plane is flying across the water dragging a 1-mile long wire that has a weight attached to it. The wire is deflected back at a 22° angle and the weight is skimming the top of the water. How high is the airplane?   (Round to the nearest foot.)

3) Tom sees an enormous thundercloud approaching from the west. He sees a lightning flash at the top of the cloud and hears thunder 15 seconds later. His angle of sight to the top of the cloud is 65°. How high is the top of the thundercloud off the ground?

4) Greg wanted to know the height of a
tree in his yard. When he is 300 feet
away, his angle of sight to the top of
the tree is 18°. If Greg is 5' tall,
how tall is the tree?

5) While Maria is looking through binoculars, she sees an avalanche
at the top of a mountain. The sound reaches her ears 20 seconds
later. If her angle of sight is 30°, how much higher in elevation is
the mountain than the elevation where she is standing?

6) You are standing 500 feet away from a tall building. When you
look up, your line of sight needs to be a 20° angle in order to see the
top of the building. If you are 6 feet tall, how tall is the building?

7) Roman soldiers needed to build an earthen ramp to attack a
fortress on the top of a cliff that sat in the desert. If the cliff was 990
feet tall and the soldiers wanted the ramp built at an angle of 10°,
how far away from the cliff should they start building the earthen
ramp? (Round to the nearest foot.)

8) Matt is trying to measure the height of a tree using trigonometry. He is having trouble because of the terrain around the tree. The horizontal distance from the tree to Matt's eyes is 120 feet. The angle of depression from the horizontal is 30°. Matt's angle of sight to the top of the tree is 23°. What is the height of the tree? (Round to the nearest foot.)

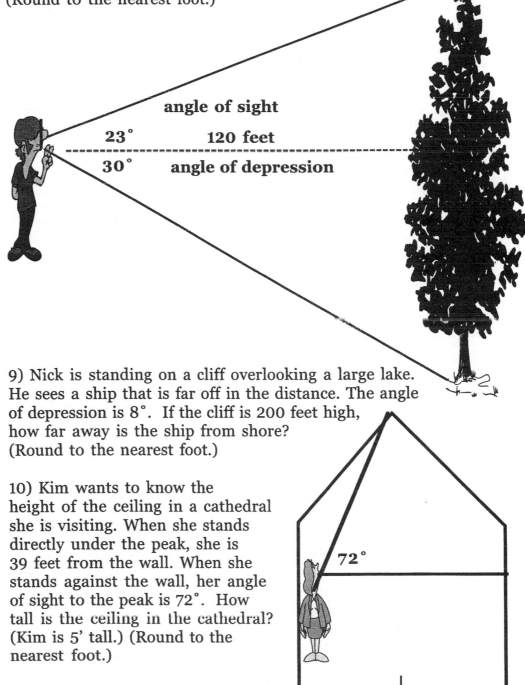

angle of sight

23°   **120 feet**

30°   **angle of depression**

9) Nick is standing on a cliff overlooking a large lake. He sees a ship that is far off in the distance. The angle of depression is 8°. If the cliff is 200 feet high, how far away is the ship from shore? (Round to the nearest foot.)

10) Kim wants to know the height of the ceiling in a cathedral she is visiting. When she stands directly under the peak, she is 39 feet from the wall. When she stands against the wall, her angle of sight to the peak is 72°. How tall is the ceiling in the cathedral? (Kim is 5' tall.) (Round to the nearest foot.)

72°

Trigonometry Table

Angle	Sine	Cosine	Tangent
1°	.0175	.9998	.0175
2	.0349	.9994	.0349
3	.0523	.9986	.0524
4	.0698	.9976	.0699
5°	.0872	.9962	.0875
6	.1045	.9945	.1051
7	.1219	.9925	.1228
8	.1392	.9903	.1405
9	.1564	.9877	.1584
10°	.1736	.9848	.1763
11	.1908	.9816	.1944
12	.2079	.9781	.2126
13	.2250	.9744	.2309
14	.2419	.9703	.2493
15°	.2588	.9659	.2679
16	.2756	.9613	.2867
17	.2924	.9563	.3057
18	.3090	.9511	.3249
19	.3256	.9455	.3443
20°	.3420	.9397	.3640
21	.3584	.9336	.3839
22	.3746	.9272	.4040
23	.3907	.9205	.4245
24	.4067	.9135	.4452
25°	.4226	.9063	.4663
26	.4384	.8988	.4877
27	.4540	.8910	.5095
28	.4695	.8829	.5317
29	.4848	.8746	.5543
30°	.5000	.8660	.5774
31	.5150	.8572	.6009
32	.5299	.8480	.6249
33	.5446	.8387	.6494
34	.5592	.8290	.6745
35°	.5736	.8192	.7002
36	.5878	.8090	.7265
37	.6018	.7986	.7536
38	.6157	.7880	.7813
39	.6293	.7771	.8098
40°	.6428	.7660	.8391
41	.6561	.7547	.8693
42	.6691	.7431	.9004
43	.6820	.7314	.9325
44	.6947	.7193	.9657
45	.7071	.7071	1.000

Angle	Sine	Cosine	Tangent
46	.7195	.6947	1.0355
47	.7314	.6820	1.0724
48	.7431	.6691	1.1106
49	.7547	.6561	1.1504
50	.7660	.6428	1.1918
51	.7771	.6293	1.2349
52	.7880	.6157	1.2799
53	.7986	.6018	1.3270
54	.8090	.5878	1.3764
55	.8192	.5736	1.4281
56	.8290	.5592	1.4826
57	.8387	.5446	1.5399
58	.8480	.5299	1.6003
59	.8572	.5150	1.6643
60	.8660	.5000	1.7321
61	.8746	.4848	1.8040
62	.8829	.4695	1.8807
63	.8910	.4540	1.9626
64	.8988	.4384	2.0503
65	.9063	.4226	2.1445
66	.9135	.4067	2.2460
67	.9205	.3907	2.3559
68	.9272	.3746	2.4751
69	.9336	.3584	2.6051
70	.9397	.3420	2.7475
71	.9455	.3256	2.9042
72	.9511	.3090	3.0777
73	.9563	.2924	3.2709
74	.9613	.2756	3.4874
75	.9659	.2588	3.7321
76	.9703	.2419	4.0108
77	.9744	.2250	4.3315
78	.9781	.2079	4.7046
79	.9816	.1908	5.1446
80	.9848	.1736	5.6713
81	.9877	.1564	6.3138
82	.9903	.1392	7.1154
83	.9925	.1219	8.1443
84	.9945	.1045	9.5144
85	.9962	.0872	11.4301
86	.9976	.0698	14.3007
87	.9986	.0523	19.0811
88	.9994	.0349	28.6363
89	.9998	.0175	57.2900
90	1.0000	.0000	∞

Probability

In the 1950's and 1960's, many juries in the south were almost entirely white, even though the make-up of juries is supposed to be done by picking randomly from a list of citizens who live in the area. Several individuals who were found guilty of committing crimes argued that they should get new trials because the jurors for their trial were not picked at random. A sample case that is similar to those that were argued in the South between 1950 and 1970 is presented below.

> *An African American who was convicted of a crime, is claiming that the jury that heard his case was not picked at random. He is claiming that there was racial bias involved in the jury selection process. His lawyer presented these facts:*
> *(1) 50% of those eligible to serve on the jury were African Americans.*
> *(2) Of the 100 people picked as potential jurors, only 5 were African American.*
> *(3) The final jury was all white.*

While the convicted man argued to the judge that he thought there was racial bias, the prosecutor argued that the fact that only 5 African Americans were in the 100-person jury pool was just a coincidence.

I'm confused. The convicted man makes a good point, but coincidences happen all the time. I wish I knew more about probability so I could determine how likely it is that this was just a coincidence.

This sounds like a job for Einstein!

The probability of this being a coincidence is 1 out of 600,000,000,000,000,000. The chance that this jury panel was picked at random is about the same as if I was playing cards and drew 4-of-a-kind, five times in a row. Not very likely!!

A statistician, who is an expert in probability, was able to prove that it was very unlikely that the jury panel was picked at random. The judge decided that there was indeed racial bias and ordered a new trial.

Einstein, you are a genius. I hope you continue to fight against bias and for fair random selection!

The official definition of probability is **"The formal study of the laws of chance"**. Today we use probability in almost all areas of modern civilization, including engineering, medicine, and weather prediction. For most of human history though, probability was used almost exclusively for one purpose:

Gambling!!

Probability Equations: Let's look at a sample problem to see how to write and solve probability equations:

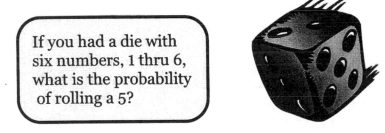

If you had a die with six numbers, 1 thru 6, what is the probability of rolling a 5?

Just as in algebra, we can express our problem using letters and numbers.

P(5) = ?

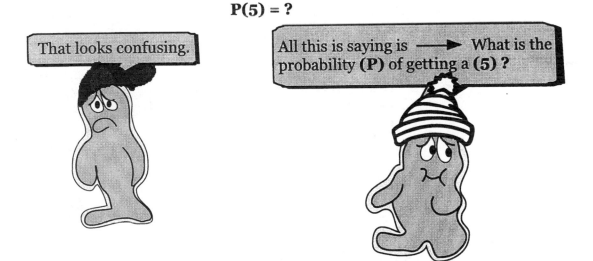

That looks confusing.

All this is saying is ⟶ What is the probability **(P)** of getting a **(5)** ?

To solve the equation, you need to determine the number of possible outcomes of your roll of this die. Finding the outcomes means finding all the different possibilities when you roll a die. You also need to find out how many of those outcomes or possibilities would be a 5.

That's easy. I can get 6 different numbers. Either a 1,2,3,4,5 or 6.

Since only one of those numbers is a 5, then the probability of getting a 5 is **1 in 6. P(5) = 1/6**

**P(5) = 1/6   or
"The probability of
getting a 5 is 1 out of 6".**

Let's look at a slightly harder problem:

> **If you had two dice and rolled them once, what is the probability of rolling a 5?**

Before the probability can be determined, we must first determine all the possible outcomes when you roll two dice.

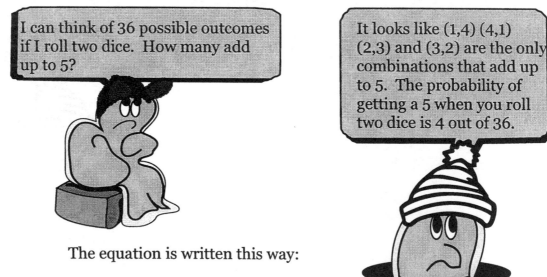

I can think of 36 possible outcomes if I roll two dice. How many add up to 5?

It looks like (1,4) (4,1) (2,3) and (3,2) are the only combinations that add up to 5. The probability of getting a 5 when you roll two dice is 4 out of 36.

The equation is written this way:

P(5) = 4/36

Probabilities are usually given as fractions. If you can reduce them, go ahead. In this case, 4/36 can be reduced to 1/9. In addition, many scientists who deal with probabilities change fractions into decimals. In this case 1/9 turns into .111. The probability of rolling two dice and getting a 5 is .111.

Write probability equations for the following problems:
(The first three are done for you.)

1) Flipping a coin and getting heads ⟶ **P(heads) = 1/2 or .5**

2) Rolling two dice and getting double
one's or double two's ⟶ **P(double 1's or 2's)=2/36 or 1/18 .0555**

3) Probability of flipping two coins
and both being tails ⟶ **P(tails,tails) = 1/4 or .25**

4) What is the probability of rolling two dice and getting 12?

5) What is the probability of guessing the month a friend was born?

6) What is the probability of guessing the day of the month a friend was born on if you already know she was born in December?

7) What is the probability of flipping three coins and getting all tails?

8) Write a probability equation for your father saying that your chances of going to the mall are 1 in a million.

It seems like probabilities are never greater than one or less than zero.

We can write an equation that's says exactly that:
$$0 \leq P \leq 1$$

This can be shown with two examples:

1) What is the probability of rolling a three when you roll a die with only three's on it?

I predict that I'm going to roll a 3.

I'd say the probability of you being right is 100% or $P(3)=1$

2) What is the probability of rolling an 8 when you roll one die with numbers that only go up to 6?

I don't think my chances are very good.

They're worse than not very good. As a matter of fact, your chances of rolling an 8 are 0. $P(8) = 0$

Now that you have learned to write and solve probability equations, we will move on to three types of probability problems. The first one deals with adding probabilities.

Adding Probabilities

Adding probabilities is best shown by looking at a problem:
**What is the probability of drawing an
ace or a red king?**

I know the probability of getting an ace is 4/52 and since there are 2 red kings, that probability is 2/52. I wonder what I do next?

Since this section is about adding probabilities, I bet you just add 4/52 + 2/52 The answer is 6/52.

P(ace or red king) = 4/52 + 2/52 = 6/52 ⟶ 3/26 ⟶ .115

Another example: What is the probability of rolling a 7 or an 11 when you roll two dice? **P(7 or 11) = ?** We learned earlier that there are 36 possible outcomes when you roll 2 dice.

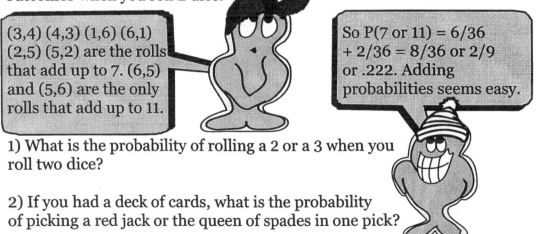

(3,4) (4,3) (1,6) (6,1) (2,5) (5,2) are the rolls that add up to 7. (6,5) and (5,6) are the only rolls that add up to 11.

So P(7 or 11) = 6/36 + 2/36 = 8/36 or 2/9 or .222. Adding probabilities seems easy.

1) What is the probability of rolling a 2 or a 3 when you roll two dice?

2) If you had a deck of cards, what is the probability of picking a red jack or the queen of spades in one pick?

3) If there was 1 black marble and 9 white marbles, what is the probability of picking the black marble if you are allowed to pick one marble?

4) There is a pile of 85 marbles with 40 black, 25 white, 17 green, and 3 red. What is the probability of picking a red or white marble if you had 1 pick?

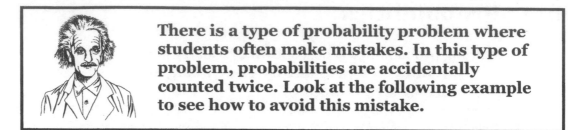

There is a type of probability problem where students often make mistakes. In this type of problem, probabilities are accidentally counted twice. Look at the following example to see how to avoid this mistake.

Say you were finding the probability of picking a king or a queen from a deck of cards.

That's easy because kings are never queens and queens are never kings.
P(king or queen) = 4/52 + 4/52 = 8/52 ⟶ reducing 2/13

What if the problem was finding the probability of picking a diamond or a queen from a deck of cards? At first glance you might think the answer is
P(diamond or queen) = 13/52 + 4/52 = 17/52.

There's a problem here. The queen of diamonds was counted twice because it is a queen and a diamond. So we must make sure we only count it once.
P(diamond or queen) = 13/52 + 3/52 = 16/52 or 4/13

1) What is the probability of picking a heart or a red jack from a deck of cards?

2) A jar contains 10 black marbles, 5 red marbles, 10 black cubes, and 10 red cubes. If you had one pick, what would be the probability of picking something red or picking a marble?

Tree Diagrams or Multiplying
to Determine Probabilities

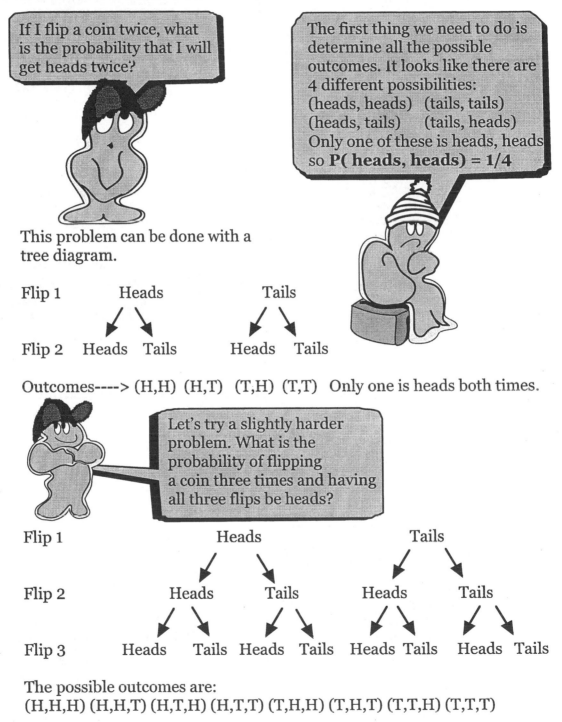

If I flip a coin twice, what is the probability that I will get heads twice?

The first thing we need to do is determine all the possible outcomes. It looks like there are 4 different possibilities:
(heads, heads)   (tails, tails)
(heads, tails)   (tails, heads)
Only one of these is heads, heads so **P(heads, heads) = 1/4**

This problem can be done with a tree diagram.

Flip 1   Heads   Tails

Flip 2   Heads   Tails   Heads   Tails

Outcomes----> (H,H) (H,T) (T,H) (T,T)   Only one is heads both times.

Let's try a slightly harder problem. What is the probability of flipping a coin three times and having all three flips be heads?

Flip 1   Heads   Tails

Flip 2   Heads   Tails   Heads   Tails

Flip 3   Heads   Tails Heads   Tails   Heads Tails   Heads Tails

The possible outcomes are:
(H,H,H) (H,H,T) (H,T,H) (H,T,T) (T,H,H) (T,H,T) (T,T,H) (T,T,T)

Since there are 8 possible outcomes and only one is (H,H,H), then
P (Heads, Heads, Heads) = 1/8

What if we wanted to know the probability of heads occurring at least once in those 3 flips?

Look at your tree diagram. Of the 8 possible outcomes, there is a head in 7 of them. **P(Heads at least once) = 7/8**

Tree diagrams are too time consuming for most probability problems. You can get the same answer by simply multiplying.

What is the probability of getting heads three times with three coin flips? We found that the answer was 1/8 when we used tree diagrams. We also could multiply: $\frac{1}{2} \times \frac{1}{2} \times \frac{1}{2} = \frac{1}{8}$

A couple has decided to have four children. What is the probability that they will be all boys?

The probability of the first child being a boy is 1/2.

Since there are going to be four children, the probability will be
$\frac{1}{2} \times \frac{1}{2} \times \frac{1}{2} \times \frac{1}{2} = \frac{1}{16}$
Wow, that was much easier than using tree diagrams.

Try the following probability problems:

1) What is the probability of flipping a coin 5 times and having all five flips be heads? **P(H,H,H,H,H) =**

2) What is the probability of rolling a die and having a 6 come up 5 times in a row? **P(6,6,6,6,6) =**

3) What is the probability of getting a total of three, 4 times in a row, when you roll two dice? **P(3,3,3,3) =**

4) If you have two decks of cards and pick one card from each, what is the probability of getting two aces? **P(Ace, Ace)**

5) If you have a coin, a die, and a deck of cards, what is the probability of getting heads, a 6, then the king of hearts?
P(Heads, 6, King of hearts)

6) If you draw two cards from a deck, what is the probability of getting a pair? What is the probability of getting a pair of 3's?

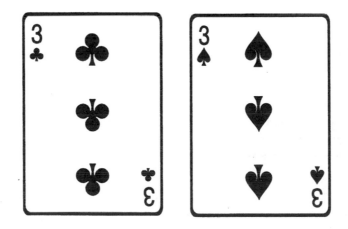

Probability of Something Not happening

I'm going to roll this die 4 times. If I get at least one 6, I'll buy you lunch. Before I roll the die though, I need to know the probability of buying you lunch. I know the probability for one roll is 1/6. Should I add 1/6 + 1/6 + 1/6 + 1/6?

That sounds reasonable, but if you rolled the die 8 times, then your probability would be 8/6, which is more than one and therefore impossible. I think we need Einstein's help.

This is a tricky type of problem that needs to be approached in a different way. We need to ask ourselves about the probability of each roll not being six. Each time you roll the die, the probability of rolling a 6 is 1/6. Therefore the probability of not rolling a 6 must be 5/6.

If you roll the die 4 times then:

$$P(\text{not } 6) = \frac{5}{6} \times \frac{5}{6} \times \frac{5}{6} \times \frac{5}{6} = \frac{625}{1296} \text{ or } .482$$

If the probability of not rolling a 6 in 4 rolls is .482, then the probability of rolling a 6 in 4 rolls must be 1 minus .482 or .518.

You are going to have to remember to subtract the probability of something not happening from one to get the probability of something happening.

1) What is the probability of getting at least one 5 in five rolls of a die?

2) What is the probability of getting at least one head if you flipped a coin 10 times?

3) You get to roll a single die 3 times. You win a free lunch if a 1,2,3 or 4 is rolled in any of the three rolls. What is the probability of getting a 1,2,3 or 4 at least once if you rolled a die 3 times?

4) If your chance of dying on a trip to the summit of Mt. Everest is 1 in 12, what are your chances of dying if you took 4 trips to the summit?

5) If your probability of being in a car accident in any particular year is 1 in 50, what are your chances of being in a car accident over a 3-year period?

Expected Value or Outcome

 **You are about to learn an exciting use for probabilities ⟶ Making predictions. If you know the probability of an event occurring, say getting heads on a coin flip, then you can predict the outcome of any number of events ⟶ 100, 1000, or even a million coin flips.**

To make a prediction, you would find the probability of the event occurring. If you flipped a coin once, what is the probability of getting heads?

In the example given above, the probability of getting heads would be $\frac{1}{2}$ or .5.   **P(heads) = .5**   The number **.5** is the number we use to make predictions. Now it is a simple matter of multiplying **.5** by the number of coin flips that are going to occur. For example:

If we are going to flip a coin 18 times, we would multiply .5 x 18.

.5 x 18 = 9

If we flip a coin 18 times, we can predict that we will get heads 9 times.

A coin is then flipped 500 times. The results are:

Heads----253

Tails------247

Let's try another problem that is a little harder:

There is one black ping pong ball in a box with 999 other white balls. How many times would we expect to pick the black ball if we pick a ball (and then put it back) 100,000 times?

We need to know two things:
1) The probability of picking a black ball in one pick.
2) The number of picks that will take place.

The answer to number 1 is easy. The probability of picking a black ball is 1 in 1000 or .001. The number of picks is 100,000, so we get our expected outcome by multiplying .001 by 100,000, which equals 100. 100 is our **mathematical probability.**

If we actually tried this and picked a ball 100,000 times, the actual number of black ping pong balls we picked would be the experimental probability. The result would probably not be 100, but it would most likely be very close to 100.

1) If you rolled two dice 789 times, how many times would you expect to get double ones? (Round to the nearest whole number.)

2) If you picked one card from a deck, and then put it back, 1 million times, how many times would you expect to pick the ace of spades?

3) If the health department said that they expect 2 out of 9 students to get the flu, how many students would you predict would come down with the flu in a school of 1161 students?

4) If 3 out of 17 climbers who attempt to scale Mt. Everest make it to the summit, how many climbers would you predict will have a successful climb in a year when 221 attempts are made?

5) What is the difference between mathematical and experimental probability?

Probability
Level 1

1) If you flip a coin 7 times, what is the probability that you will get heads on every flip?

2) If you are planning to roll two dice a thousand times. How many of those rolls would you expect to equal 7?

3) A jar is filled with nickels and pennies. The value of the nickels is $5 and the value of the pennies is $1. If you picked a hundred coins, what is your expected outcome?

4) If you pick one card from a deck, what is the probability that the card will be a diamond or the ace of spades?

5) If the probability of getting the flu is 2 out of 3, how many flu cases would you project for a school with 741 students?

6) If Sean rolls three dice, what is the probability of rolling three ones?

7) A gambler was watching coin tosses at a casino. He knows that the probability of flipping 10 heads in a row is 1 out of 1024. He decided that he would wait until he saw 9 head flips in a row and then bet $1000 that the next toss would be tails. Is his logic flawed? Why or why not?

8) Eric and Mike are playing a game with coins and dice. Eric is tossing three coins in the air. If he gets three heads, he is the winner. Mike is rolling two dice. If he rolls a seven, he wins. Is this a fair game?

9) Two children are playing a game to decide who is going to do the dishes. Daniel has one die and his sister has two dice. They decided that if Daniel rolls a three before Rachel rolls a seven, he would win. If Rachel rolls a seven before Daniel rolls a three, she would win. Is this a fair game?

10) If a newly married couple decided they were going to have five children, what is the probability that they will have five boys?

Probability
Level 2

1) In a jar of quarters, nickels and pennies, the value of the quarters is $10. The value of the nickels is $10, and the value of the pennies is also $10. If you picked one coin, what is the probability of getting a penny?

2) If you picked one card from a deck, what is the probability that it will be a spade or a king?

3) A couple has four children and they are all boys. They are going to have two more children. What is the probability that they will have at least one girl?

Questions 4-8 are based on the following information:

Tay-Sachs disease is a genetic disorder that is almost always fatal in early childhood. If both parents are carriers of the disease, the probability that a child will be born with the disease is 1 in 4. A man and a woman, who are both carriers of the disease, are trying to determine the probability of having children born with Tay-Sachs disease.

4) If they decide to have three children, what is the probability that all three children will have Tay-Sachs?

5) If they decide to have three children, what are the chances that no child will have Tay-Sachs?

6) If they decide to have three children, what is the probability that at least one child will be born with Tay-Sachs?

7) If the couple has identical triplets, what are the chances that all three children will have the disease?

8) If they have triplets that are not identical, what are the chances that all three children will have the disease?

9) What is the probability of somebody having a birthday of February 29th?

10) If the probability of getting polio from a vaccine is .00003, how many cases of polio would you expect per year if 1,350,000 children are being vaccinated each year?

Einstein Level

1) If you pick one card from each of 5 different decks, what is the probability that you will pick at least one spade?

2) When a state has a lottery, it usually has a player pick five numbers from the sequence 1-49. If the numbers drawn match the player's chosen numbers, in any order, then he would win a substantial amount of money. What is the probability of winning this type of lottery?

3) A different type of lottery requires the participant to pick six numbers from the sequence 1-49. The first five picks can be in any order, but the sixth number is called a **super-number** and must match the sixth number drawn by lottery officials. For example:

> Player's numbers---2,5,6,19,30 super number **17**
> Winning numbers---6,2,5,17,30 super number **19**

Even though the player has chosen the winning numbers, he would not win because the sixth number was not a 19. Again, the first five numbers can be in any order, but the sixth must match the sixth number drawn by lottery officials. What is the probability of winning this type of lottery?

4) A poker player would have a royal flush if she was dealt the 10-jack-queen-king-ace of one suit. If she picked five cards from a deck, what is the probability of her getting a royal flush?

5) The probability of getting in a car accident in a particular year is 1 in 50. What is the probability of being involved in a car accident over a 5-year period?

6) A young couple decided to have six children. They did not care if their children were boys or girls. The only wish that they had was that they would have at least one girl and at least one boy. What is the probability that this couple, after having six children, would have at least one boy and at least one girl?

7) There is a fatal disease that occurs in only 1 in 1000 people in the United States. A blood test that is available to diagnose the disease is 99% accurate. This means that in 1 out of 100 tests, the test results will say that a person has the disease, when in actuality he does not have the disease. This is called a false positive. The test never misses the disease though. In other words, if you have the disease, the test will always detect it.

If you test positive for the disease, what is the probability that you do have the disease?

8) In a heart disease study, 11,034 men over the age of 35 took an aspirin a day for five years, while 11,037 men took a fake pill (placebo). Of those who took the aspirin, 139 had heart attacks while 239 of the men who took the fake pills had heart attacks. Using the data from this experiment, predict how many lives would be saved over a five year period if 50 million men in the United States who are over the age of 35 took an aspirin a day.

9) If you pick three cards from a deck of cards, what is the probability that you will get three of a kind?

10) If you pick three cards from a deck of cards, what is the probability that you will pick three aces?

Statistics

If you lived in London, England in 1840, one of the diseases that you would have been terrified of was cholera. Cholera was a mysterious disease that would suddenly appear in cities, kill thousands, and then disappear. There was no known cure and no one knew what caused the disease. What was especially frustrating was that it was unclear why some people contracted the disease while others did not.

A dramatic discovery occurred in 1840 that would forever change how cholera was viewed by the people of London and the world. In 1840, during a major cholera epidemic, London doctor John Snow placed dots on a map of London to represent each cholera death. This famous map was one of the most powerful weapons in the fight against cholera because it clearly showed a connection between cholera deaths and one water pump on Broad Street in London. This connection was strengthened even further when Dr. Snow found that one cholera death that occurred far from the Broad Street pump was of a woman that liked Broad Street water so much that she paid to have it delivered to her home. It became very clear that something was contaminating the water at this pump and killing thousands of people.

The statistics Dr. Snow gathered about cholera deaths in London not only taught us the importance of sanitation in preventing illness, but it also showed us the importance of organizing and analyzing data. Dr. Snow's use of statistics clearly led to changes that saved thousands of lives.

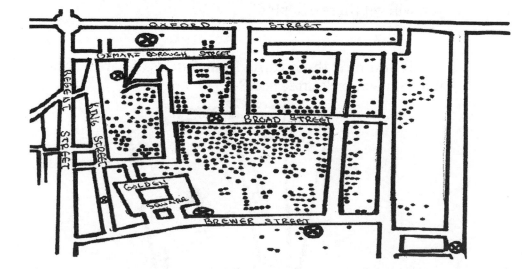

Data

Data is the raw material that statisticians and scientists use to try to answer important questions about our world. Put simply ⟶ **Data** is information.

I have superstitions, flawed thinking, and ignorance that are keeping me from understanding what is true and what is not true. I need help to determine what reality really is!!!!

I have just the thing for you. You need data!

When we collect data and interpret it, we can make important decisions that can have a profound impact on our lives. Think of the dramatic effect that collecting and analyzing data had on the health of the people of London. The dramatic improvements in sanitary conditions would not have happened if this data was not collected and studied.

Let's look at what happened when a group of students collected **data** from their school. We will see how **data** can be interpreted, or in some cases misinterpreted. The **data** we will be looking at concerns the family income of 15 children who are all in one 5th grade classroom. The questions that we will be trying to answer are:

◇ Is this a class of rich students?
◇ If a new student was added to this class, could we predict by looking at our data, the family income of that student?
◇ What is the family income of a typical student in this classroom?
◇ Could we use our data to make predictions on the family income of the other 100 children at our school?

This is the data the children collected:

Family income of our class	
Student	**Family Income**
1	$10,000
2	$5,000
3	$15,000
4	$10,000
5	$20,000
6	$20,000,000
7	$25,000
8	$10,000
9	$20,000
10	$15,000
11	$20,000
12	$30,000
13	$30,000
14	$20,000
15	$20,000

Before we can analyze this data, we need to organize it so it is easier to understand. We do this by finding six different measurements of data:

□ **Mean**.........The mean is another word for average. To find the average income for our 15 students, we need to add up all the family incomes and divide by the number of students (15). In this case we find that the average family income in this class is $1,350,000.

❑ **Median**........The median of a set of data is the number in the middle. To find the median, we need to line up all the data from lowest to highest and then take the middle number.

5000 10,000 10,000 10,000 15,000 15,000 20,000 ⟨20,000⟩
20,000 20,000 20,000 25,000 30,000 30,000 20,000,000

The median makes this class look poor, but the mean makes it look rich. I'm getting confused.

Maybe one of these measures isn't a good one to use when we try to determine whether this is a rich class.

If the list of data is an even number, then there will not be a middle number to use for the median. In that case, take the middle two numbers and average them. That will be your median. For example: (4, 8, 9, 10, 15, 20) The median of this set of numbers is the average of 9 and 10 which is 9.5.

❑ **Range**........Another measure that is helpful when we analyze data is the range. If all the families had incomes of $20,000, there would be a range of $0. In this case, the incomes go from $5000 to $20,000,000. This is a range of $19,995,000!!

This is a very significant range!! When a range is this large, it warns us that we probably won't get useful data from the average.

□ **Mode**.........The mode in a set of data is the number that occurs the most. In our data, $20,000 occurs five times and is therefore the mode.

□ **Frequency Table**.........After we collect data, it is helpful to make a frequency table so we can see at a glance how many families make how much money.

Frequency Table

Income	Number of Families
$0 - $10,000	4
$10,001 - $20,000	7
$20,001 - $30,000	3
$30,001 - $40,000	0
$40,001 - $50,000	0
Over $50,000	1

□ **Relative Frequency**........This is really not as confusing as the name *relative frequency* makes it appear. This is a very important measurement number that allows us to make predictions. Since these measurements are used to make predictions, they are often called by their simpler name ——▶ Predictor numbers.

To find predictor numbers, start by copying the frequency table. Then make a fraction comparing the number of families at each income level to the total number of families ——▶In this case 15 families. Statisticians then turn that fraction into a decimal. That decimal is your predictor number.

Frequency Table

Income	Number of Families	Fraction	Predictor Number
$0 - $10,000............................4		4/15	.267
$10,001 - $20,000..................7		7/15	.467
$20,001 - $30,000.................3		3/15	.2
$30,001 - $40,000.................0		0/15	0
$40,001 - $50,000.................0		0/15	0
Over $50,000........................1		1/15	.067

Say we wanted to predict the family incomes of the rest of our students. Instead of going to the trouble of asking all 100 students, we could use predictor numbers to make fairly good guesses. To find out how many of those 100 students have families that have an income of $0 - $10,000, we simply multiply the $0 - $10,000 predictor number by the 100 students.

.267 x 100 = 26.7 students.

We can predict that there will be approximately 27 families with an income of $0 - $10,000.

These predictions aren't guaranteed to be accurate, but they usually are pretty close.

Let's answer the four questions we talked about at the beginning of the chapter:

◇ Is this a class of rich students? **Clearly it is not!!**

◇ If a new student was added to this class, could we predict by looking at our data, the family income of that student? **If a new student was added to this class, his family income would most likely be in the neighborhood of $20,000.**

◇ What is the family income of a typical student in this classroom? **The median, mode, and predictor numbers would point to a typical income of $20,000.**

◇ Could we use our data to make predictions on the family income of the other 100 children at our school? **Yes. By using predictor numbers, we would predict:**

- **0 - $10,000 ....26.7 families**
- **$10,001 - $20,000........46.7 families**
- **$20,001 - $ 30,000.......20 families**
- **$30,001 - $40,000........0 families**
- **$40,001 - $50,000........0 families**
- **Over $50,000...............6.7 families**

Data can be used to find truth, or it can be used to give a distorted picture of the truth. In our example of school children and family income, someone intent on showing that this class was rich, could truthfully claim that the average income of these students was $1,350,000. Truthful yes ⟶ But also very misleading. Data must always be looked at very carefully.

Pretend that you are going to write an article for your school newspaper about allowances of 6th graders at Einstein Elementary School. There are four 6th grade classrooms in the school with a total of 75 students. You have decided that you only have time to gather data from one classroom. The data you collected is shown below:

Student	Allowance	Student	Allowance
1	$2	10	$5
2	$3	11	$4
3	$3	12	$3
4	$2.50	13	$10
5	$2.50	14	$150
6	$10	15	$8
7	$10	16	$1.50
8	$1	17	$2
9	$3	18	$5

Your task is to organize the data into the six different measures ➤ **Mean, median, mode, range, frequency table, relative frequency**. After you have done that, answer the following questions. Note: When you do the frequency table, use the following ranges:

$0 - $2.50
$2.51 - $5.00
$5.01 - $7.50
$7.51 - $10.00
$Over $10.00

1) What is a normal allowance for 6th graders at this school?

2) Predict how many of the 75 students in grade 6 would have allowances in the range of $0 - $5. Predict how many would have allowances of over $5.00.

3) The average student has an allowance of over $10 per week. Can you say that this class has students with fairly high allowances?

Predicting by Using Samples

When you studied probability, you had a very easy way of predicting an outcome. If you wanted to predict how many 6's you would get in 1000 rolls of a die, you would simply multiply 1/6 or .167 times 1000.

I can predict how many times I'll get a 6 if I roll this die 1000 times. It is 1000 x .167 or 167 times.

I can predict that you have very little going on in your life if you are going to sit and roll that die 1000 times.

Pretend that you are the president of the French club at your high school. The club is going to sell candy to raise money to finance a trip to Paris. The candy is made especially for your school and it is in the shape of your school mascot: Herbie the Parrot. You need to make $5 per parrot and the club needs $1500 for the trip. It would be very helpful if there was some way to predict how many parrots would sell so the club doesn't order too many, because the candy company certainly will not take back any unsold Herbies.

Whose idea was it to sell chocolate parrots?

I don't know, but I'm predicting that we'll only raise enough money to buy a map of Paris, not go there.

Since you cannot ask all 2000 students in your school whether they would buy a chocolate parrot, you could ask a sample of students and make predictions based on the data you collect from them. You wanted your sample to be random, so you wrote down all 2000 student's names and put them in a hat. Fifty names were picked and each one of those students was called and asked whether they would be interested in buying a chocolate parrot. This is the data that was collected:

> **Definitely buying..............7**
> **Definitely not buying.......39**
> **Maybe...............................4**

We should have picked our friends for the sample, then we would be sure of getting a lot of students that were interested in buying chocolate parrots.

The important thing is that our sample be a fair test of the students' wishes, not that it look good.

Now you need to make predictor numbers by making fractions.

	Predictor Fraction	Predictor Number
Definitely buying..............7	7/50	.14
Definitely not buying........39	39/50	.78
Maybe...............................4	4/50	.08

Remember that the denominator in your fraction is the total number of students in your sample.

To find out how many candy bars to order, you would multiply .14 x 2000 students. Now you know that approximately 280 candy bars will sell.

I thought we were in trouble when only 7 students said they were interested in buying a chocolate Herbie.

It looks like predicting by using samples is something important to learn. I wonder if they know about it in Paris?

Answer the following questions using predictor numbers:

1) Chad decided to try and predict how many people in the United States would pick soccer as their favorite sport. He picked 100 people at random and asked them the following question: What is your favorite sport?

Or if you want to impress your friends, call them relative frequencies.

Data Collected:

Baseball.........38
Football.........26
Basketball......28
Soccer............8

If the population of the United States is 250,000,000 people, use predictor numbers to estimate how many people have soccer as their favorite sport?

2) A doctor had a theory that if adults took an aspirin a day, they would get fewer heart attacks. He did an experiment where 11,034 men over the age of 35 took an aspirin a day for five years. At the same time, he gave 11,037 men a fake pill (called a placebo) that looked like an aspirin. Of those who took aspirin, 139 had heart attacks while 239 of the men who took the fake pills had heart attacks. Analyze this data and predict how many lives could be saved if 50 million men over the age of 35 took an aspirin a day.

3) Dungeons and Dragons is a game that was popular with teenagers in the 1980's. As the game grew in popularity, the news media started reporting a possible link between Dungeons and Dragons and teenage suicide. In several instances, the news media reported this connection in a very sensationalistic manner. They focused on two points:

☐ There were over three million teenagers playing Dungeons and Dragons in one particular year.
☐ There were 28 cases of suicide in that year involving teenagers who played Dungeons and Dragons.

Look at the data below and decide whether there was a strong connection between playing Dungeons and Dragons and teenage suicide. How many suicides would you expect to occur among the three million Dungeons and Dragons players, even if Dungeons and Dragons had no connection at all with teenagers committing suicide?

United States suicide rate for ages 12 to 24 ....12 per 100,000
Suicides of teenage Dungeon and Dragon players................28 in one year

In 1986, seven astronauts died in the explosion of the space shuttle Challenger. After the disaster, an investigation turned up evidence that Challenger was launched in 29° weather, even though several engineers warned against the launch. Even more disturbing was the fact that the launch took place without a study of data on shuttle performance at low temperatures. Data is important, but it must be analyzed carefully to be useful. When performance data was finally studied after the Challenger explosion, it predicted that the potential for serious problems was very real at temperatures near or below freezing.

Statistically Significant

When scientists do experiments, they normally use a **factor** to try and decide whether a theory they have is true.

On the previous page, we talked about a study concerning heart attacks and aspirin. In that study, the factor was aspirin. The theory was that taking aspirin would help prevent heart attacks. The experiment showed that the scientist's theory was right ➤The data from the experiment was statistically significant.

If the aspirin takers had 235 heart attacks while the ones taking the placebo had 237 heart attacks, then the results would have shown that aspirin was not effective in preventing heart attacks. In other words, the results would not have been statistically significant.

The idea behind a factor being statistically significant can be more easily explained by proposing a simple theory and then doing an experiment. What if someone thought that if he held his nose during a coin flip, he could influence the outcome of the flip and make the result turn out heads?

The outcome is heads both times, but did that happen by chance or was nose holding the reason both flips were heads?

Before we can judge whether these results are statistically significant, we need to use what we learned in the probability chapter to see what the chances are that two coin flips would both turn out heads, even without someone holding his nose.

P(heads, heads) = 1/2 x 1/2 = 1/4

The probability of flipping a coin two times and getting two heads is 1 in 4. Is the fact that the two coins turned out heads statistically significant? No it isn't because this result would often happen by chance ⟶ 1 in 4 times!

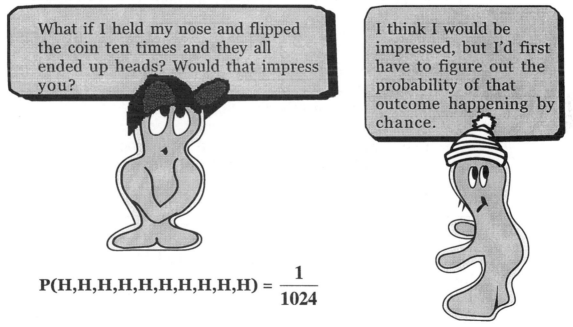

What if I held my nose and flipped the coin ten times and they all ended up heads? Would that impress you?

I think I would be impressed, but I'd first have to figure out the probability of that outcome happening by chance.

$$P(H,H,H,H,H,H,H,H,H,H) = \frac{1}{1024}$$

Would 10 heads in a row be statistically significant? Yes it would be, because getting ten heads in a row would only happen by chance 1 in 1024 times. This outcome is very significant!!!

Even though these results would be very significant, they would not prove that holding your nose causes a coin flip to be heads. It would cause us to take this theory a little more seriously though.

1) In the early 1990's, the claim was made that cellular phones might cause brain cancer. This theory arose from the fact that hundreds of cellular phone users, from all over the country, were getting brain cancer on the side of their head where they held their cellular phone. Look at the data listed below and then try and answer the questions.

Normal brain cancer occurrence
in the United States....................................20,000 cases per year

Cellular phone use in the United Sates...........1 out of every 8 people

Population of the United States......................250,000,000

Cellular phone users diagnosed with brain cancer.......2500

◇ What is the factor in this situation?

◇ How many cell phone users would you expect to get brain cancer every year, even if cell phones did not cause cancer?

◇ Is this data statistically significant?

2) You are a scientist investigating a significant number of brain cancers that have occurred at a chemical research center. You know the following:
• The city where the research facility is located has a population of 38,000.
• The research center employs 552 workers.
• There are four floors at the center with 138 employees on each floor.
• During the years 1990 - 1998, there were seven cases of brain cancer at the research facility, with six of those cases occurring on the third floor.
• The brain cancer rate in 1996 for the general population of the United States was 7.2 cases per 100,000 population.

From the data that is available, you are to determine the following:

◇ How many brain cancer cases would you expect to occur in a population of 38,000 over the nine-year period from 1990 - 1998?

◇ How many brain cancer cases would you expect to occur at the research facility over this same nine - year period?

◇ How many brain cancer cases would you expect to occur over this same nine-year period on the third floor of the research facility?

◇ Is the brain cancer rate at the facility close to the expected rate? If not, how many times greater than the expected rate is the actual rate of brain cancer?

Experimental Bias

Experimental bias is a fancy way of saying that an experiment was done unfairly.

I just proved that taping magnets to your head will make colds go away much faster than they normally do. I had my grandparents, parents, two uncles, and four friends try it and they all said the magnets helped their colds.

Something about your experiment doesn't seem quite right.

There are several obvious flaws in this experiment:

- The participants should have been picked at random. The people who took part in the experiment were limited to friends and relatives. The participants were biased!!
- The experiment should have had a control group. This means that there should have been an equal sized group of people with colds who were given a fake magnet.
- The people with colds and the person doing the experiment should both have been *blind* to who had the real magnets and who had the fake magnets. That way wishful thinking would not influence the results.

 **A control group is a very important part of experiments. This is the group who thinks they are getting the magnet, medicine, aspirin, or whatever the experiment is testing. If the experiment was set up in this manner, then the experimenter and the participants would not be influenced by wishful thinking, or their belief or non-belief in the power of magnets. In other words they would not be biased.**

Read the description below of a poorly designed experiment. The data that was gathered from the experiment led some people to jump to conclusions that were not accurate. Explain why this experiment is flawed.

The Bayside Vitamin Store decided to test whether vitamin C helps cure the common cold. To conduct their experiment, Bayside gave free vitamin C to 100 of its customers who had colds. A week later, they asked the participants whether the vitamin C helped their colds. When the experiment was finished, it turned out that 95% of the participants thought that the vitamin C helped their colds. The owner of the Bayside Vitamin Store then announced that he had proven that vitamin C helps cure the common cold.

Occam's Razor

A man was walking down a road late at night when he heard a loud roar and saw lights hovering above him. He became more and more worried as he searched for some kind of explanation for the strange lights. He looked at his watch and it read 10:00 P.M. He then looked back up at the lights. The next thing he knew, he was bruised and bloody and lying in a ditch beside the road. His watch now said 2:00 A.M. He could not account for his missing time or the obvious beating he had endured. He began searching through his memory of recent X-files episodes to try and explain what happened to him.

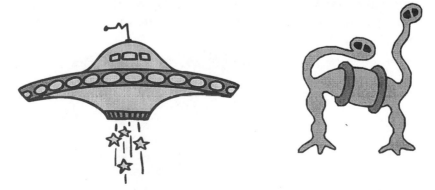

There is a rule in science called the **"rule of parsimony"** or **Occam's Razor.** These are fancy names for a very simple rule:

> **If you are searching for an explanation for an event that is perplexing or unusual, the correct explanation is usually the most basic or down to earth explanation.**

Put simply, this rule suggests that you try to explain unusual events by first using all the possible normal explanations before you resort to aliens, UFOs and other bizarre explanations.

Keeping Occam's Razor in mind, give this distraught individual some suggestions as to what happened to him. After you've done that, read the following true stories and try to think of some explanations that follow Occam's Razor.

Clever Hans

Clever Hans was a horse that lived in Germany in the early 1900s. He appeared to be able to answer math problems by tapping out answers with his hooves. His owner would ask questions such as 15 divided by 3. Clever Hans would then tap his hoof 5 times. He could even answer square roots. If he was asked the square root of 81, he would tap his hoof nine times. Clever Hans traveled all over the world making thousands of dollars for his owner.

Was Clever Hans really able to answer math questions, or was he secretly being cued by his owner? Well-known scientists from Germany were convinced that no trickery was involved and that Clever Hans was really capable of solving math problems. Other researchers were not sure if Clever Hans was really a horse prodigy, or if something else was going on that made it appear like the horse was answering math questions. How do you think Clever Hans was able to figure out the answers to the math problems?

Sir Edmund Digby and the Healing Salve

Early in the 1600s, wars were raging all over Europe. The injuries from these battles were horrific, but most deaths occurred because of infection. When a wounded soldier would be brought in for treatment, a common practice by battlefield doctors was to cover the wounds with a salve that they carried in a large bucket. Doctors felt that this salve helped heal wounds. Needless to say, most soldiers ended up dying from massive infections.

Sir Edmund Digby had an idea that he thought would help treat the wounded soldiers more effectively. He thought that if he put the salve on an enemy soldier's gun, instead of the wounded soldier, his patients might be more likely to be healed. Sir Edmund's idea was not accepted very well by the other doctors. They thought the idea of putting healing salve on enemy guns instead of wounds was ridiculous.

Even though he was laughed at, Sir Edmund decided to try his new treatment. Much to the surprise of his fellow doctors, Sir Edmund Digby's patients soon started recovering at rates much higher than the other doctor's patients. Month after month, Sir Edmund's patients lived, while other doctor's patients died. The doctors finally had to accept the fact that patients getting this bizarre treatment were living, while their patients were dying. They soon began treating guns with the healing salve instead of treating their patients' wounds. Soon their patients began surviving in large numbers, just like Sir Digby's.

Was there something magic about putting salve on the guns? Using Occam's Razor, come up with the most likely explanation for the success of the treatment.

Crop Circles

In the early 1970's, strange shapes began appearing in farm fields all over England. Soon there were reports of similar occurrences in the United States and several other countries. There were mixed opinions as to how and why these "crop circles" were made.

One school of thought expressed a strong belief that the complexity of the shapes made it unlikely that the "crop circles" could have been done by people. This group was of the opinion that "visitors from outer space" was the most likely explanation for these events.

Another group of investigators thought it very unlikely that the crop circles were anything more than the work of very sophisticated pranksters. This group of investigators could not explain how all of the shapes were made, but they still thought the work was more likely to be the "irrational acts of terrestrials instead of the rational acts of extraterrestrials."

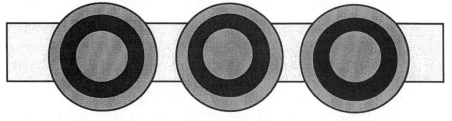

Statistics Questions

1) What does picking at random mean?

2) You have 50 bean plants growing in pots. You want to find out whether talking to plants makes them grow better. Describe an experiment you would set up.

3) In the early and mid 1900's, the numbers on millions of watches were coated with a radioactive material so that they would glow in the dark. The workers who painted these numbers would use a fine paintbrush that they would curl with their tongues to make the point of the brush sharp enough to paint clearly. In the process of doing this, these workers would get radioactive material on the tips of their tongues. If there were 100 workers at the plant, approximately how many cancers of the tip of the tongue would it take to make you fairly certain that you could place the blame for these cancers on the practice of workers putting radioactive paintbrushes in their mouths? What additional information would you need to help you make your decision?

4) Give an example of experimental bias.

5) It is late at night in a small town in Iowa. A young man suddenly wakes up because he hears the sound of elephants trumpeting outside his window. Using Occam's Razor, come up with some possible explanations for this strange event.

6) Explain how predictor numbers are useful.

7) What is the difference between mean and median.

8) Why is a control group important?

9) A person claims to be able to pick a heart from a deck by chanting hearts before the pick. If this person then picks a heart, is this statistically significant? Why or why not?

10) If an unknown object is seen shooting at high speed across the sky, what kinds of explanations should be considered first?

Distance = Speed x Time

Isaac Newton probably had the finest scientific mind the world has ever seen. Newton's discoveries about motion allowed humankind to accomplish many things, including putting a man on the moon. Two of Newton's greatest discoveries were laws that explain how objects move in the universe. Newton's first law:

When an object is at rest, it tends to stay at rest. An object in motion tends to stay in motion at a constant velocity and in a straight line.

If all objects tend to stay in motion, then why doesn't a car continue rolling when it runs out of gas? If no other force was acting on the car, it would continue rolling, but friction causes it to slow down and eventually stop. All objects resist change, whether they are in motion or not. This is called inertia. The amount of inertia a body has depends on its mass. An 80,000 pound semi going 60 mph has a large amount of inertia that wants to keep the truck moving. This same truck, when it is motionless, also has a large amount of inertia that makes it not want to move. A fly moving at 2 mph has very little inertia and therefore it takes very little force to stop the fly. (And it takes very little force to get a motionless fly moving.)

It's not fair, you have more inertia than I do.

Newton's third law: ***For every action, there is an equal and opposite reaction.***

If an astronaut was outside the space shuttle and her tether was cut, Newton's third law describes how she could get back to the shuttle. If she threw one of her tools in the opposite direction that she wanted to go, she would be propelled back towards the shuttle. She would have to be careful though, because if the hammer was thrown too hard, or in the wrong direction, she would be in serious trouble.

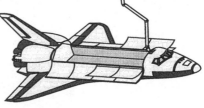

Anna was planning to visit her mother at Christmas time. She knew she had to drive 715 miles and she also knew that she usually drives, on average, 55 miles per hour.

Anna predicted her time of arrival by using the formula:

> **Distance = Speed x Time**

715 Miles = 55 MPH x Time
(Distance)   (Speed)   (Unknown)

$$715 = 55t \longrightarrow t = 13$$
Anna's trip would take 13 hours.

 **This formula is used millions of times each day by astronauts, airline companies, bus companies, train companies, and ordinary families. This equation helps you find distances, speed, or time. If you know two of the three pieces of information, it is a simple algebra problem to find the missing piece.**

Let's look at a much harder problem:

> **Dan and Luke decided to take part in a twenty mile race. Luke runs at 5 mph, while Dan runs at 4 MPH. When Luke crosses the finish line, how far will Dan be from finishing?**

The first thing we need to do is find out how long it took for Luke to reach the finish line.

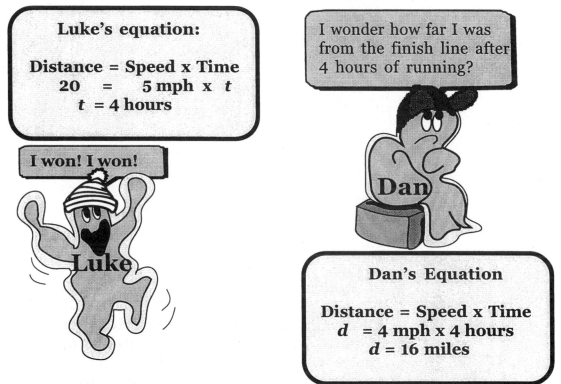

Luke's equation:

Distance = Speed x Time
$$20 = 5 \text{ mph} \times t$$
$$t = 4 \text{ hours}$$

I won! I won!

I wonder how far I was from the finish line after 4 hours of running?

Dan's Equation

Distance = Speed x Time
$$d = 4 \text{ mph} \times 4 \text{ hours}$$
$$d = 16 \text{ miles}$$

Dan's distance run was 16 miles or 4 miles from the finish line.

You only beat me by 4 miles, I think you were lucky.

1)A trip to Chicago from Dubuque, Iowa is 180 miles. If the roads allow for a speed of 50 mph, how long would the trip take?

2) Isaac will be attending a meeting 252 miles from his home. If he sets his cruise control at 48 mph, how much driving time should he plan for?

3) Juan rode a bus across the entire country at an average speed of 60 mph. If the trip took him 48 hours, how many miles did the bus cover?

4) One train leaves the station at 10:00 A.M. and arrives at its destination at 2:30 P.M. If the distance the train traveled was 405 miles, what was its average speed?

5) Train A leaves the station heading north at 80 mph. At the same time and from the same station, train B heads south at 65 mph. How far apart are the trains after 3 hours?

A Different Kind of Average Speed

If Jay walked a mile at 2 mph and then rode his bike for another mile at 10 mph, what would be his average speed?

It seems like you would just add 2 + 10 and then divide by 2. I have a feeling that is wrong.

I know you cannot figure averages like you normally do. Let's ask Einstein to show us how to do these.

When you are figuring speed averages, you must think differently. You must think in blocks of time. Since 2 mph is five times slower than 10 mph, the time Jay spent walking was 5 times longer than the time he spent riding his bike. Because of this, you must give walking five blocks of time.

Walking | 2 | 2 | 2 | 2 | 2

Biking | 10

To find the average speed, you simply add up the numbers inside the blocks and then divide by 6 (the number of blocks of time).

$$20 \div 6 = 3\frac{1}{3}\text{mph}$$

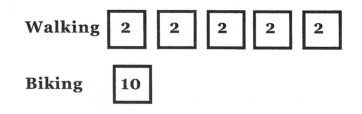

Another Example:

> If Michelle walked halfway to school at 5 mph, and then ran the rest of the way at 10 mph, what was her average speed?

 **Since Michelle spent twice as long walking, make sure walking gets two blocks of time and running gets one.**

Walking ☐ 5 ☐ 5   **Running** ☐ 10

Adding and dividing gives you

$$5 + 5 + 10 = 20 \div 3 = 6\frac{2}{3}\text{mph}$$

Let's try a slightly harder problem:

> A student was driving to school at 50 mph. A quarter of the way there he ran out of gas. If he ran the rest of the way at 10 mph, what was his average speed?

Let's draw a picture to represent his trip.

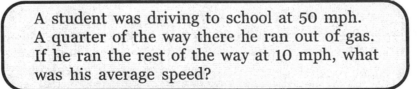

As you can see, the student spent a lot of time going 10 mph, and very little time going 50 mph. When you look at the picture, it is clear that each 10 mph section should have 5 blocks of time.

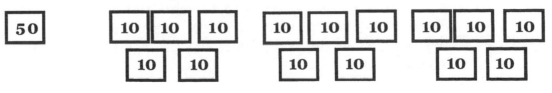

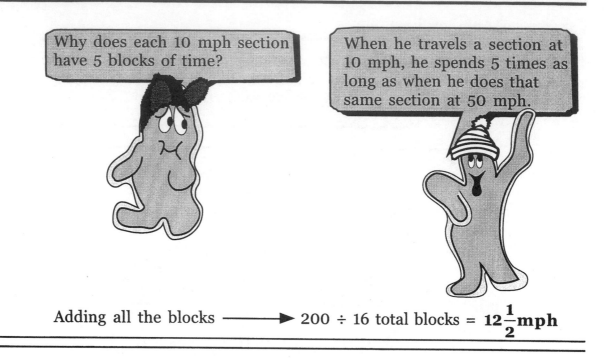

Why does each 10 mph section have 5 blocks of time?

When he travels a section at 10 mph, he spends 5 times as long as when he does that same section at 50 mph.

Adding all the blocks ⟶ 200 ÷ 16 total blocks = **12$\frac{1}{2}$mph**

1) If Sara walks to school at 4 mph and runs home at 12 mph, what is her average speed?

2) If Mark skates across a lake at 20 mph and then walks back at 4 mph, what is his average speed?

3) If Kristin hikes up a mountain at 2 mph and hikes down at 5 mph, what is her average speed?

4) Minnie canoes with the current at a speed of 8 mph. On her return trip she paddles against the current so her speed drops to 2 mph. What is her average speed for the trip?

5) Claire was riding her bike to school at a speed of 12 mph. When she was 2/3 of the way there, she got a flat tire. Her mother drove her the rest of the way at a speed of 48 mph. What was her average speed?

Distance = Speed x Time
Level 1

1) A family took a trip to Pittsburgh from Cleveland. Their average speed was 60 mph and the trip took $3\frac{1}{2}$ hours. What is the distance between the two cities?

Use the distance chart below for questions 2 - 5

	Boston	Chicago	Denver	New York	Miami
Boston	*	860	1766	204	1139
Chicago	860	*	907	721	1188
Denver	1766	907	*	1627	1716
New York	204	721	1627	*	1092
Miami	1139	1188	1716	1092	*

2) Jayme drove from Miami to Denver at an average speed of 55 mph. How long did the trip take?

3) Adam rode his bike from New York to Boston. If it took him 8 hours and 30 minutes, what was his average speed?

4) Kyle drove from Chicago to New York. The first 450 miles were driven at an average speed of 65 mph. Because of engine problems, the remaining distance was driven at an average speed of 45 mph. How long did Kyle's trip take?

5) If a car averages 55 mph, how long will a round trip take between Denver and New York?

6) Two trains start at the same train station and travel in opposite directions. One train travels at 35 mph and the other travels at 45 mph. How far apart are they in 8 hours?

7) Michelle hiked up a mountain trail at a constant speed of 3 mph. She borrowed a mountain bike at the top of the mountain and rode down at a speed of 12 mph. What was her average speed?

8) Mark leaves for school at 8:00 and walks at 4 mph. His sister, who is riding her bike, leaves at 8:15 and travels at 8 mph. If school is 2 miles away, who will arrive first?

9) Kristin rode the 5 miles to school with her dad at 50 mph. She then jogged home at 10 mph. What was her average speed?

10) On January 15, 1999 a spacecraft was launched from earth on a mission to Mars. If the average speed is 17,500 mph, and the distance traveled by the spacecraft will be 51 million miles, in what month and year will the spacecraft reach Mars?

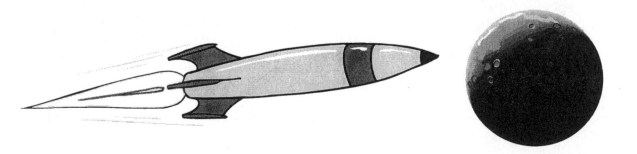

Distance = Speed x Time
Level 2

1) Two brothers are planning to run in a 20 mile race. Since the older brother runs at 7 mph, and the younger brother runs at 5 mph, they decided that the slower runner should get a one hour head start. How far apart are they 2 1/2 hours after the younger brother starts the race?

2) Two children run in opposite directions. One runs at a speed of 4 mph while the other runs at a speed of 6 mph. How long will it take before they are 5 miles apart?

3) Martha leaves from home and travels toward school at 4 mph. At exactly the same time, Kristin leaves from school and travels towards home at a speed of 12 mph. If the distance between home and school is 4 miles, and they both leave at 8:00, what time will they meet?

4) Kirsten is planning a bike trip of 408 miles across Iowa. She plans to travel an average of 8 hours a day at a speed of 12 mph. If food cost $8 per day, how much will the food cost for her trip?

5) Michelle walks at 3 1/2 mph. If she enters a tunnel that is 2 miles long, approximately how many seconds will it take her to go through the tunnel?

6) Ben has a new 15-speed bike. He wants to see how fast it will go down a hill near his home. The bike doesn't have a speedometer, but Ben knows the hill is 4.4 miles long, and he also knows that it takes him exactly 9 minutes to travel down the hill. How fast does his bike travel?

7) Michelle's bike can go 12 mph. She needs to be at a soccer field at 10:00 A.M.. If the field is 20 miles from her home, what time will she need to leave?

8) Ellen needed to ride her moped to school because she missed the bus. School is 6.3 miles away and her moped can travel at a constant speed of 23 mph. If school starts at 9:00 and it is now 8:45, will Ellen get to school on time? Explain why.

9) Martin was jogging to school at a speed of 10 mph. Unfortunately, when he was halfway there, he sprained his ankle and his mom had to give him a ride the rest of the way at 40 mph. After school Martin rode the bus home at an average speed of 20 mph. What was Martin's average speed on his round trip to school and back?

10) A family is trying to find the fastest way from their school to their home. One choice is a 6 mile trip where they can travel at 60 mph. The other possibility is a 5.5 mile trip that can be traveled at a speed of 50 mph. Which route should they pick if they wanted to get home in the shortest amount of time? If they chose the slower route, how much more time will it take them?

Einstein
Level

1) A train, whose speed is 75 mph, takes 3 minutes to pass a car that is going 60 mph in the same direction. How long is the train?

2) A peregrine falcon can reach speeds of 200 mph while it is diving. If a peregrine falcon that is circling a rabbit at an altitude of 1320 feet, turns and dives at a speed of 200 mph, how long until it reaches the rabbit?

3) Gabe is driving toward San Francisco at a speed of 48 mph. If his dad left an hour later at a speed of 72 mph, how long will it take for Gabe's dad to catch him?

4) A speed boat went up the Mississippi River at a speed of 40 mph. It then turned around and traveled downstream to the original starting point at a speed of 60 mph. What was the boat's average speed?

5) Warren is riding his bike at 15 mph on a road adjacent to railroad tracks. A train traveling at 90 mph in the opposite direction as Warren, takes 20 seconds to pass him. How long is the train?

6) In a recent 50-yard Olympic swimming event, the 1st place finisher beat the 2nd place finisher by 1/100 of a second. If the winning time was 26.80 seconds, how many inches behind was the 2nd place finisher when the race ended? (Round to the nearest inch.)

7) Carolyn drove from her home to school at 40 mph and was 10 minutes late. The next day she drove to school at 60 mph and was 10 minutes early. How far is Carolyn's school from her home?

8) In a recent running of the 100-yard dash, the winner won the race with a time of 9.87 seconds. The 2nd place finisher had a time of 9.92 seconds. When the winner crossed the finish line, how far behind was the 2nd place finisher? (Give your answer in yards.)

9) Susan rode her bike alongside a train that was traveling at a speed of 24 mph. If she was traveling at a speed of 12 mph and it took the train 2 minutes 24 seconds to pass her, what is the length of the train?

10) Mack drove the 1 mile distance to his place of work at 30 mph. If Mack wanted to average 60 mph on his round trip, (home to work and then back home) how fast would he have to travel on his way home? (The answer is not 90 mph.)

Simultaneous Equations

We have seen how helpful algebra is when solving confusing word problems.

Four times a number is equal to 2 times the number plus 17.

I can make an equation and solve that problem in less than a minute.

$$4n = 2n + 17$$
$$2n = 17$$
$$n = 8.5$$

Up to now we have been solving equations with only one unknown. We are now going to work with problems and equations that have two unknowns.

 **We have been using the letter n to take the place of our unknown. Mathematicians call these letters variables. In this chapter, we will be using the letters x and y as our variables.**

I'm going to start calling unknowns variables. That way I'll sound much smarter than I am.

I have been using n as my variable. I wonder if using x for a variable will make me appear more sophisticated.

Solving Equations By Elimination

Look at the two equations shown below. What values of *x* and *y* will make both these equations true?

Equation 1 ➤ **x + y = 11**
Equation 2 ➤ **2x - y = 7**

We could use trial and error by finding all the numbers that make the first equation true and then seeing if any of those also make equation 2 true.

I can think of many combinations that make equation 1 true:

x=10 y=1	x=5 y=6
x=9 y=2	x=4 y=7
x=8 y=3	x=3 y=8
x=7 y=4	x=2 y=9
x=6 y=5	x=1 y=10

I can think of even more combinations such as:

$x = \dfrac{1}{2}$ $y = 10\dfrac{1}{2}$

$x = \dfrac{1}{4}$ $y = 10\dfrac{3}{4}$

I think there is an infinite number of solutions for equation 1.

There are an infinite number of solutions for **x + y = 11**, but there is only one solution that will make both equations true. We do not want to use trial and error to solve these equations because of the time it would take, so we will use a special method called the elimination method.

Look at the two equations again:

$$x + y = 11$$
$$2x - y = 7$$

One of the most basic rules of algebra is that you can add or subtract the same thing from each side of an equation. Since **2x - y** and 7 are equal to each other, we can add the two equations. Notice that something very interesting happens.

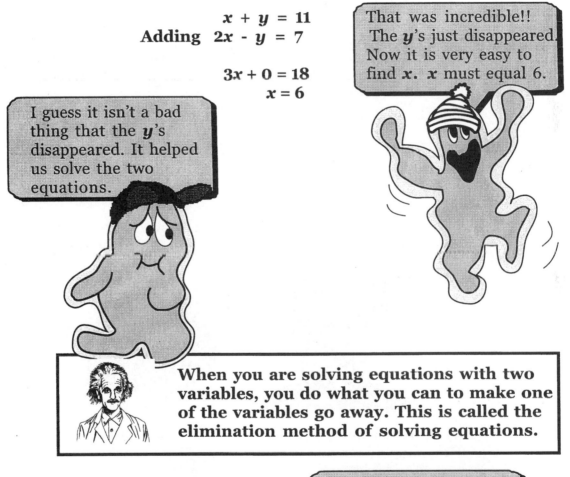

$$x + y = 11$$
Adding $2x - y = 7$

$$3x + 0 = 18$$
$$x = 6$$

That was incredible!! The **y**'s just disappeared. Now it is very easy to find **x**. **x** must equal 6.

I guess it isn't a bad thing that the **y**'s disappeared. It helped us solve the two equations.

When you are solving equations with two variables, you do what you can to make one of the variables go away. This is called the elimination method of solving equations.

Look at the two equations below:

$$7x + y = 52$$
$$4x + y = 31$$

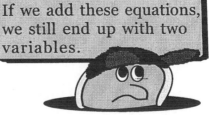

If we add these equations, we still end up with two variables.

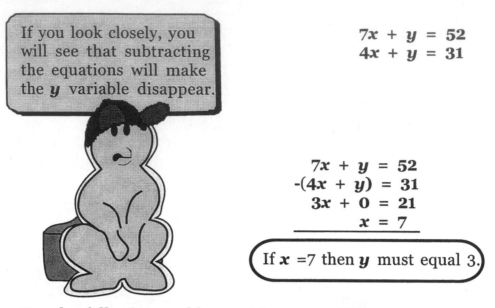

If you look closely, you will see that subtracting the equations will make the **y** variable disappear.

$$7x + y = 52$$
$$4x + y = 31$$

$$7x + y = 52$$
$$-(4x + y) = 31$$
$$3x + 0 = 21$$
$$x = 7$$

If $x = 7$ then **y** must equal 3.

Try the following problems with two variables:

1) $4x + 3y = 55$
   $4x + y = 45$

2) $3x + y = 29$
   $7x + y = 65$

3) Sam bought two hats and one coat at a cost of $92. Laura bought two hats and two coats at a cost of $140. What was the cost of each hat?

4) A pencil and a pen cost $1.58. A pen minus a pencil cost $.40. How much does one pencil cost?

5) $4x + y = 10$
   $2x + y = 9$

Sometimes the elimination method calls for some extra work. Look at the two equations below:

$$4x + y = 23$$
$$2x + 3y = 29$$

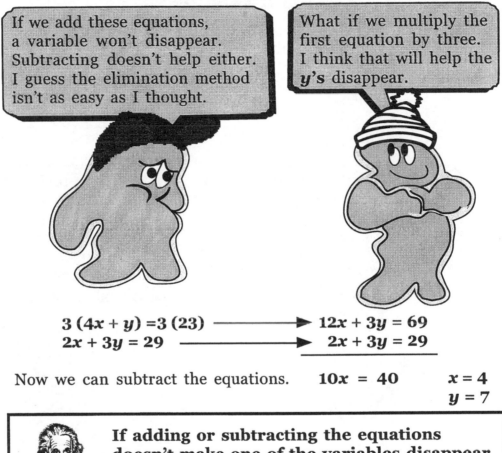

If we add these equations, a variable won't disappear. Subtracting doesn't help either. I guess the elimination method isn't as easy as I thought.

What if we multiply the first equation by three. I think that will help the y's disappear.

$$3(4x + y) = 3(23) \longrightarrow 12x + 3y = 69$$
$$2x + 3y = 29 \longrightarrow 2x + 3y = 29$$

Now we can subtract the equations. $10x = 40$ $x = 4$
$y = 7$

 **If adding or subtracting the equations doesn't make one of the variables disappear, then you are going to have to change one of the equations, or both of the equations.**

Look at the following two equations:

$$3x + y = 38$$
$$x + 4y = 31$$

Adding or subtracting will not make one of the variables disappear.

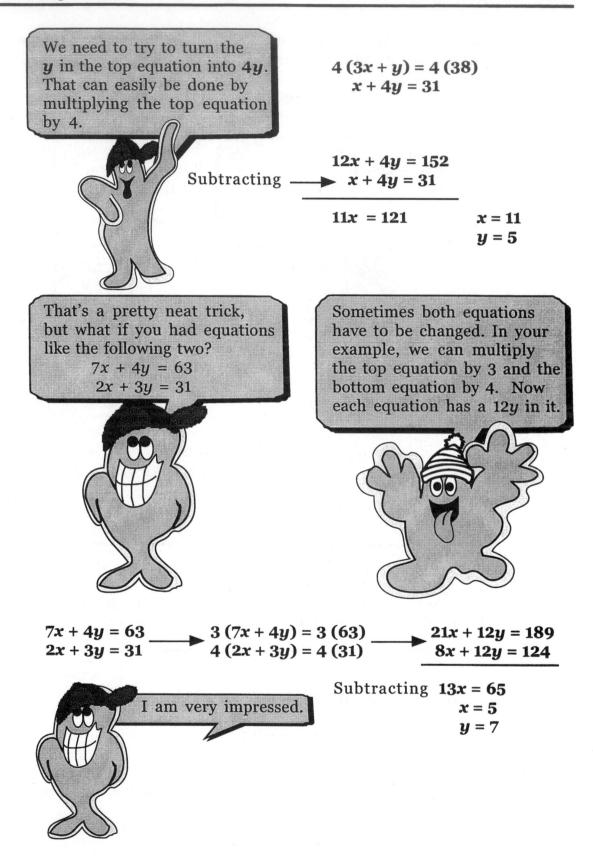

We need to try to turn the **y** in the top equation into **4y**. That can easily be done by multiplying the top equation by 4.

$$4(3x + y) = 4(38)$$
$$x + 4y = 31$$

Subtracting ⟶
$$12x + 4y = 152$$
$$x + 4y = 31$$
$$\overline{}$$
$$11x = 121 \qquad x = 11$$
$$y = 5$$

That's a pretty neat trick, but what if you had equations like the following two?
$$7x + 4y = 63$$
$$2x + 3y = 31$$

Sometimes both equations have to be changed. In your example, we can multiply the top equation by 3 and the bottom equation by 4. Now each equation has a 12y in it.

$$7x + 4y = 63$$
$$2x + 3y = 31$$
⟶
$$3(7x + 4y) = 3(63)$$
$$4(2x + 3y) = 4(31)$$
⟶
$$21x + 12y = 189$$
$$8x + 12y = 124$$
$$\overline{}$$

I am very impressed.

Subtracting
$$13x = 65$$
$$x = 5$$
$$y = 7$$

Use the elimination method to solve the following equations:

1) $x + y = 10$
       $3x + 5y = 36$

2) $2x + 3y = 55$
       $9x + 4y = 105$

3) Three pairs of shoes and two pairs of socks cost $123, while three pairs of socks and two pairs of shoes cost $89.50. What does a pair of socks cost?

4) There are two numbers. If the first number is added to three times the second, you will get 35. If the second number is added to three times the first, you will get a value of 33. What are the two numbers?

5) Mark's age plus three times Nik's age is equal to 54. Twice Mark's age plus four times Nik's age is equal to 80. How old is Nik?

Substitution Method

Another way mathematicians solve equations with two variables is by using the substitution method. When you use the substitution method, it is important to get x all alone on one side of one of the equations. Look at the two equations below:

$$x + y = 10$$
$$3x + 4y = 38$$

What is x equal to?

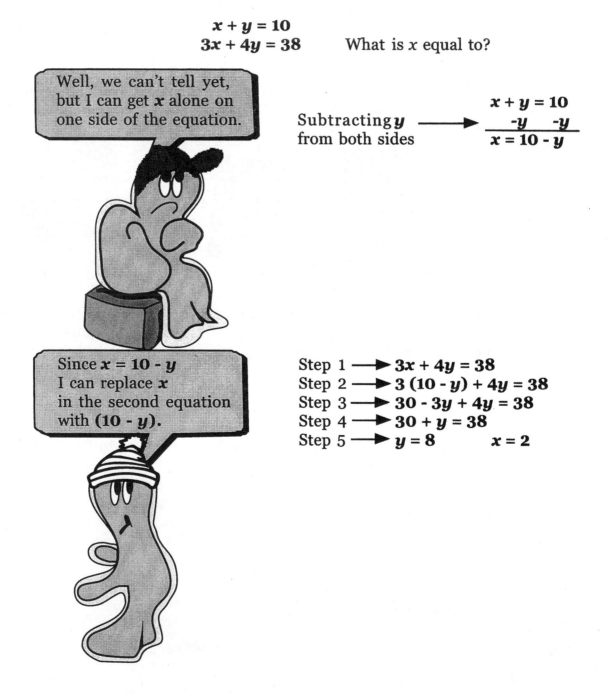

Well, we can't tell yet, but I can get x alone on one side of the equation.

Subtracting y from both sides ⟶

$$x + y = 10$$
$$\underline{-y \quad -y}$$
$$x = 10 - y$$

Since $x = 10 - y$ I can replace x in the second equation with $(10 - y)$.

Step 1 ⟶ $3x + 4y = 38$
Step 2 ⟶ $3(10 - y) + 4y = 38$
Step 3 ⟶ $30 - 3y + 4y = 38$
Step 4 ⟶ $30 + y = 38$
Step 5 ⟶ $y = 8$ $x = 2$

Let's try another example:

2x + y = 21
7x - 3y = 2

Step 1 (Isolating a letter)   **y = 21 - 2x**

Step 2 (Replacing y with 21 - 2x)   **7x - 3 (21 - 2x) = 2**

Step 3 (Do multiplication)   **7x -63 + 6x = 2**

Step 4 (Solve)   **13x -63 = 2**
                                                                  13x = 65
                                                                  x =5

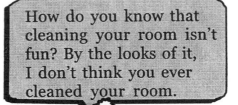

Try the following problems using the substitution method.

1) $x + y = 16$
   $2x + 3y = 44$

2) $2x + y = 21$
   $x + 2y = 12$

3) $2x + 4y = 100$
   $6x + 10y = 264$

4) $x + y = 10$
   $7x + 9y = 70$

5) $2x - y = 14$
   $3x + 2y = 19$

Hint: Don't be shocked if a variable is
      equal to zero.

Having Fun
With Variables

A pet store is owned by an eccentric mathematician who does not list the prices of the animals in his store. Instead of prices, he has written a number of equations to express the value of each animal.

> **2 Turtles + 2 Hamsters = Dog**
> **2 Cats + 4 Turtles = Dog**
> **2 Dogs - 2 Cats = 4 Hamsters**

Eric bought a dog at the store that he is having a problem with. (It has bitten him 7 times since he bought the dog.) Eric would like to trade the dog for some cats. Using the equations, determine how many cats Eric will receive in trade for his dog.

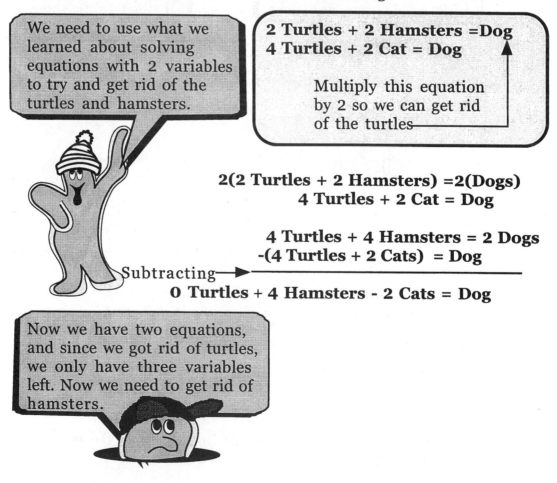

We need to use what we learned about solving equations with 2 variables to try and get rid of the turtles and hamsters.

2 Turtles + 2 Hamsters =Dog
4 Turtles + 2 Cat = Dog

Multiply this equation by 2 so we can get rid of the turtles

2(2 Turtles + 2 Hamsters) =2(Dogs)
4 Turtles + 2 Cat = Dog

4 Turtles + 4 Hamsters = 2 Dogs
-(4 Turtles + 2 Cats) = Dog

Subtracting⟶ _____

0 Turtles + 4 Hamsters - 2 Cats = Dog

Now we have two equations, and since we got rid of turtles, we only have three variables left. Now we need to get rid of hamsters.

4 Hamsters - 2 Cats = Dog
2 Dogs - 2 Cats = 4 Hamsters ◄── Let's use what we know about algebra to move the dogs to the right side of the equation and the hamsters to the left side.

+ **4 Hamsters - 2 Cats = Dog**
      -4 Hamsters - 2 Cats = -2 Dogs ◄── Now we can add the equations to make the hamsters disappear.

-4 Cats = - Dog
or
4 Cats = Dog

1)   Dog = Cat + Snail
      Horse = Dog + Cat   How many cats equal 1 dog?
      2 Horses = 3 Snails

2)   Banana + Pear = Apple   How many pears would it
      3 Bananas = Apple   take to make 2 apples?

3)   Car - Truck = 2 Bikes
      2 Trucks = Car + 8 Unicycles   How many bikes are
      Bike = 2 Unicycles   equal to a car?

4)   Triangle - Square = 2 Circles
      2 Circles + 5 Rectangles = Triangle   How many circles
      2 Squares = Triangle   equal one square?

5)
Math	Science		English	Social Studies		Math	Social Studies
Math	Science		English	Science		Math	Social Studies

How many social studies books equal an English book?

Simultaneous Equations:

1) $3x + y = 40$ $x =$_____

   $5x - y = 48$ $y =$_____

2) $9x - y = 39$ $x =$_____
   $2x - 2y = 22$ $y =$_____

3) Michael bought 3 pencils and 2 rulers at a total cost of $2.30. Nancy bought 3 rulers and 2 pencils for $2.00. What would be the cost of one pencil?

4) Sara wanted to buy fish for her aquarium. She determined that 9 goldfish plus 3 angelfish would cost $8.70. If she bought 6 angel and 4 goldfish, the cost would be $8.30. What is the cost of one goldfish?

5) If you have two numbers and add the first number to 4 times the second, you would get 30. If the second number is added to 4 times the first, you would get 15. What are the two numbers?

6) Travis bought 6 soccer balls and returned two shirts. He was charged $70.50. (The value of the shirts was subtracted from what he owed for the soccer balls.) Isaac bought the two shirts Travis returned plus 4 soccer balls. He was charged $84.50. What is the price of a soccer ball?

7) Andrea has two employees who are paid according to the chart below:

Employee	Hourly Pay	Daily Bonus
Carol	$6 per hour	$5
June	$4 per hour	$10

It is clear from the chart that each employee is paid a different hourly wage and is also paid a different daily bonus. Andrea wants both Carol and June to end each day working the same number of hours and she also wants them to receive the same amount of money. How many hours should Andrea have them work? Hint: Call the number of hours worked **x,** and make the total pay each employee receives equal to **y.**

8) Cat = 2 Dogs + Hamster
   3 Hamsters = Cat + 2 Dogs

How many dogs equal a cat?

9)   Dog = Cat + Mouse
     Horse = Dog + Cat
     2 Horses = 3 Mice

How many cats would it take to equal a dog?

10)   Math Book = 2 English Book
      4 Science - Social Studies = Math
      3 English = Science + Social Studies

How many social studies books equal a math book?

Graphing Equations

In the early 1600's, a mathematician named Descartes invented a way to find a spot on a grid. Say you wanted to direct people to the buried treasure on the grid below. You would simply give them the X and Y coordinates ——➤ (5,4). Now they would know exactly where the treasure was buried.

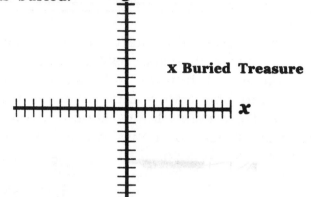

We not only use coordinate graphs for finding locations on grids, but also for graphing equations. Graphing equations allows us to solve problems and make predictions about many things such as distance traveled, speed, and acceleration. Look at how easy it is to make a prediction about distance traveled when we look at a time-distance graph for a spacecraft on its way to the moon. How far will the spacecraft go in 8 hours?

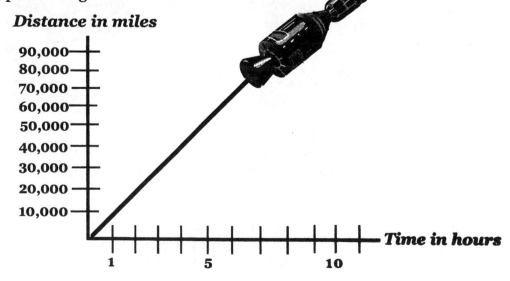

We even apply coordinate systems to the earth. Longitude and latitude lines are a form of grid that allows us to find locations on a map or globe. For example, Denver, Colorado is located at 40° north latitude and 105° west longitude. Knowing these two coordinates allows us to go to a globe and quickly find the city of Denver.

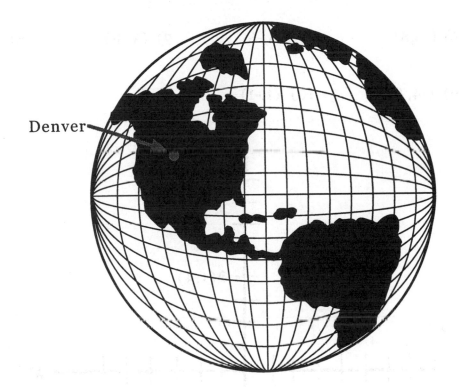

Denver

Place the following points on the graph shown below. The first one is done for you.

1) (1,4)   2) (2,-4)   3) (0,0)   4) (-4,-8)

5) (-6,8)   6) (-6,-6)   7) (3,-8)   8) (-2,-2)

9) (-4,7)   10) (1,-1)

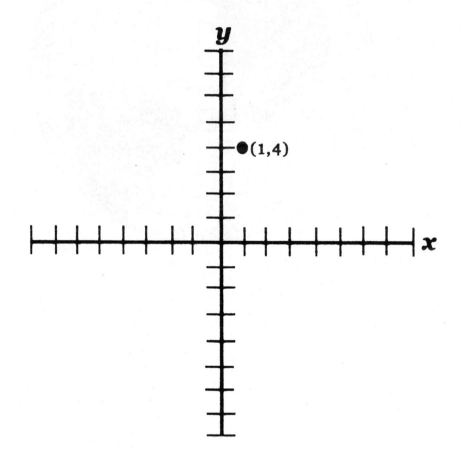

Name each point: A (3,2)

B_____

C_____

D_____

E_____

F_____

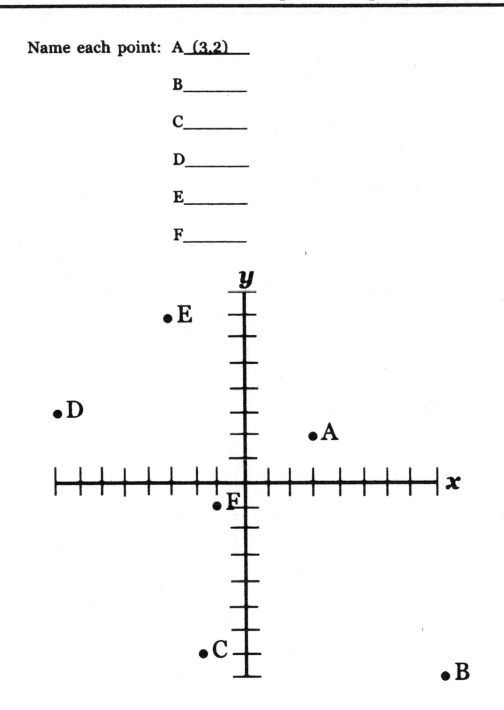

In addition to finding points on a graph, we can also graph equations. Look at the equation **2x + 1 = y.**

If *x* is equal to 1, then *y* must equal 3.
If *x* is equal to 2, then *y* must equal 5.
If *x* is equal to 3, then *y* must equal 7.

Try graphing the equation $x + 5 = y$. Before you graph the equation, make a chart so you will have points to connect.

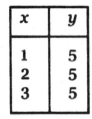

x	y
1	6
2	7
3	8

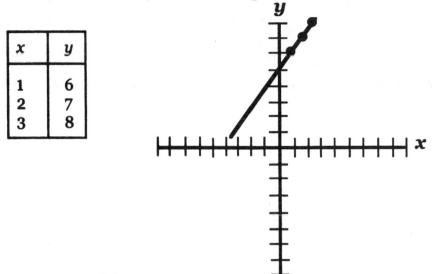

Some equations appear strange, but they are really quite simple. Look at the equation $y = 5$. Make a chart for several values of x.

x	y
1	5
2	5
3	5

As you can see, whatever value of x you chose, y will always be equal to 5.

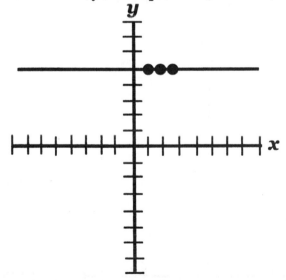

Try graphing the following equations on the graphs that are provided on the next page.

1) $x+6=y$ 2) $2x-1=y$ 3) $3x-5=y$

4) $y=4$ 5) $2x+y=10$ 6) $x=-8$

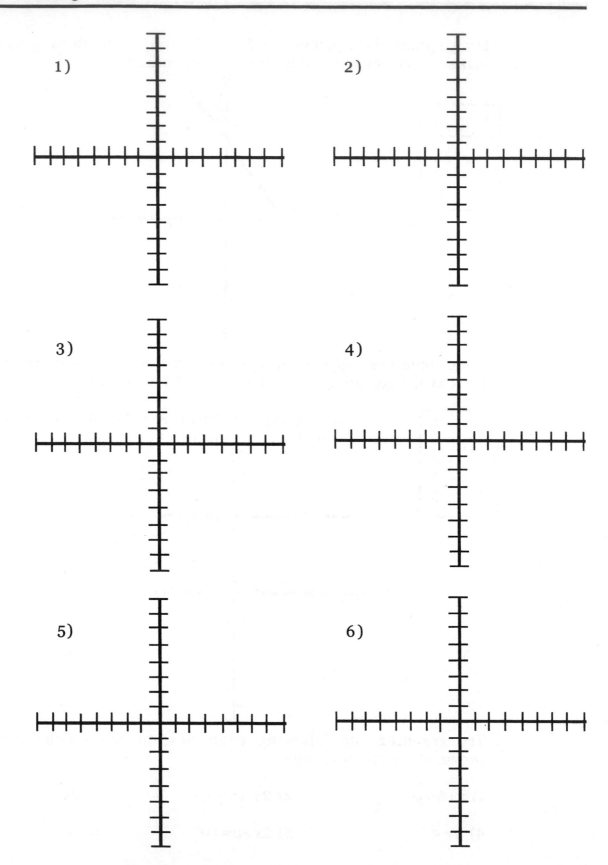

When you are graphing an equation, you are showing a relationship between x and y. Look at the graph below that shows information about a trip Isaac took with his family.

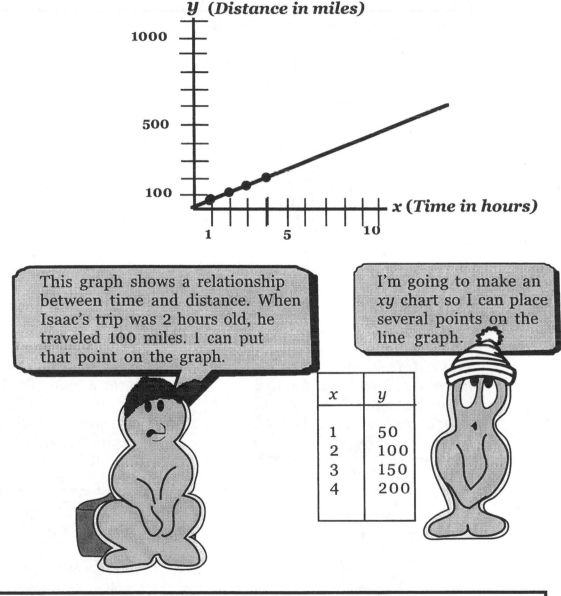

This graph shows a relationship between time and distance. When Isaac's trip was 2 hours old, he traveled 100 miles. I can put that point on the graph.

I'm going to make an xy chart so I can place several points on the line graph.

x	y
1	50
2	100
3	150
4	200

We could make predictions by using this graph. If Isaac traveled for 10 hours, he would go 500 miles. We can even write an equation showing the relationship between time and distance: $50x = y$

Travis also went on a trip, but he went by plane. Look at the graph below. Notice how it also shows a relationship between time and distance. Just like Isaac's trip, the relationship between time and distance on Travis's trip can be expressed by writing an equation. For every hour Travis travels, the distance he covers is 400 miles, so the equation would be $400x = y$.

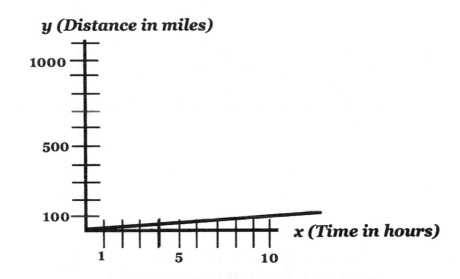

When two things have a relationship, such as time and distance, a graph can usually be drawn. Sometimes the graphs are straight lines, and sometimes they are curved. Draw graphs for the following situations. The first one is done for you.

1) A math teacher gathered data comparing the amount of time her students studied and the grades they received on their end of the year test. The teacher found that those students who studied an hour received an average test score of 65%, while those students who studied two hours received an average test score of 70%. Look at the graph the teacher compiled and then make a graph to show the relationship between study time and test scores. Do you think the graph will continue to head up, or will it level off?

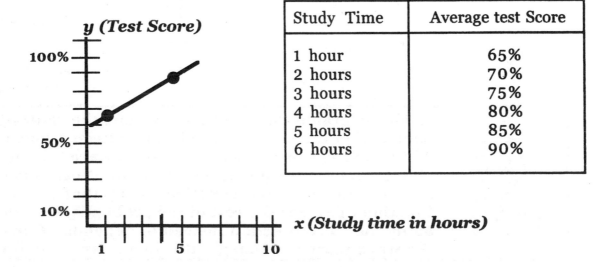

Study Time	Average test Score
1 hour	65%
2 hours	70%
3 hours	75%
4 hours	80%
5 hours	85%
6 hours	90%

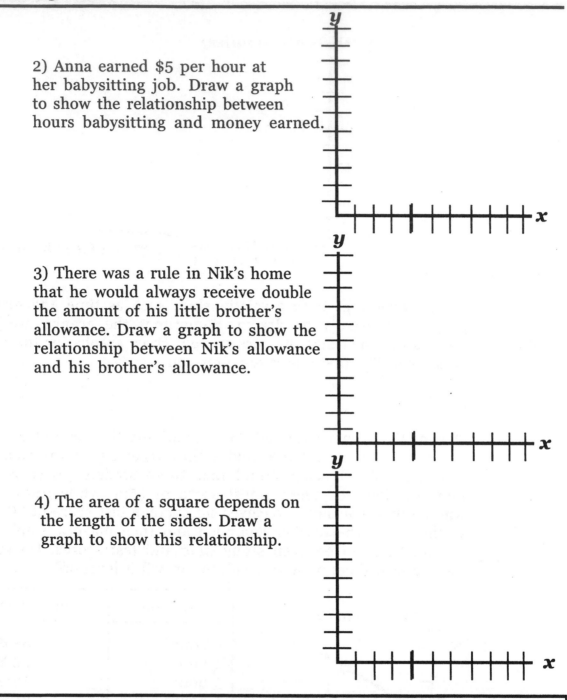

2) Anna earned $5 per hour at her babysitting job. Draw a graph to show the relationship between hours babysitting and money earned.

3) There was a rule in Nik's home that he would always receive double the amount of his little brother's allowance. Draw a graph to show the relationship between Nik's allowance and his brother's allowance.

4) The area of a square depends on the length of the sides. Draw a graph to show this relationship.

In all the graphs you have done so far, the value of *y* depends on the value of *x*. Mathematicians normally don't use the word depends when they are talking about a relationship between *x* and *y*. When *y* depends on the value of *x*, mathematicians say that *y* is a function of *x*. For the rest of the problems, we will be using the word function instead of depends. Don't let the word scare you though; it is just a fancy math word.

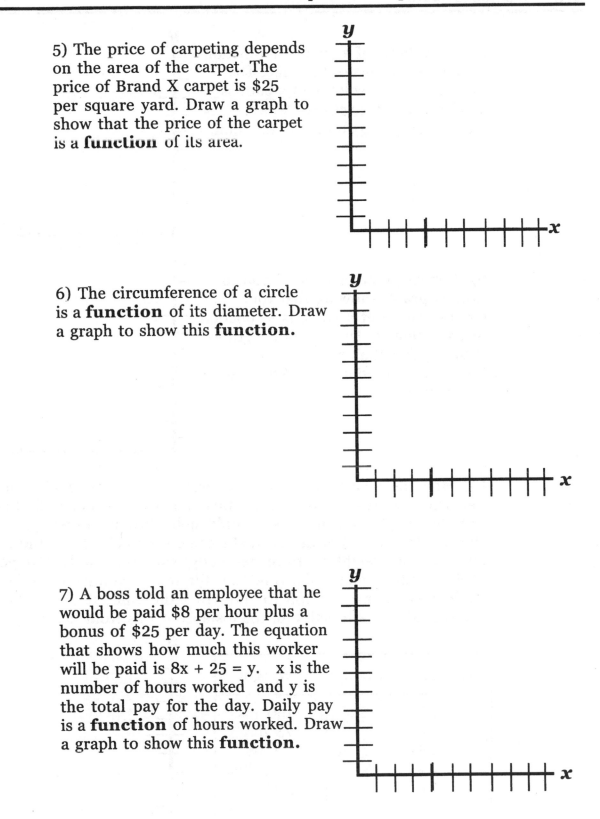

5) The price of carpeting depends on the area of the carpet. The price of Brand X carpet is $25 per square yard. Draw a graph to show that the price of the carpet is a **function** of its area.

6) The circumference of a circle is a **function** of its diameter. Draw a graph to show this **function.**

7) A boss told an employee that he would be paid $8 per hour plus a bonus of $25 per day. The equation that shows how much this worker will be paid is 8x + 25 = y.   x is the number of hours worked and y is the total pay for the day. Daily pay is a **function** of hours worked. Draw a graph to show this **function.**

8) The volume of a cube is a function of the dimensions of the cube. The formula for the volume of a cube is **V = side x side x side** or V=s³. Draw a graph to show this function.

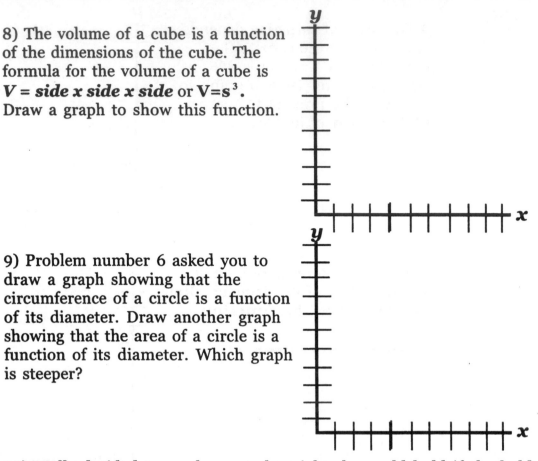

9) Problem number 6 asked you to draw a graph showing that the circumference of a circle is a function of its diameter. Draw another graph showing that the area of a circle is a function of its diameter. Which graph is steeper?

10) Molly decided to see how much weight she could hold if she held her arm out straight. She found that the closer to her body that she put the weight, the more she could hold. When the weight was all the way to the end of her arm, she could only hold 30 pounds. When she put the weight 6" from her body, she could hold 150 pounds. Molly made a chart showing the different amounts of weight she could hold. Draw a graph to show that the amount of weight Molly could hold was a function of the distance it was from her body.

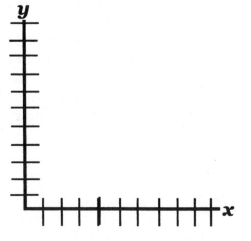

Distance from body	Weight
6"	150 lbs.
12"	75 lbs.
18"	50 lbs.
24"	37.5 lbs.
30"	30 lbs.

Slope of a Line

The slope of a line tells us how steep the line is and in what direction it is pointing. Look at the following lines and the description of their slopes.

This line has a very steep slope.

This line is flat and has 0 slope.

This line has a medium slope. Because the line is pointing down, it is said to have a negative slope.

This line is so steep that there is no number to describe the slope, so we say it has an infinitely steep slope. Because there is no number to describe this, we say that a vertical line has no slope. Be very careful though because no slope is obviously very different than 0 slope.

Earlier in the chapter we looked at line graphs that showed the relationship between time and distance for trips taken by Isaac and Travis.

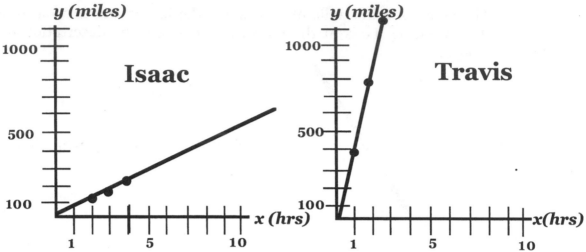

We also saw that the slope of Travis's graph was much steeper than the slope of Isaac's graph. We guessed that steeper slopes meant faster speeds.

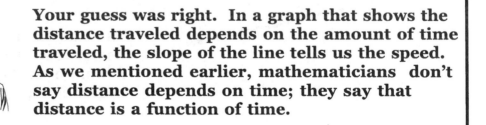

Your guess was right. In a graph that shows the distance traveled depends on the amount of time traveled, the slope of the line tells us the speed. As we mentioned earlier, mathematicians don't say distance depends on time; they say that distance is a function of time.

I know that the slope of Travis's graph is very steep so he must have traveled at a very fast speed. If I can find the slope of Travis's line graph, then I'll know his speed. How do I find the slope?

I think we should ask Einstein.

The first thing you need to do when you are determining slope is to pick two points on the graph. On Travis's graph, we will pick the points (1,400) and (2,800). Now you are just about ready to find the slope of a line, but before do, you need to know the meaning of two words ———————▶   **Rise** and **Run.**

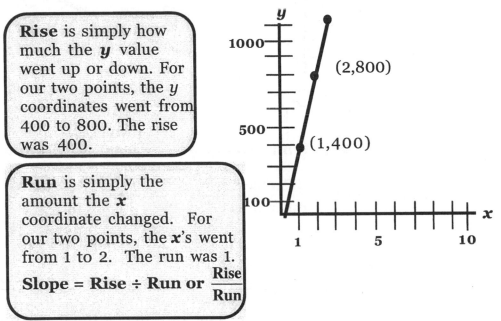

Rise is simply how much the y value went up or down. For our two points, the y coordinates went from 400 to 800. The rise was 400.

Run is simply the amount the x coordinate changed. For our two points, the x's went from 1 to 2. The run was 1.

Slope = Rise ÷ Run or $\dfrac{\textbf{Rise}}{\textbf{Run}}$

Let's review. To find the slope, you simply make a fraction:

$$\frac{\textbf{Amount of rise}}{\textbf{Amount of run}}$$ ———▶Then divide the fraction.

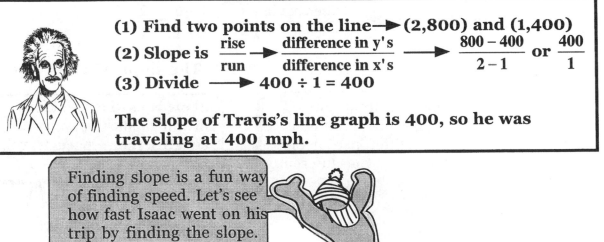

(1) Find two points on the line━▶ **(2,800) and (1,400)**

(2) Slope is $\dfrac{\textbf{rise}}{\textbf{run}}$ ➞ $\dfrac{\textbf{difference in y's}}{\textbf{difference in x's}}$ ———▶ $\dfrac{800-400}{2-1}$ **or** $\dfrac{400}{1}$

(3) Divide ———▶ **400 ÷ 1 = 400**

The slope of Travis's line graph is 400, so he was traveling at 400 mph.

Finding slope is a fun way of finding speed. Let's see how fast Isaac went on his trip by finding the slope.

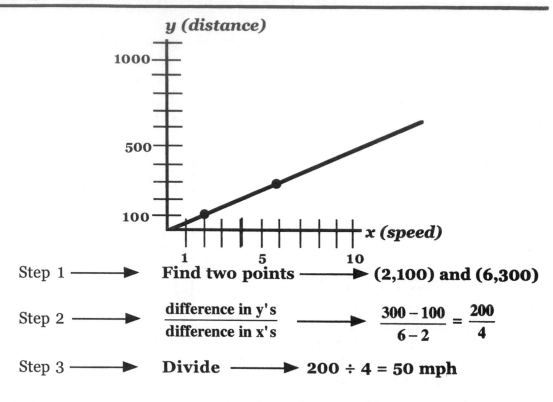

y (distance)

x (speed)

Step 1 ⟶ **Find two points** ⟶ **(2,100) and (6,300)**

Step 2 ⟶ $\dfrac{\textbf{difference in y's}}{\textbf{difference in x's}}$ ⟶ $\dfrac{\textbf{300}-\textbf{100}}{\textbf{6}-\textbf{2}} = \dfrac{\textbf{200}}{\textbf{4}}$

Step 3 ⟶ **Divide** ⟶ **200 ÷ 4 = 50 mph**

Let's look at how to find the slope of a line without making a graph.
Example: Find the slope of the equation **2x + 4 = y.**

Step 1 ⟶ Find two points   (1,6) and (2,8)

Step 2 ⟶ $\dfrac{\text{Difference in y's}}{\text{Difference in x's}}$ $\dfrac{8-6}{2-1} = \dfrac{2}{1}$

Step 3 ⟶ Divide   2÷1=2 **The slope of 2x +4 = y is 2.**

Now I am beginning to see that the slope of a line is simply the difference in the rise, divided by the difference in the run.

Slope is used for all kinds of things such as construction, space travel, and engineering.

Find the slope of the following equations. The first one is done for you.

1) $x+5=y$

Step 1 $(1,6)$ and $(2,7)$

Step 2 $\dfrac{7-6}{2-1}=\dfrac{1}{1}$

Step 3 $1 \div 1 = 1$ Slope = 1

2) $3x-1=y$

3) $2x+5=y$

4) $x-y=5$

5) $6x+5=y$

6) The distance a train travels is a function of the amount of time it is traveling. One particular train's travel equation is $20x+15=y$. x stands for the number of hours traveled and y is the distance traveled. What is the average speed of the train?

7) Match each of the seven lines with the phrase describing its slope.

No slope

Steep positive slope

0 slope

Very steep negative slope

Gradual negative slope

Gradual positive slope

Medium negative slope

8) What is the speed of the vehicle represented by the graph below?

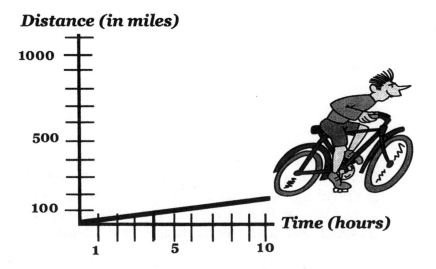

The slope of a time-distance graph gives you speed. The slope of a time-speed graph gives you acceleration. Use this information to answer questions 9 and 10.

9) What is the acceleration of the car represented by this graph?

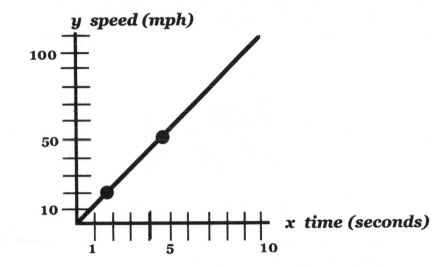

10) Write an equation and draw a graph to represent the acceleration of a vehicle traveling at a constant speed of 60 mph.

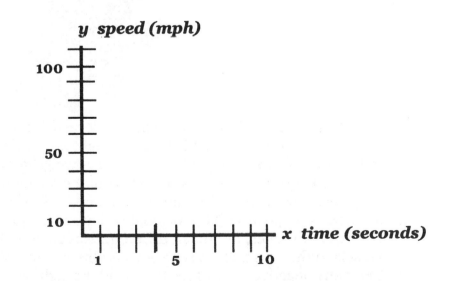

Chapter 18

Acceleration

G-forces are the forces of acceleration that pull on you when you suddenly change your speed and/or direction. People are typically exposed to 1-G, which is the force of gravity when you are engaged in normal activity. Pilots encounter high G's when they are engaged in sudden maneuvers. The effects on pilots when they are experiencing high G's are substantial.

When pilots are exposed to 8 G's, their heads, which normally weigh 10-12 pounds, will weigh 80 pounds. High G-forces will also push blood towards their feet. The heart then has an extremely difficult time pumping the blood back to the head. The first symptoms that a pilot feels are tunnel vision and loss of color. Eventually, if the G-forces continue, the pilot will lose consciousness. This is called *"Gravity Induced Loss of Consciousness"*

The G-forces that a pilot feels when making sudden climbs and turns are positive G-forces. If a pilot is flying straight and suddenly pushes the nose of the aircraft down, he will experience a weightless feeling. What he is feeling are negative G-forces. These act in the opposite way of positive G-forces. Negative G-forces push the blood back into the head. People can be exposed to positive 9 G's without serious consequences. Negative G-forces, however, are much different. Negative 2 G's can rupture blood vessels in the eyes and cause serious problems for a pilot. A pilot who pulls too many negative G's will see the world through blood-shot eyes.

Acceleration is often confused with speed. Acceleration is not the speed of an object, it is the change in speed. The idea of acceleration can be best explained by taking the example of a car being driven on a highway. If the driver turns on the cruise-control and maintains his speed at 60 mph, we say that his acceleration is zero————▶In other words, the speed of the car is not changing. If the driver speeds up to 75 mph to pass another vehicle, then we say he has a positive acceleration. If he brakes and slows to 25 mph, we say that he is experiencing negative acceleration or deceleration.

When our driver speeds up to pass a car, we know that his acceleration is a positive number, but we need to know how to determine what that number is. When you are calculating acceleration, you use a very simple formula:

$$Acceleration = \frac{Change\ in\ Speed}{Time}$$

> For example: *If a car went from 10 mph to 60 mph in 10 seconds, what was the acceleration of the car?*

Since the speed went from 10 mph to 60 mph, the change in speed was 50 mph (subtraction). The time was 10 seconds, so:

$$Acceleration\ =\ \frac{50}{10}\ or\ 5\ ???$$

That was pretty easy, but what is the label when you are talking about acceleration?

The car increased its speed by 5 miles per hour every second, so we say the acceleration is 5 mph per second.

Another example: If the space shuttle went from the launch pad to a speed of 6000 mph in 2 minutes, what was its acceleration?

$$\text{Acceleration} = \frac{6000 - 0 \text{ (change in speed)}}{2 \text{ minutes (time)}}$$

$$\text{Acceleration} = \frac{6000}{2} = 3000 \text{ miles per hour} \longrightarrow \text{per minute}$$

> When I run, I can go from standing still to a speed of 12 feet per second in only 6 seconds. What is my acceleration?

> Using the acceleration formula, your acceleration must be 12 ÷ 6 or 2 feet per second per second.

1) What is the acceleration of a car that goes from a standstill to 65 mph in 13 seconds?

2) A car is traveling at a speed of 60 mph. Because of road construction, it takes 5 seconds for it to slow to 30 mph. What is this car's deceleration?

3) A rock is dropped from the top of a building. After 2 seconds, it is traveling at a speed of 64 feet per second. After 5 seconds, it is traveling at a speed of 160 feet per second. What was the acceleration of the rock between the 2 second mark and the 5 second mark?

When scientists deal with acceleration, they often use speed measurements that are different from miles per hour. When we deal with acceleration in this chapter, we will also work with other ways to measure speed. One that we will use quite often will be ***feet per second***.

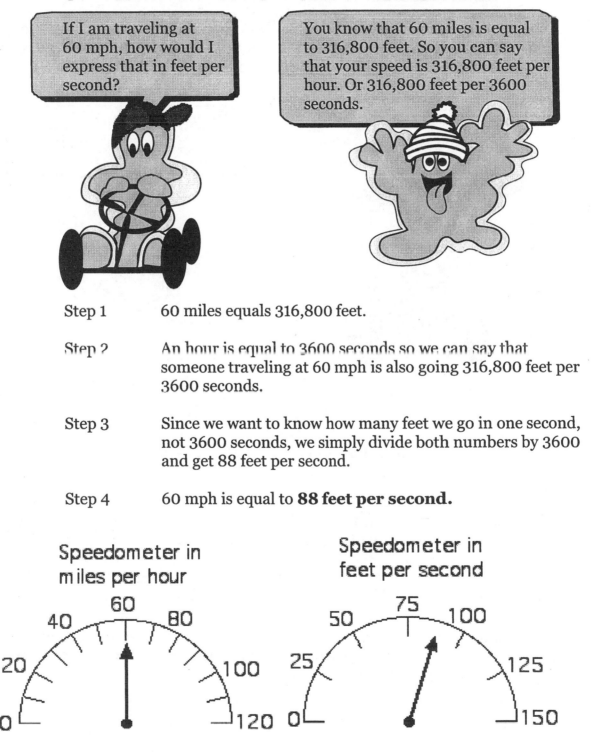

If I am traveling at 60 mph, how would I express that in feet per second?

You know that 60 miles is equal to 316,800 feet. So you can say that your speed is 316,800 feet per hour. Or 316,800 feet per 3600 seconds.

Step 1   60 miles equals 316,800 feet.

Step 2   An hour is equal to 3600 seconds so we can say that someone traveling at 60 mph is also going 316,800 feet per 3600 seconds.

Step 3   Since we want to know how many feet we go in one second, not 3600 seconds, we simply divide both numbers by 3600 and get 88 feet per second.

Step 4   60 mph is equal to **88 feet per second.**

Speedometer in miles per hour

Speedometer in feet per second

Another example: When a car has a speed of 75 miles per hour, what is its speed in feet per second?

Since 75 miles is equal to 396,000 feet and an hour is equal to 3600 seconds, then the car's speed in feet per second is found by dividing both numbers by 3600 ——▶ 110 feet per second.

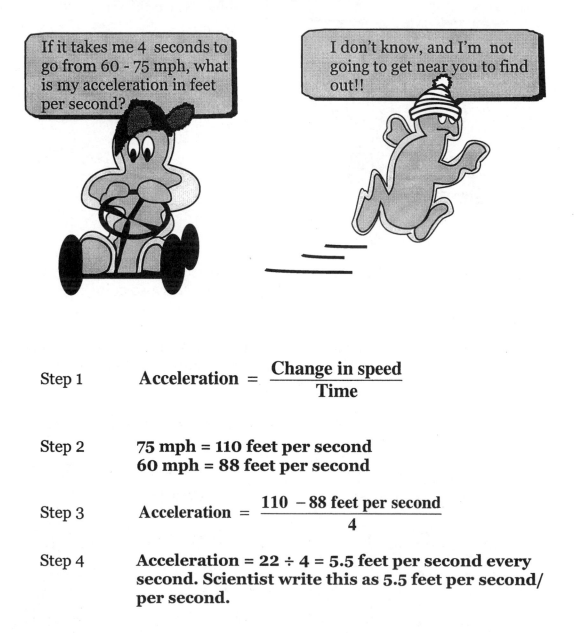

If it takes me 4 seconds to go from 60 - 75 mph, what is my acceleration in feet per second?

I don't know, and I'm not going to get near you to find out!!

Step 1   Acceleration = $\dfrac{\text{Change in speed}}{\text{Time}}$

Step 2   **75 mph = 110 feet per second**
60 mph = 88 feet per second

Step 3   **Acceleration** = $\dfrac{110 - 88 \text{ feet per second}}{4}$

Step 4   **Acceleration = 22 ÷ 4 = 5.5 feet per second every second. Scientist write this as 5.5 feet per second/ per second.**

Let's try another problem: When our driver brakes and has negative acceleration, he goes from 60 mph to 25 mph in 4 seconds. What is his deceleration in feet per second?

The first thing we need to do is find out what those speeds are in feet per second.

60 mph = 88 feet per second (We know this from a previous problem.)

$$25 \text{ mph} = \frac{25 \times 5280}{3600} = \frac{132,000}{3600} = 36\frac{2}{3} \text{ feet per second}$$

Step 1 $$\text{Acceleration} = \frac{\text{Change in speed}}{\text{Time}}$$

Step 2 $$\text{Acceleration} = \frac{88 - 36\frac{2}{3}}{4}$$

Step 3 $$\text{Acceleration} = \frac{51\frac{1}{3}}{4} = 12.8$$

Our driver has a negative acceleration of 12.8 feet per second/per second.

Problems:

1) What is the speed, in feet per second, of a car traveling at 30 mph?

2) What is the speed, in feet per second, of a car traveling at 15 mph?

3) If a car traveled 450 feet in two seconds, what is its speed in feet per second?

4) If a car increases its speed from 44 feet per second to 100 feet per second over an eight second time span, what is the car's acceleration?

5) What is the acceleration of a car traveling at a constant speed of 80 mph?

6) If speed increases from 20 mph to 80 mph in 4 seconds, what is the acceleration?

7) If a driver traveling at 75 mph suddenly slams on her brakes and slows to 10 mph, what is the rate of deceleration if the amount of time it took to slow to 10 mph was three seconds?

8) Using the formula for acceleration, prove that a car traveling at 50 mph for one minute has an acceleration of 0.

9) What is the acceleration of a car that goes from 0 to 60 mph in 4 seconds? (Use feet per second per second.)

10) If a car traveling at 80 mph hits a tree and decelerates to 0 mph in 1/3 second, there will be such a rapid negative acceleration that the potential for injury is very high. What is the acceleration in this example? (Use feet per second per second.)

Almost every car has a speedometer to measure speed.

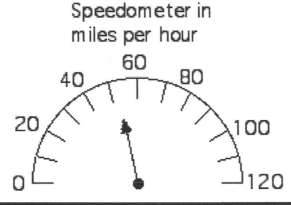

Speedometer in
miles per hour

You can also make a simple device to measure your acceleration. If you attached a string to a metal ball and suspended it from the ceiling of your car, you would notice that the hanging ball changes position depending on whether your acceleration is positive, negative, or zero.

The ball swings back when you accelerate.

The ball swings forward when you decelerate.

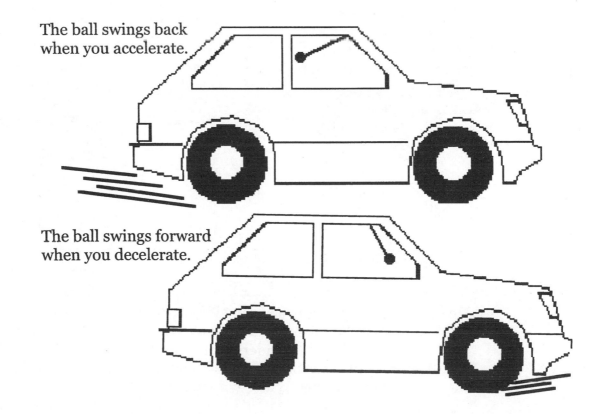

The ball hangs vertically when you are moving at a constant speed.
(0 acceleration means 0°)

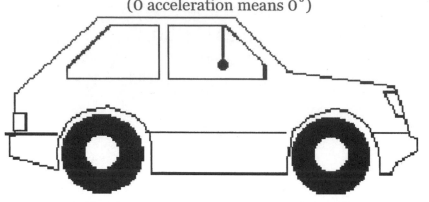

If you look at the string and the metal ball, you will see that something very interesting happens with the angle of the string and ball. The faster the acceleration or deceleration, the larger the angle. There is a formula that we can use that will tell us the acceleration of our vehicle. This formula is based on the angle of the hanging ball:

Acceleration = g   x   tangent of the angle.

I can find the tangent of any angle by looking up the angle in my trigonometry table, but what is **g** ?

I don't know why, but I know **g** is equal to 32 feet per second per second. Maybe Einstein can explain what **g** is.

Understanding what **g** is and why it is 32 feet per second per second is a little confusing. You can use the formula without understanding **g**, but if you would like to try and understand what it is, read what Einstein has to say. If your mind is starting to overload and is in danger of exploding, skip the explanation and come back to it later.

g stands for the acceleration of objects near the surface of the earth when they are in free fall. This sounds complicated, but it is really quite simple. Galileo discovered that if you don't count air resistance, all objects fall with the same acceleration, regardless of their weight. What is that acceleration?

It is g ————————▶ 32 feet per second per second. Look at the following chart which shows the speed of a bowling ball that is dropped from a tall building:

Time	Speed
0 seconds.....................0 feet per second
1 second........................32 feet per second
2 seconds....................64 feet per second
3 seconds....................96 feet per second
4 seconds....................128 feet per second

Remember, acceleration is the change in speed. The change in speed in this example is 32 feet per second every second. Every second the bowling ball drops, it goes 32 feet per second faster.

Let's try using the formula to determine the acceleration of a car whose hanging string and ball show an angle of 40°.

Acceleration = g _x_ tangent of angle

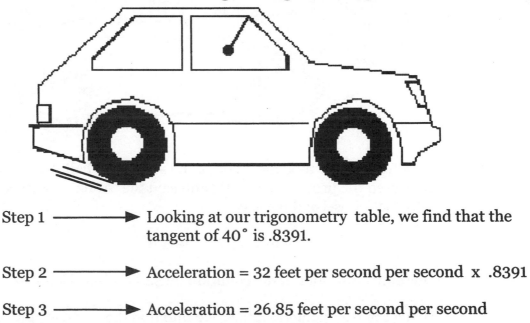

Step 1 ————————▶ Looking at our trigonometry table, we find that the tangent of 40° is .8391.

Step 2 ————————▶ Acceleration = 32 feet per second per second x .8391

Step 3 ————————▶ Acceleration = 26.85 feet per second per second

Let's try another problem by going to the problem on page 284 and seeing what angle our acceleration meter would have for a car accelerating from 60 mph to 75 mph. We have already determined that the acceleration is 5.5 feet per second per second. Using the formula:

Acceleration (5.5) = 32 feet per second per second x tan A

(A stands for our unknown angle)

5.5 = 32 x tan A

$$\frac{5.5}{32} = \tan A$$

.1718 = tan A

Looking in our trigonometry table, we find that this would be an angle of about 10°. Our acceleration meter would show an angle of approximately 10°.

Let's try an extreme example to show why large accelerations or large decelerations mean large angles on our acceleration meter. Look back to problem 10 on page 286. The question dealt with a car that crashed at a speed of 80 mph.

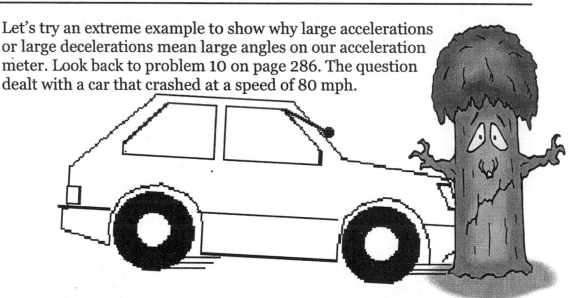

Let's try to determine the angle of the string and ball. Hopefully you answered the problem correctly and said the car had an acceleration of -352 feet per second per second.

-352 = 32 x tan A

Dividing both sides of the equation by 32 ⟶ tan A = 11

Using the trigonometry tables, we find that the angle is approximately 85°.

Acceleration:

1) What is the acceleration of a car with an acceleration meter angle of 60°?

2) What is the acceleration of a car with an acceleration meter angle of 30°?

3) If a car goes from 50 mph to 55 mph in 5 seconds, what is the angle of the acceleration meter?

4) There is something special about the acceleration of a car that has an acceleration meter that registers 45°. Why is this a special acceleration?

5) If a drag racer goes from 0 mph to 250 mph in 5 seconds, what is the angle of the acceleration meter?

6) A car that is traveling at 25 mph has a partially filled fish bowl resting on its seat. If the car accelerates to 50 mph in 5 seconds, draw a picture showing what happens to the water during the acceleration?

7) If a car accelerates from 60 mph to 90 mph in a span of 10 seconds, what is its acceleration? (Give your answer in feet per second per second.)

8) If a wheelchair racer accelerates from 10 mph to 50 mph on a 1 minute trip down a steep hill, what is his acceleration? (Give your answer in feet per second per second.)

9) A car holds a cubic container with sides of 8 inches that is half filled with water. The car accelerates smoothly from 0 mph to 100 mph in 5 seconds. Will any water spill during the acceleration? Why or why not?

10) If the angle on the acceleration meter is at a negative 30° and the car slowed to a stop over a 5 second period of time, what was the approximate speed of the car before the deceleration started?

Calculus

Calculus is not only one of the most mysterious and misunderstood areas of mathematics, but it is also one of the most important. Without calculus, most of the advances in technology and space exploration would not have been possible.

In 1665, Isaac Newton left the city of London to escape the bubonic plague and spent two very productive years at his family's farm. During these years, Newton not only produced his three laws of motion, but he also invented calculus. Newton invented calculus because he needed to find a way to determine the speed and acceleration of each planet at any point in its orbit. Because the planets' orbits around the sun are elliptical, the force of gravity exerted by the sun on the planets was constantly changing. Because of this, the speed and acceleration of the planets was also constantly changing. With calculus, Newton could overcome this problem and accurately determine speed and acceleration.

In this chapter, we will be using calculus to find the speed of a train at many points along its journey. This train, like the planets, has a speed that is constantly changing. This chapter will introduce you to calculus and show you some of the extraordinary things that it can do.

A math contest was being held for all elementary schools in the United States. As the contest entered the final round, three schools were tied for first place. The Einstein Elementary school was one of those three schools. The final round consisted of three problems.

Problem 1:

The graph below shows the relationship between time and distance for a car traveling from Chicago to Boston. The equation that represents this relationship is $y = 50x$. At what speed is the car traveling?

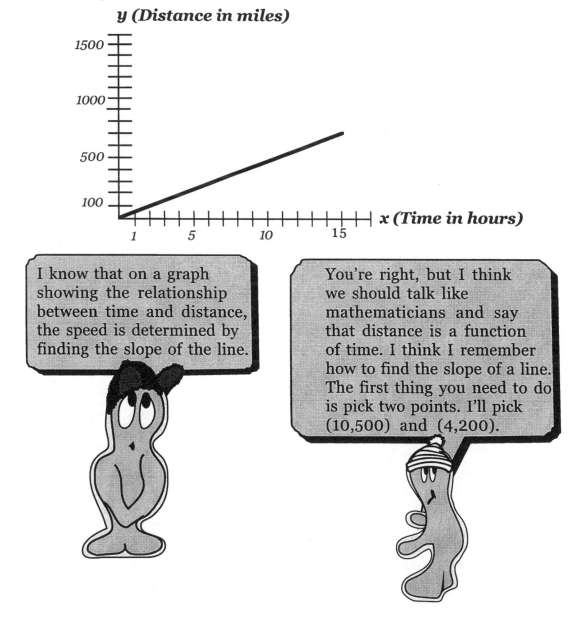

I know that on a graph showing the relationship between time and distance, the speed is determined by finding the slope of the line.

You're right, but I think we should talk like mathematicians and say that distance is a function of time. I think I remember how to find the slope of a line. The first thing you need to do is pick two points. I'll pick (10,500) and (4,200).

The chapter on graphing equations told us that there are three steps we need to take when we are trying to find the slope of a line. The first step is to pick two points.

I already picked them: (10,500) and (4,200).

Step 2 (Make a fraction)

$$\frac{\text{Amount of the rise}}{\text{Amount of the run}} \longrightarrow \frac{\text{Subtract y's}}{\text{Subtract x's}}$$

Step 3 (Divide the fraction)

That's easy: 300 miles ÷ 6 hours = 50. The speed of the car is 50 mph. I think we might win this contest.

That's easy:
$$\frac{500 - 200}{10 - 4} = \frac{300}{6}$$

Problem 2:

A freight train had a very serious problem with its engine. It could only start very, very slowly and gradually pick up speed. The engineer kept a time/distance chart so he could determine the average speed of the train. The engineer noticed an interesting relationship between x and y.

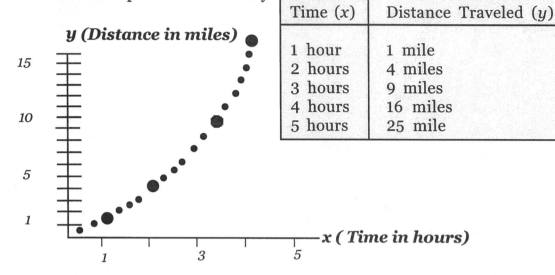

Time (*x*)	Distance Traveled (*y*)
1 hour	1 mile
2 hours	4 miles
3 hours	9 miles
4 hours	16 miles
5 hours	25 mile

(a) Write an equation to show the relationship between x and y.
(b) What was the train's average speed for the 5 hour trip?
(c) What was the train's average speed between the 2 hour and the 4 hour mark?

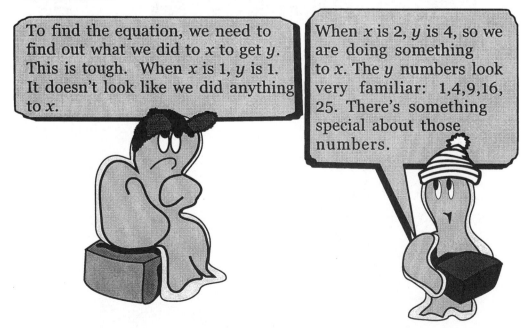

To find the equation, we need to find out what we did to x to get y. This is tough. When x is 1, y is 1. It doesn't look like we did anything to x.

When x is 2, y is 4, so we are doing something to x. The y numbers look very familiar: 1,4,9,16, 25. There's something special about those numbers.

Problem 3:

The engineer in problem 2 is facing a perplexing situation. He knows how to find the average speed of his train after he has gone a certain distance, but because the train's speedometer is broken, he never knows how fast he is traveling. You need to help the engineer by determining how fast the train is traveling at each of the hour marks.

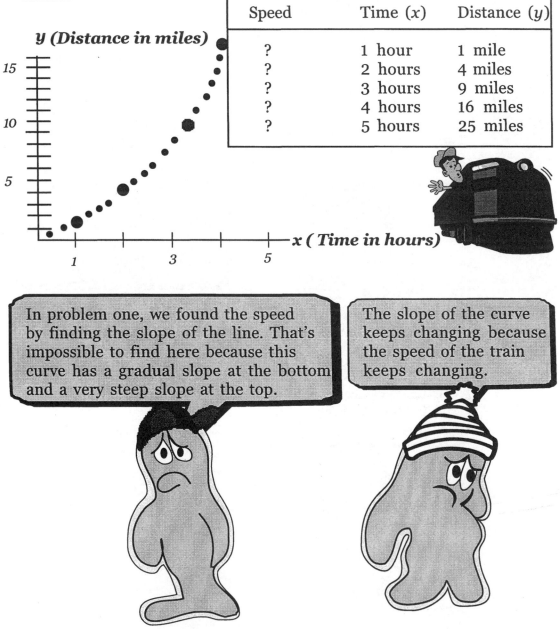

Speed	Time (x)	Distance (y)
?	1 hour	1 mile
?	2 hours	4 miles
?	3 hours	9 miles
?	4 hours	16 miles
?	5 hours	25 miles

y (Distance in miles)

x (Time in hours)

In problem one, we found the speed by finding the slope of the line. That's impossible to find here because this curve has a gradual slope at the bottom and a very steep slope at the top.

The slope of the curve keeps changing because the speed of the train keeps changing.

If we could find the slope of a point, we could easily find the speed of the train at any place on the curve. But a single point doesn't have a slope, does it?

I know we can't find the slope of a point, but we can find the slope of a line near a point. Let's start by looking at hour mark C. I'll draw a line from C to D and find the slope of that line.

y (Distance in miles)

D (4,16)

C (3,9)

15

10

5

B

A

1

1   3   5

x (Time in hours)

The slope of CD is easy. $\dfrac{16-9}{4-3}=7$

I know that 7 mph is pretty close to the speed of the train at point C. Even though it is close, I know that it is not the exact speed. If we want to win the contest, we'll have to find a way to determine the exact speed.

Why don't we draw another line with a point even closer to C. Let's try the point (3.5, 12.25). The slope of that line is $\dfrac{12.25-9}{3.5-3}=6.5$

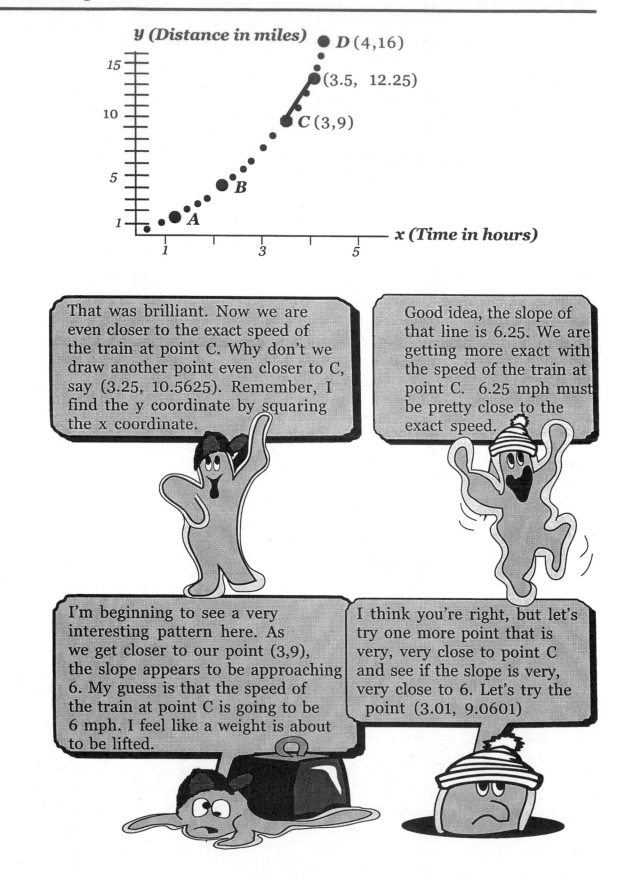

That was brilliant. Now we are even closer to the exact speed of the train at point C. Why don't we draw another point even closer to C, say (3.25, 10.5625). Remember, I find the y coordinate by squaring the x coordinate.

Good idea, the slope of that line is 6.25. We are getting more exact with the speed of the train at point C. 6.25 mph must be pretty close to the exact speed.

I'm beginning to see a very interesting pattern here. As we get closer to our point (3,9), the slope appears to be approaching 6. My guess is that the speed of the train at point C is going to be 6 mph. I feel like a weight is about to be lifted.

I think you're right, but let's try one more point that is very, very close to point C and see if the slope is very, very close to 6. Let's try the point (3.01, 9.0601)

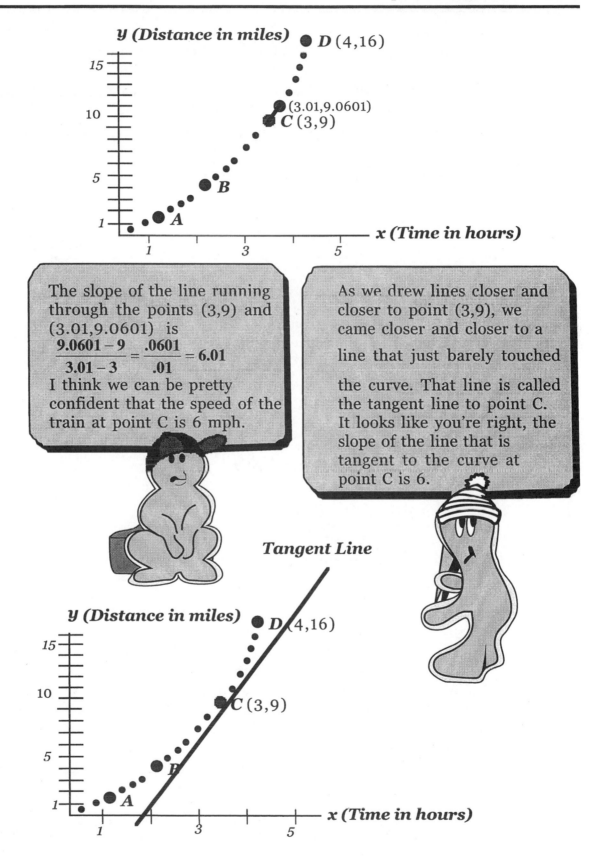

y (Distance in miles)

D (4,16)

(3.01,9.0601)

C (3,9)

B

A

x (Time in hours)

The slope of the line running through the points (3,9) and (3.01,9.0601) is

$$\frac{9.0601 - 9}{3.01 - 3} = \frac{.0601}{.01} = 6.01$$

I think we can be pretty confident that the speed of the train at point C is 6 mph.

As we drew lines closer and closer to point (3,9), we came closer and closer to a line that just barely touched the curve. That line is called the tangent line to point C. It looks like you're right, the slope of the line that is tangent to the curve at point C is 6.

Tangent Line

y (Distance in miles)

D (4,16)

C (3,9)

B

A

x (Time in hours)

We have our answer for point C, but we are running out of time. I wonder if we have to do all the calculations for every point. It seems like there must be a rule to help us find the slope of the line tangent to the curve at each point.

Let's see if Einstein knows if there is a rule.

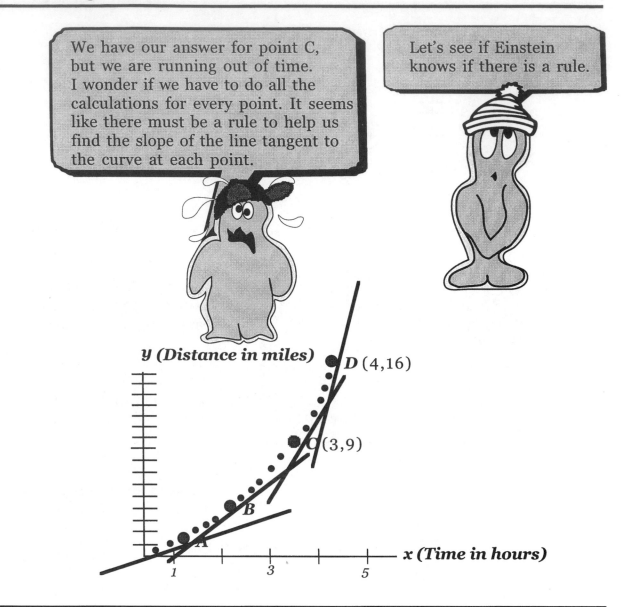

y (Distance in miles)

D (4,16)

C (3,9)

B

A

1   3   5

x (Time in hours)

Einstein isn't very good at this kind of math, but I, Calculus Man am here to help. You are right, there is a rule that will help you determine the slope of the line tangent to the curve at a single point. The slope of the tangent line for the function $y = x^2$ is $2x$.

This makes our task easier. The slope of the tangent line at each point can be figured by taking the x value and multiplying by 2.

Point	Slope	Speed
(1,1)	$2x=2$	2 mph
(2,4)	$2x=4$	4 mph
(3,9)	$2x=6$	6 mph
(4,16)	$2x=8$	8 mph
(5,25)	$2x=10$	10 mph

If you want to impress people, instead of calling your answer the slope of the tangent line, you can talk like calculus students and call it the derivative.

If people ask me how we figured the speed of the train at the 5 points, I'm going to say that we simply found the derivative.

I wonder if Einstein thinks he's fooling anyone by wearing sunglasses and a hat and calling himself Calculus Man.

It's not that I don't trust Calculus Man, but let's check one more point the same way we checked point C. I want to make sure Calculus Man's rule works.

Let's take another point that is very close to point E, say (5.01, 25.1001) If Calculus Man is right, then the slope of the line going through (5,25) and (5.01, 25.1001) will be very close to 10.

$$\frac{25.1001 - 25}{5.01 - 5} = \frac{.1001}{.01} = 10.01$$

It works!! Let's get these answers turned in and get our trophy.

To find the derivative of the function $y = x^2$, you simply take the value of x and multiply by 2. (The derivative of $y = x^2$ is $2x$.)

1) What is the speed of the train 10 hours after it leaves the station?

2) What is the speed of the train 5 hours and 30 minutes after it leaves the station?

3) How many hours until the train reaches a speed of 60 mph?

4) What is the speed of the train 30 minutes after it starts?

5) Look at the time/speed curve for a moving car that is shown below. Remember that acceleration can be determined by finding the slope of an equation that is a function of time and speed. What do you think the equation is for this graph?

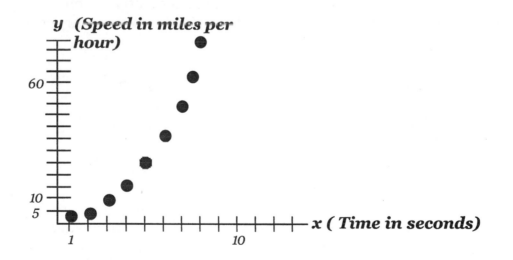

6) What is the speed of the car seven seconds after it starts?

7) What is the acceleration of the car 7 seconds after it starts?

8) How many seconds will it take for the car to hit 100 miles per hour?

9) If the car continues to accelerate at the same pace, how many seconds will it take for the car to reach an acceleration of 50 mph per second?

10) We know that the derivative of $y = x^2$ is 2x. The derivative of $y = x^3$ is $3x^2$. In the function $y = x^3$, what is the derivative at the point (4,64)?

Look at the functions and their derivatives that are given below. See if you can figure out how Newton found the derivative of each function.

$y = x^2$ -------- 2x $y = 5x^3$ ---------- $15x^2$

$y = x^3$ -------- $3x^2$ $y = 11x^4$ --------- $44x^3$

$y = 4x^2$ ------- 8x $y = 11x^2$ --------- 22x

See if you can find the derivatives for the following functions :

1) $y = x^4$ 2) $y = 7x^2$ 3) $y = 5x^3$

4) $y = 10x^6$ 5) $y = 3x^3$ 6) $y = 5x^1$

1) An eastbound train, traveling at 40 mph, left a train station at 10:00 A.M.   A northbound train, traveling at 30 mph, also left the train station at 10:00 A. M.   Three hours later, both trains stopped. If a bird flew directly from one train to the other, how far would it fly?

2) Mary, who is 5 feet tall, casts a 6 foot shadow. At the same time, an oak tree in her yard has a shadow of 88.5 feet. How tall is the oak tree?

3) The area of the square is 144 sq. in. What is the area of the shaded part?

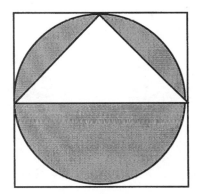

4) A bat and a ball together cost $10. If the bat cost $9 more than the ball, what is the cost of the bat?

5) An $80 computer is on sale for 45% off. What is the new price?

1) If Kristin can read $1\frac{1}{4}$ pages per minute, how long will it take her to read $123\frac{3}{4}$ pages?

2) Eric bought a guitar that cost $152.25, including tax. The sales tax is 5% in his state. What was the cost of the guitar before the tax was added?

3) If you roll four dice, what is the probability of rolling four ones?

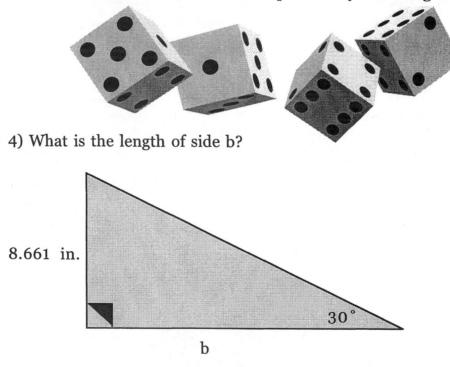

4) What is the length of side b?

8.661 in.

30°

b

5) What is the volume of a quarter?
(The diameter of a quarter is $\frac{15}{16}$ of an inch and the height is $\frac{1}{16}$ of an inch.)

1) Bob's age is 4 times Michelle's age and Sara's age is half Bob's age. If their ages add up to 84, what is Michelle's age?

2) What is the area of the shaded part?

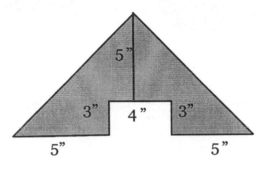

3) A micron is a thousandth of a millimeter. How many microns are in 8 meters?

4) A family leaves their house on Monday at 8:15 A.M. for a 1530 mile trip. If they average 42.5 mph, on what day and at what time will they arrive at their destination?

5) A certain kind of orange soda is made of 5 ounces of orange juice and 7 ounces of mineral water. If you had 134.75 ounces of mineral water, how much orange juice would you need to make the orange soda?

1) Bill and Steve decided that they would always have a money ratio of 9:7 (Bill to Steve). If Steve has $129.50, how much money should Bill have?

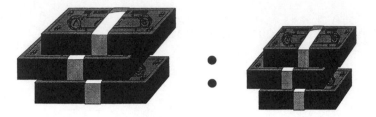

2) Can the fraction $\dfrac{1678194}{94328163}$ be reduced. How can you tell?

3) What is the probability of picking a pair of jacks if you are allowed two picks from a deck of cards?

4) The diameter of the circle is 5" and the length of the rectangle is twice its width. What is the area of the shaded part?

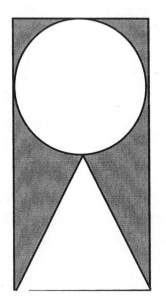

5) How far does light travel in the month of December?

1) There is a pile of coins that consists of quarters, dimes, and nickels. There are twice as many dimes as nickels and 8 times as many quarters as there are dimes. If the value of the pile is $29.75, how many quarters are in the pile?

2) How many times will a 15" diameter bike tire turn when a bike has traveled a mile?

3) Jill was dealt two cards from a standard 52 card deck. Her mother told her that if neither of the cards was hearts, she would double Jill's allowance. What is the probability that Jill will not be dealt any hearts?

4) A truck driver took $55\frac{5}{9}$ hours to travel 3000 miles. What was his average speed?

5) A store was having a December 26th special on freshly cut Christmas trees. Trees that normally sold for $25 were selling for 98% off the regular price. What was the sale price for the trees?

1) Bill takes 4 hours to paint a fence. Molly can paint the same fence in 2 hours. How long will it take them if they work together?

2) The diameter of the circle is 8 inches. What is the area of the shaded part?

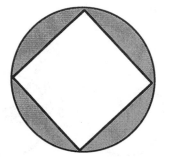

3) Sasha rode her bike halfway to school at a speed of 12 mph. Unfortunately, she rode over a nail and had to be driven the rest of the way by her dad. What was her average speed on her way to school if her dad drove at 60 mph?

4) A coat that normally sells for $84 is on sale for 40% off. The owner of the store decided that any coats that were left after the sale would have an additional 10% taken off the discounted price. What will be the price of the leftover coats?

5) Seven students in one class are planning to vacation in Europe. Fifteen students in the class are going to vacation in California while five students are planning to vacation in both Europe and California. Eight students are not taking any vacation. How many students are in the class?

1) What is the 500th term of the following sequence?

$$0,7,14,21,28\ldots\ldots\ldots\ldots$$

2) Sara wouldn't tell anyone her age, but she did agree to give it as an algebra problem.

"Nine times my age, divided by 12 is equal to 36".

3) Comet and Rudolph decided to race for 60 yards. Comet beat Rudolph by 10 yards. If they continued at the same speed for a 100 yard race, by how many yards would Comet beat Rudolph?

4) Visitors from another planet don't use seconds for time, they use gorgos. A gorgo is the amount of time it takes light to travel 2,790,000 miles. How many gorgos are in our 24-hour day?

5) Rachel rode her trail bike halfway up a mountain at 12 mph. She then walked the rest of the way up the mountain at 2 mph. Rachel then ran down the mountain at 6 mph. What was her average speed?

1) A sled that normally cost $60 is on sale for 20% off. The sales tax in this state is 5%. What is the cost of the sled including tax?

2) What is the area of the unshaded part if the area of the square is 64 square inches?

3) There are 8 students in a sixth grade class who have a dog as a pet. Twelve students have a cat as a pet and 5 have both as pets. If 11 children in the class have neither a dog or a cat, how many children are in the class?

4) A ladder is leaning against the very top of a building. The ladder is leaning at a 60° angle to the ground, and the bottom of the ladder is 15 feet from the building. How tall is the building?

5) What term in this sequence is the number 3136?

1   4   9   16   25...3136

1st   2nd   3rd   4th   5th   ?

1) Sixteen construction workers finished half a road in 10 days. If 4 more workers are added to the crew, how long will it take to finish the road?

2) Dave is running from one side of a circular lake to his cabin on the other side. (He is running around the lake.) If the lake is 7.6433 miles across, and he is running at 6 mph, how long will it take him?

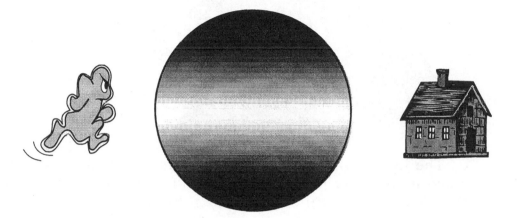

3) I have 7 times as many quarters as I do nickels. If the total value of the quarters and nickels is $19.80, how many quarters do I have?

4) How many squares of any size are in this figure?

5) What is the probability of getting a pair if you are dealt two cards from a standard deck?

1) What is the next number in this sequence?   1, 2, 6, 15, 31, ?

2) A family decided to hike to the top of Mt. Washington and then take the train down. They climbed the mountain at 3 mph and the train traveled at a speed of 21 mph. What was the average speed for their trip?

3) The light that comes from the sun must travel a long distance to reach earth. How far would a car with a speed of 60 mph go in the time it takes for light to travel from the sun to the earth?

4) Gabe incorrectly set the dial on his time-machine and ended up face to face with a Tyrannosaurus Rex. Gabe was 400 yards away from the dinosaur when it started to chase Gabe. Gabe's stride is 6 feet and the Tyrannosaurus Rex's stride is 36 feet. If they both take one stride every 1.5 seconds, how long until Gabe is caught?

5) Dave's age is three times Dan's age. Dan is 4 years older than Sara, and their ages add up to 91. How old is Sara?

1) Suppose six days before the day before yesterday is a Saturday, what day of the week is tomorrow?

2) Alex has a pile of money worth $42.40. He has dimes, quarters, and $5 bills. The number of quarters is twice the number of dimes, and the number of $5 bills is the same as the number of quarters. How many dimes does Alex have?

3) The converting machine for meters to inches is shown below. How many cubic inches are in a cubic meter?

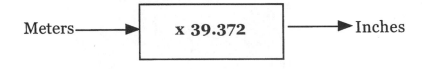

Meters ———→ | **x 39.372** | ——→ Inches

4) Isaac's car gets 28 miles per gallon of gas. If Isaac is going on a trip of 3164 miles and gas cost $1.28 per gallon, what would be the cost of gas for the trip?

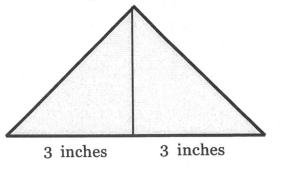

5) The altitude of the triangle is 4 inches. What is its perimeter?

3 inches   3 inches

1) The two lines are 8 feet long and are diameters of the circle. What is the area of the shaded part?

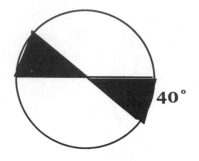

40°

2) A full swimming pool is 8 meters by 5 meters by 10 meters. How many liters of water does the pool hold?

3) An iron cost $42. If sales tax is 7%, what is the total cost of the iron?

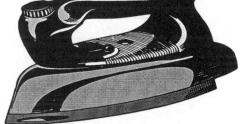

4) A 20 foot telephone pole casts a shadow of 16 feet. If Eric casts a shadow of 5 feet, how tall is he?

5) How long is side a? (The tangent of 35° is .7002)

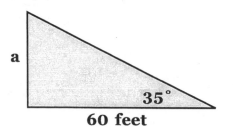

a

35°

60 feet

1) If a couple has 5 children, what is the probability that they will have all girls?

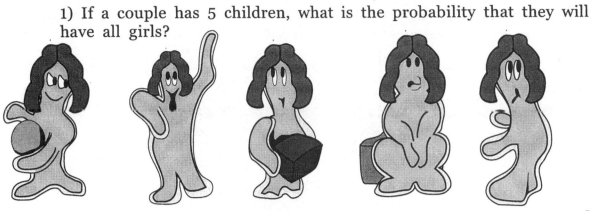

2) Michelle bowled four games with scores of 125, 155, 165, and 185. If she needs to have an average score of 150, and she has one more game to bowl, what must she score in her final game?

3) A train took 1 hour and 20 minutes to travel 48 miles. What was the trains average speed?

4) The scale on a map is 2cm: 20 miles. How long would 54 miles be on the map?

5) $5x + 3y = 27$
       $8x - 3y = 12$

What is the value of x and y?

1) The area of the square is 121 square feet. What is the circumference of the circle?

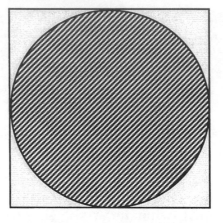

2) A family took a canoe trip on the Mississippi River. When they were going with the current, their speed was 5 mph. On the return trip they traveled against the current at a speed of 3 mph. What was their average speed?

3) What is the slope of the line represented by the equation $4x + 9 = y$

4) If a car started at 0 mph and took 9 seconds to reach 54 mph, what is its acceleration? (Label must be correct.)

5) What is the area of a circle with a $\frac{1}{11}$ inch radius? Use $\frac{22}{7}$ for pi.

1) $4^{x-2} = 8^{x-4}$ What is the value of x?

2) The altitude of the figure below is 12 inches. What is its area?

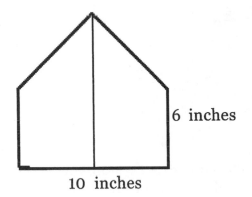

6 inches

10 inches

3) What is the ratio of a circle's circumference to its diameter?

4) When Grace was in 3rd grade, she was 4 feet tall. When she started high school, she was 5 1/2 feet tall. By what percent did she increase in height?

5) $\dfrac{1}{5\dfrac{1}{2\frac{1}{4}}} = \dfrac{?}{?}$

1) A class of 30 children has 11 students home with the flu. If the proportion of students home with the flu in this class holds true for the entire school's 432 students, how many students in the school are home with the flu? (Round to nearest whole number.)

2) The following 4-digit numbers each have one number that has been replaced with a letter.

122**P** is a perfect square
694**R** is a multiple of 10   What is the value of the number **PRM**?
948**M** is a multiple of 9

3) Determine the mean, mode, median, and range for the following salaries.

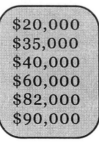

$20,000
$35,000
$40,000
$60,000
$82,000
$90,000

Mean_____
Mode_____
Median_____
Range_____

4) How many squares are in the 85th row?

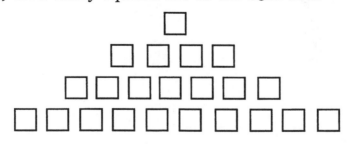

5) If the number of left-handed people in the United States is 1 out of 7, how many left-handed students would you expect in a school with 623 students?

1) Six consecutive numbers add up to 615. What is the smallest number?

2) Thunder was heard 17 1/2 seconds after a flash of lightning. Ten minutes later, the thunder and lightning occurred at the same time. How fast was the storm moving?

3) A clothing store sold a leather coat at a 40% discount on Monday. It then took another 40% off the discounted price on Tuesday. If Tuesday's price was $54, what was the regular price of the coat?

4) Due to an accident, the selling price of a car went from $15,000 to $10,000. What was the percent of decrease?

5) Michelle has a square piece of wood with 12.4 inch sides. Kristin has a circular piece of wood with an identical area. What is the length of the radius of Kristin's wood? (Round to the nearest whole number.)

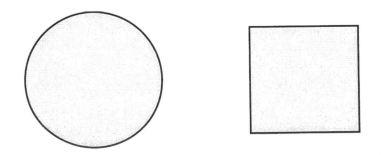

1) In a school of 320 students, 90% went to the school dance. If 80% of the boys and 220 girls were in attendance, how many boys are there in the school?

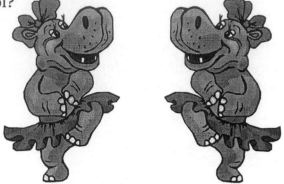

2) A gas tank was 2/5 full. When 12 gallons were added, the tank went to 4/5 full. What is the size of the tank?

3)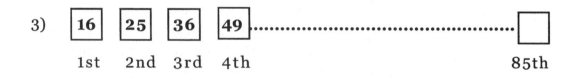

| 16 | 25 | 36 | 49 | .... | □ |

1st   2nd   3rd   4th   85th

4) A quart container holds a drink that is made of milk and tomato juice that are in a proportion of 7:5. A quarter of the drink was lost when the container was knocked over. If tomato juice is used to fill the container again, what is the new proportion of milk to tomato juice?

5) If the radius of a circle is doubled, the area of the new circle is how many times larger than the area of the old circle?

1) Jessica went on a 10-day shopping trip. The amount of money she spent increased by $10 each day. If the total amount of money she spent was $600, how much did she spend the first day?

2) The length of the rectangle is twice the width, and the area is 72 square inches. What is the area of the shaded part?

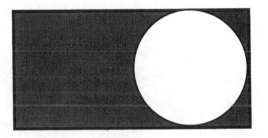

3) What is the acceleration of a car that increases its speed from 30 mph to 63 mph in 11 seconds? (Label must be correct.)

4) $x + 3y = 17$ What are the values of x and y?
      $12y - x = 13$

5) How many cubic millimeters would fit inside a cubic meter?

1) Travis had a circle with a radius of 10. He multiplied the area of the circle by a number we'll call **P**. Mark had a square with sides equal to 3. He multiplied the area of the square by a number we'll call **T**. Travis and Mark both ended up with the same product. What is the value of **P**? What is the value of **T**? (**P** is a whole number between 0 and 10)

2) It took 8 people 6 hours to unload watermelons from 3 identical pickup trucks. How long will it take 10 people to unload 2 more trucks?

3) A cubic inch is what fraction of a cubic foot?

4) A block is made up of nickel and copper in a ratio of 7:11 (weight). If the block weighs 2034 pounds, what is the weight of the nickel?

5) In a state with a sales tax of 6%, a book cost $19.61, including tax. What was the price of the book before the tax was added?

Note to teacher: The answers students arrive at may be different than what is shown in the solutions below. If an answer is based on a different but acceptable estimate, then the answer should be considered correct. For example: If a student uses 186,200 miles per second for the speed of light instead of the standard estimate of 186,000, the answer should be considered correct.

Chapter 1
Page 10

1) 5,280,000,000
2) 6,696,000,000
3) 368,460,000,000

Page 12

1) 25,120 miles
2) 6280 miles
3) 2,512,000 miles
4) 26,878 miles

Level 1
1) 500 seconds
Light travels 186,000 miles each second.
The sun is 93,000,000 miles from the Earth.
93,000,000 ÷ 186,000 = 500 seconds.

2) 5,865,696,000,000 miles
There are 60 seconds in a day; 3600 seconds in an hour; 86,400 seconds in a day; and 31,536,000 seconds in a year.
To find the number of miles traveled in a year, simply multiply 31,536,000 times 186,000.
Remove the zeroes: 31,536 times 186 = 5,865,696
Replace the zeros: 5,865,696,000,000

3) $1\frac{1}{2}$ miles

Because sound takes 5 seconds to travel one mile, the shout traveled 3 miles.
The sound traveled to the rock wall and back, so the distance to the wall is 1.5 miles.

4) $5\frac{1}{2}$ miles
27.5 divided by 5 seconds per mile is 5.5 miles.

5) 1.52 miles
24 x 365 = 8760 hours in a year
11 inches x 8760 hours = 96,360 inches in a year. This is equal to 8030 feet. 8030 feet divided by 5280 feet in a mile equals 1.52 miles.

6) 518,400,000,000,000,000,000,000 electrons
There are 24 x 3600 = 86,400 seconds in a 24 hour period.
86,400 x 6,000,000,000,000,000,000 = 518,400,000,000,000,000,000,000

7) 26,784 times
Light travels 186,000 (miles per second) x 3600 (seconds) = 669,600,000 miles in an hour.
669,600,000 ÷ 25,000 (circumference of the Earth) = 26,784

8) 87,985,440,000,000 miles
There are 60 x 60 x 24 x 365 x 15 seconds in 15 years. (473,040,000)
473,040,000 x 186,000 miles per second = 87,985,440,000,000 miles

9) 10 billion years
Light travels 5,865,696,000,000 miles in one year. (Problem #2)
58,656,960,000,000,000,000,000 ÷ 5,865,696,000,000 = 10,000,000,000 years

10) 7.2 miles
The light traveled to Rachel's eyes almost instantaneously.
The sound took 36 seconds. Because sound takes 5 seconds to travel one mile, the distance the sound traveled was 36 ÷ 5 = 7.2 miles.

Level 2
1) 1042 miles per hour
The circumference of the Earth is 25,000 miles.
25,000 ÷ 24 hours is equal to 1042 miles each hour.

2) 9:00
If the asteroid is 1,004,400,000 miles from Earth, then light from the asteroid takes 1,004,400,000 ÷ 186,000 seconds to reach the Earth.
5400 seconds is equal to 90 minutes. The asteroid exploded at 9:00 and it took 1.5 hours for the light to reach Earth.

3) 1,595,120 miles
The diameter of the orbit circle is 508,000 miles. (The diameter of the Earth plus two distances of 250,000 miles.) 508,000 x π = 1,595,120 miles

4) 24 miles per hour
When the thunder takes 30 seconds to reach your ears, the storm is 30 ÷ 5 = 6 miles away.
When the thunder and lightning occur simultaneously, the storm has traveled the 6 miles to where you are.
Traveling 6 miles in 15 minutes is the same as traveling 24 miles in 60 minutes.

5) Distance
A light year is a measurement of the distance light travels in one year.

6) 3 miles

It took 30 seconds for sound to travel to one mountain peak and back. The round trip distance the sound traveled was 6 miles, therefore the distance from one mountain to the other is half that distance or 3 miles.

7) 2400 miles per hour

We learned in problem #3 that the moon travels 1,595,120 miles during one orbit of the Earth.
27 days and 8 hours is equal to 656 hours. 1,595,120 ÷ 656 = 2431 miles per hour.

8) 2006

Light travels 46,925,568,000,000 miles in 252,288,000 seconds.
(46,925,568,000,000 miles ÷ 186,000 miles per second = 252,288,000 seconds.)
252,288,000 seconds ÷ 31,536,000 seconds in a year is equal to 8 years.

9) 8 miles

It took the sound a total of 80 seconds to make the round trip between the two rock walls. Because it takes sound 5 seconds to travel one mile, it traveled 16 miles during the round trip. The distance between the rock walls is half of that, or 8 miles.

10) 18 quintillion

900,000 parsecs is equal to 3.26 x 900,000 = 2,934,000 light years.
There are 5,865,696,000,000 miles in one light year.
5,865,696,000,000 miles x 2,934,000 light years can be rounded to 6 trillion times 3 million.

Einstein Level

1) 5,280,000,000 years old

The first piece of information that is needed is the distance to the moon in inches. One mile has 12 x 5280 = 63,360 inches. The Earth is 250,000 miles away from the moon so there are 250,000 x 63,360 = 15,840,000,000 inches to the moon. If the tree grows at a rate of 3 inches per year, it will take 15,840,000,000 ÷ 3 = 5,280,000,000 years to grow to the moon.

2) 20 mph

At the first flash, the storm is 1.5 miles away. (The sound took 7.5 seconds to reach your ears) 12 minutes later the storm is 2.5 miles away because it took the sound 12.5 seconds to reach your ears. The storm traveled 4 miles in 12 minutes, which is a speed of 20 miles in one hour.

3) 27,632 mph

The circumference of Jupiter is 88,000 x 3.14 = 276,320 miles. It takes the planet 10 hours to rotate once. It travels 276,320 ÷ 10 = 27,632 miles in one hour.

4) 66,958 mph

The Earth is approximately 93,000,000 miles from the sun. If we pretend the orbit is circular, then the diameter of the circle is 93,000,000 miles plus the diameter of the sun (800,000 miles) plus 93,000,000 miles. This equals 186,800,000 miles.

186,800,000 x 3.14 =586,552,000 miles in one orbit.
There are 365 x 24 =8760 hours in a year.
The speed is 586,552,000 ÷ 8760 = 66,958 miles per hour

5) 8:35

Light takes one second to travel 186,000 miles. The light leaving the clock on Earth takes 3,348,000,000÷186,000 = 18,000 seconds to reach Pluto. 18,000 seconds is equal to 5 hours. Because it takes 5 hours for the light to reach Pluto, the Plutonian is looking at the clock as it appeared 5 hours ago------8:35.

6) 7.5° is 1/48 of the entire circumference of the Earth (360°÷7.5°is equal to 48) If 7.5° is equal to 500 miles, then 360° is equal to 48 x 500 = 24,000 miles.

7) 1835

A parsec is equal to 3.26 light-years. An area that is 50 parsecs away is 3.26 x 50 = 163 light-years away. 1998 minus 163 = 1835

8) 123 orbits

The diameter of the orbit is 250 + 8000 + 250 = 8500 miles.
The circumference of the orbit is 8500 x 3.14 = 26,690 miles.
3,282,870 miles divided by the distance in one orbit is equal to 123 orbits.

9) 1000 miles

The meteor is 1/250 of the moon's diameter.
(Moon's diameter of 2000 miles ÷ 8 miles = 250)
Because they appear to be the same size, the meteor must be 250 times closer to the Earth than the moon.
The moon is approximately 250,000 miles, so 250 times closer would be 1000 miles.

10) 50 seconds

Because sound takes 5 seconds to go one mile, a meteor traveling at 100 times the speed of sound would travel 20 miles in one second.
At a speed of 20 miles per second, it would take the meteor 50 seconds to travel 1000 miles.

Super Einstein) 12.5 seconds

We know that a meteor with a diameter of 8 miles that appears to be the same size as the moon is 1000 miles away. Because the meteor appears to be four times as large as the moon, it must be four times closer than the meteor that is 1000 miles away-----250 miles.
The meteor is traveling at a speed of 20 miles per second (Problem #10) 250 ÷20 = 12.5

Chapter 2

Charts and Diagrams (Page 23)
1) 48 gallons
If 3/4 of a tank holds 36 gallons, then each of the three quarters must hold 12 gallons.

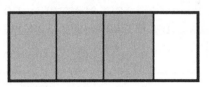

2) Wednesday
Make a box chart and pick any day to be today. Now label the days that are mentioned in the problem. They are the day after tomorrow and 5 days before the day after tomorrow---which you know is Monday. It is now obvious that yesterday must be Wednesday.

Monday		Yesterday	Today		Day after tomorrow		

3)$27
The first box shows that Tom spent 1/3 of his money.
The second box shows that Tom spent 1/3 of his remaining money.

The remaining dark boxes represent the $12 that he had left.

If those two boxes are equal to $12, then the three are equal to $18.
We now know that each 1/3 is equal to $9

4) 10:45
If Peter drives 60 miles at a speed of 40 miles per hour, it will take him 1.5 hours.
Because he arrived at 12:15, he must have left his home 1.5 hours earlier---10:45

5) Saturday
26th is a Wednesday; 19th must be a Wednesday; 12th is a Wednesday; 5th is a Wednesday.
4th is a Tuesday--3rd a Monday--2nd a Sunday--1st must be a Saturday.

6) 7 people
There had to be 5 canoes for the first trip.
If there were 4 in each canoe on the return trip, 20 people rode in canoes. Seven people were left to ride in the motorboat.

7) Wednesday
Make a box chart and pick any day to be today. Now label the days that are mentioned in the problem. They are the day before yesterday and 5 days after the day before yesterday---which you know is Saturday. It is now obvious that today must be Wednesday.

	Day before Yesterday		Today			Saturday	

8) 80 gold coins

Marilyn first gave 1/8 to her mother---(Light shaded area)
She then gave half of what remained to her brother-----(Medium shaded area)
Finally she gave 2/7 of what was left to her dad--------(Dark shaded area)
25 coins remained, therefore each box had 5 coins.
We now know that each 1/8 rectangle is equal to 10 coins.

9) Sunday
If three days ago was a Wednesday, then today must be a Saturday
52 weeks x 7 days equals 364. In 364 days, it will be a Saturday. In 365 days it will be a Sunday.

10) Einstein, Rover, Spot, Buffy, Shadow

Spot   Shadow
Einstein Rover   Buffy

Each name falls into its correct order except for Buffy. We don't know if Buffy is before Spot or after Spot. Because Buffy cannot be the third one listed, we know that Buffy must be fourth on the list.

Chapter 2 (Page 25)

Think 1
1) 6 days
Because we know that 6 people take 8 days to build the wall, we know that it will take one person 6 x 8 = 48 days

1 person---------48 days
2 people---------24 days   (48÷2)
3 people---------16 days   (48÷3)
8 people---------6 days   (48÷8)

2) 6 days
If one child took all the food, it would last 12 x 8 = 96 days
Because 2 adults are equal to 4 children, we are trying to find out how long the food will last for 16 children.

1 child--------------96 days
2 children----------48 days (96÷2)
16 children---------6 days (96÷16)

3) 2 hours
Think one hour. How much of the car can Luke paint in one hour? The answer is 1/6
How much of the car can Daniel paint in one hour? The answer is 1/3
Together, they can paint 1/3 + 1/6 = 1/2 of the car in one hour.
They can paint the whole car in 2 hours.

4) 8 days
1 man-----------------48 days
2 men-----------------24 days
6 men-----------------8 days (48÷6)

5) 1 hour
Think one hour. Because it takes 15 minutes for the hose to fill the pool, the hose will fill 4 pools in an hour.
Because it takes 20 minutes to drain the pool, the drain will empty 3 pools in one hour.
In one hour, 4 pools will be filled and 3 drained. This will leave you with one full pool.

6) 1 hour 20 minutes
Think one hour. How much of the fence can Sara paint in one hour? The answer is 1/2
How much of the fence can Daniel paint in one hour? The answer is 1/4
Together they can paint 3/4 of the fence in one hour, so each quarter takes them 20 minutes.
3/4 in one hour and the remaining quarter in 20 minutes.

7) 1.5 hours

Think one hour. The first hose fills 1/4 of the pool in one hour. The second fills 1/6 of the pool in one hour.

The third and the fourth each fill 1/8 of the pool in one hour.

In one hour the hoses together fill 1/4 + 1/6 + 1/8 + 1/8 = 16/24 = 2/3 of the pool.

Each third takes 1/2 hour, so the whole pool would take 1.5 hours.

8) 3 bags

Think one cat. One bag of food will last three cats 15 days so it will last one cat 3 x 15 = 45 days.

Food for 8 cats on a 12 day vacation is the same as food for one cat on a 8 x 12 = 96 day vacation.

Each bag of food will last 45 days, so 96 days calls for 96 ÷ 45 = 2.133 bags.

9) 72 days

Think one person. If it took 8 people 30 days to dig 1/4 of the tunnel, then it would take one person 8 x 30 = 240 days to dig 1/4 of the tunnel.

Because it would take one person 240 days for 1/4 of the tunnel, it would take one person 720 days to finish the remaining 3/4 of the tunnel.

1 person--------720 days

2 people--------360 days (720 ÷ 2 = 360)

10 people-------72 days (720 ÷ 10)

10) 8 more painters

Think one painter. Because 7 painters took 45 days to paint 1/3 of the bridge, it would take one painter 7 x 45 = 315 days to paint 1/3 of the bridge or 2 x 315 = 630 days to paint the remaining 2/3 of the bridge.

1 painter------------630 days

2 painters----------315 days for remaining 2/3 of the bridge

3 painters----------210 days for the remaining 2/3 of the bridge

? painters----------42 days

15 painters would be required to paint the remaining 2/3 of the bridge in 42 days. (630 ÷ 42 = 15 painters) Because there were already 7 painters, 8 more would need to be hired.

Venn Diagrams   (Pages 31-32)

1) 46 children

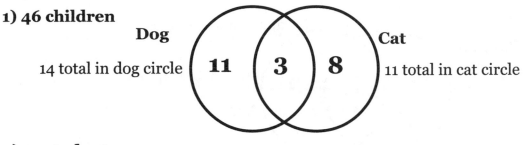

Dog

14 total in dog circle

11   3   8

Cat

11 total in cat circle

2) 13 students

17 students are in the circles, so 13 students do not take any language.

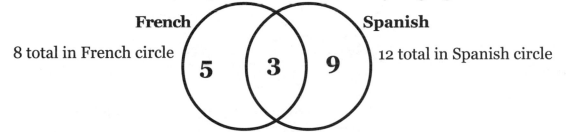

French

8 total in French circle

5   3   9

Spanish

12 total in Spanish circle

3) 10 members

10 players are in the circles, so the remaining 10 players do not have any brothers or sisters

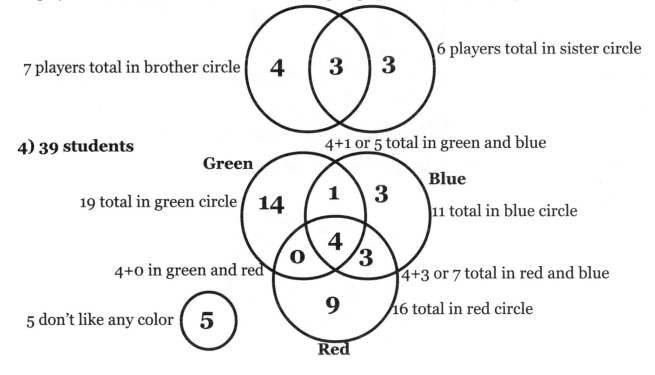

7 players total in brother circle

4   3   3

6 players total in sister circle

4) 39 students

4+1 or 5 total in green and blue

Green

19 total in green circle

14   1   3

Blue

11 total in blue circle

0   4   3

4+0 in green and red

4+3 or 7 total in red and blue

9

16 total in red circle

5 don't like any color

5

Red

5) 57 students

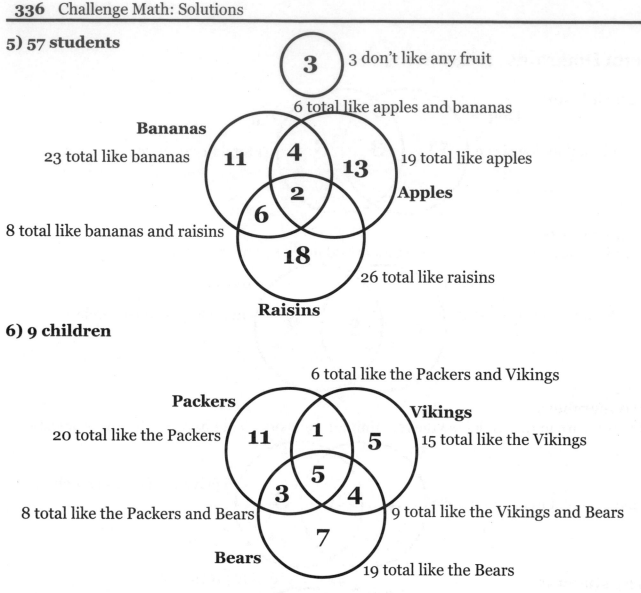

3 don't like any fruit

6 total like apples and bananas

Bananas

23 total like bananas

19 total like apples

Apples

8 total like bananas and raisins

26 total like raisins

Raisins

6) 9 children

6 total like the Packers and Vikings

Packers

20 total like the Packers

Vikings

15 total like the Vikings

8 total like the Packers and Bears

9 total like the Vikings and Bears

19 total like the Bears

Bears

45 children in class minus the 36 in the circles = 9 children.

7) 4 children

9 total in the Edgar Allen Poe circle

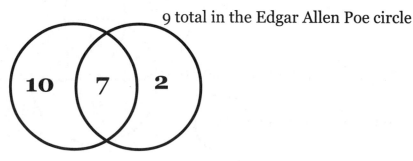

17 total in Call of the Wild Circle

23 children in the class minus 19 in the circles = 4 who didn't read any book.

8) 12 people   3 didn't eat any of the three foods

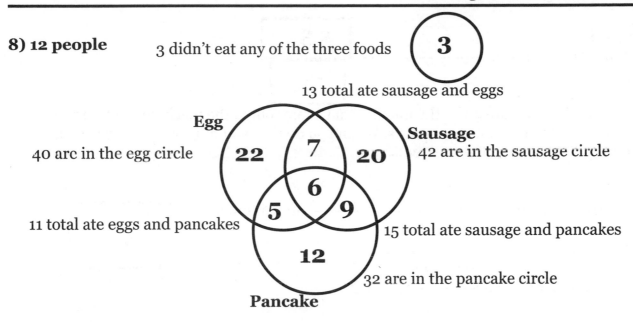

13 total ate sausage and eggs

Egg

40 are in the egg circle

Sausage
42 are in the sausage circle

11 total ate eggs and pancakes

15 total ate sausage and pancakes

32 are in the pancake circle

Pancake

There are 12 people in the "only pancakes" part of the Venn diagram.

9) 84 people
If you combine the people in the diagram and the 3 that didn't eat either eggs, pancakes or sausage, you will get an answer of 84 people.

10) 44 people
The people outside the egg circle total 41 + the 3 who didn't eat any of the three items.

Patterns, Sequences and Function Machines (Page 36)

1) 8994
The function machine is---------------------
1000 goes in the top and 8994 comes out.

X 9

-6

2) 1001
The function machine is----------------------
500 goes in the top and 1001 comes out.

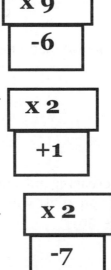

X 2

+1

3) 393
The function machine is-----------------------
200 goes in the top and 393 comes out.

X 2

-7

4) 250th
The function machine is----------------------

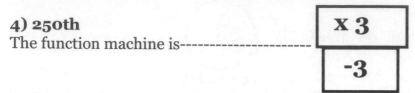

In this situation, you are given the number that comes out of the machine. To find what goes in, go through the machine backwards. When you do this, you must reverse operations. 747 plus 3 divided by 3. The answer is 250.

5) 125
The function machine is--------------------------------the number cubed

n^3

The first term is cubed------1 x 1 x 1 = 1
The second number is cubed----2 x 2 x 2 = 8
The next number is cubed------3 x 3 x 3 = 27

To find the fifth number------5 x 5 x 5 = 125

6) 4,999,996
The function machine is------------------------

1,000,000 goes in the top and
4,999,996 comes out.

x 5

-4

7) 4,000,007
The function machine is----------------------

2000 goes in and 4,000,0007 comes out.

n^2

+7

8) 5/128
Each fraction is divided by 4. Function machine is-------

9) 56
Large size triangles---1
Next size--------------3
Next size------------6
Next size------------10
We now can see the pattern is increasing one triangle each time. We can predict that the next size triangle will have 15 and the smallest will have 21. (It is easy to count the smallest triangles) 21 + 15 + 10 + 6 + 3 + 1 = 56

÷4

10) 204

8 x 8 squares----1
7 x 7 squares---------4
6 x 6 squares--------9

It is easy to see that the pattern involves squaring numbers. We can predict all the rest of the squares by using this pattern.

5 x 5 will have 16 squares
4 x 4 will have 25 squares
3 x 3 will have 36 squares
2 x 2 will have 49 squares
1 x 1 will have 64 squares

Adding all the squares 1 + 4 + 9 + 16 + 25 + 36 + 49 + 64 = 204

Chapter 3: Algebra

Page 43

1) n =7
2) n=5
3) n=9
4) n=2

Page 44

1) n=14   7) n=2
2) n=5   8) n=10
3) n=6   9) n=11
4) n=2   10) n=-11
5) n=2   11) n=10
6) n=25   12) n=11

Page 46

1) 7 quarters
2) 11 dimes
3) 8 nickels (40 cents)

Level 1   (Page 47)

1) 164 pounds
Steve: n
Bill: n + 42
Equation: 2n + 42 = 370   n = 164

2) 461
Smallest number: n
Next number: n + 1
Next number: n + 2
Largest number: n + 3
Equation: 4n + 6 = 1850   n = 461

3) $141
Youngest: n
Next: n + 10
Next: n + 20
Oldest: n + 30
Equation: 4n + 60 = 504   n = 111 (youngest)   Oldest = 111 + 30 = 141

4) 63 years old
Youngest sister: n
Next sister: n + 3
Middle sister: 2n
Next to the oldest: 3n - 2
Oldest sister: 3n
Equation: 10n + 3 - 2 = 211   n = 21(youngest)   Oldest: 3 x 21 = 63

5) 60 pounds
Kirsten: n
Dan: 2n
Jay: 2n + 20
Equation: 5n + 20 = 320   n = 60

6) 1040
Smallest number: n
Next: n + 5
Next: n + 10
Largest: n + 15
Equation: 4n + 30 = 4130   n = 1025 (smallest)   Largest: 1025 + 15 = 1040

7) $2444
First picture: n
Second: n + 28
Third: n + 56
Fourth: n + 84
Fifth: n + 112
Equation: 5n + 280 = 12,500   n = 2444

8) 12
Some number: n
Equation: 8n = n + 84   n = 12

9) $79
Daniel: n
Rachel: n + 48 - 21 or n + 27
Luke: n + 48   Equation: 3n + 75 = 168   n = 31   Luke: 31 + 48 = 79

10) $50
Saddle: n
Horse: n + 900
Equation: 2n + 900 = 1000   n = 50

Level 2   (Page 49)

1) 45 pounds
Weight of gold bar: n

Equation: $\frac{1}{3}n + 30 = n$

Subtract $\frac{1}{3}n$ from both sides: $30 = \frac{2}{3}n$ 2/3 of something equals 30   n = 45

2) $51
Amount needed to buy gold coin: n
Cheri's money: n - 23
Denzel's money: n - 28

Together they have enough to buy the gold coin. This means that together their money is equal to n.
Equation: 2n - 51 = n
Subtract n from both sides: n - 51 = 0
Add 51 to both sides: n = 51

3) 34 kg.
Weight of brick: n
Equation: 2n + 17 = 3n - 17
Subtract 2n from both sides: 17 = n - 17
Add 17 to both sides: 34 = n

4) 16 nickels
Number of nickels: n   Value of nickels: 5n
Number of dimes: 19 - n   Value of dimes: 10(19 - n) or 190 -10n
Equation: 5n + 190 - 10n = 110
Collect: -5n + 190 = 110
Add 5n to both sides: 190 = 110 + 5n
Subtract 110 from both sides: 5n = 80   n = 16

5) 21 nickels
Number of dimes : n   Value of dimes: 10n
Number of nickels: 3n   Value of dimes: 15n
Equation: 25n = 175   n = 7   Number of nickels is 3n or 21

6) 9 dimes
Number of nickels: n
Number of dimes: n
Value of nickels: 5n
Value of dimes: 10n
Value of quarters: 15n + 240
Equation: 5n + 10n + 15n + 240 = 510   30n = 270   n = 9

7) 91 pages
Number of pages in Mitchel's book: n
Jay's favorite book: 3n - 182
Equation: (Because both books have the same number of pages, we set them equal to each other.)   n = 3n - 182
Subtract n from both sides: 0 = 2n - 182
Add 182 to both sides: 182 = 2n   n = 91

8) 444th
Function machine is 5n - 2 = 2218   5n = 2220   n = 444

9) 138
Normal systolic blood pressure = 56/2 + 110   Normal = 138

10) 80.6° F

Temperature (in Celsius) = $\dfrac{159 + 30}{7}$ Temperature = 27°C

$F = \dfrac{9}{5}C + 32$ $F = \dfrac{9}{5}x27 + 32$ F = 1.8 x 27 + 32 = 80.6°

Einstein Level   (Page 51)

1) 21 years old
Mike: n
Rick: 5n
Larry: 2n
Ed: Double Larry and Mike's combined ages is 6n so Ed's age is 6n - 30
Daniel: 5n - 79
Equation: 19n -109 = 271   19n = 380   n = 20   Daniel = 5n - 79 or 21

2) 71 babies
Number of school-age children: n   Cost for school-age children: 5 x n = 5n
Number of babies: n   Cost for babies: 3 x n = 3n
Number of adults: 2n   Cost for adults: 2n x 7 = 14n
Equation: 22n = 1562   n = 71

3) 32 years old

Jim: n

Dave: 3n

Bill: 2n

Equation: $\dfrac{n + 3n + 2n}{3} = 64$ 6n/3 = 64   n = 32

4) Nick $180   Stacey $60   Lindsey $240

Stacey: n

Nick: 3n

Lindsey: 4n

Rick: $120

Equation: $\dfrac{n + 3n + 4n + 120}{4} = 150$ $\dfrac{8n + 120}{4} = 150$ $\dfrac{8n}{4} + \dfrac{120}{4} = 150$ n = 60

5) Quarter:24   Dimes: 8   Nickels: 4   Pennies: 23

Number of nickels: n

Number of dimes: 2n

Number of quarters: 3 x 2n = 6n

Number of pennies: 59 - 9n (59 coins minus the total of the nickels, dimes and quarters)

Value of the nickels: 5n

Value of the dimes: 20n

Value of the quarters: 150n

Value of the pennies: 59 - 9n

Equation: 175n + 59 - 9n = 723   166n + 59 = 723   166n = 664   n = 4

6) 72 years old

Grandfather's age: n

Half their age: 23

Equation: 23n = 1656   n = 72

7) $614.25

Amount of sales: n

Incorrect tax amount collected .06n (Total sales times 6%)

Equation: n + .06n = 620.10   1.06n = 620.10   n = 585

Total sales = $585

Correct amount of tax: .05 x 585 = $29.25 $585 + $29.25 = $614.25

8) Length: 78   Width 13   Equation: $6n^2 = 1014$

Width: n   Length: 6n

Equation: n x 6n = 1014 $6n^2 = 1014$ $n^2 = 169$ n = 13

9) 18n = 216   Length = 96
Width of rectangle: n
Length of rectangle: 8n
Perimeter: n + 8n + n + 8n = 18n
Equation: 18n = 216   n = 12

10) 28 dimes

Number of pennies: n	Value of pennies: n
Number of nickels: 2n	Value of nickels: 10n
Number of dimes: 4n	Value of dimes: 40n
Numbers of quarters: 4n - 3	Value of quarters: 25(4n -3) = 100n -75
Number of one dollar bills: 2n	Value of one dollar bills: 100 x 2n = 200n
Number of five dollar bills: 2n	Value of five dollar bills: 500 x 2n = 1000n

Equation: n + 10n + 40n + 100n - 75 + 200n + 1000n = 9382
1351n -75 = 9382   1351n = 9457   n = 7

Super Einstein Problem) 4000 miles
Time until they meet: n
Distance light travels per second: 186,000 miles
Distance rocket travels per second: 8 miles   (28,800 miles ÷ 3600 seconds per hour)
Equation: 186,000n + 8n = 93,000,000   186,008n = 93,000,000   n =500 seconds
8 miles x 500 seconds = 4000 miles

O— 8n —| ——————— 186,000n ——————————— O

Chapter 4: Metric System

Metric Length (Page 55)
1) 2700 cm.
2) .282 meters
3) 5.3 meters
4) 4.54 dm.
5) 11,000,000 mm.
6) 13 cm.
7) 1.8 meters
8) 11 km.
9) 884,800 cm.
10) 1,000,000
11) 100,000,000 viruses
12) 28
13) 3.5 meters
14) 10,000 sq. cm.
15) 80,000 sq. mm.

Volume and Weight (Page 60)
1) 2450 ml.
2) 37 grams
3) 2.4 kg.
4) 850 grams
5) .785 grams
6) 8.395 kg.
7) 12,000 mg.
8) .0094 liters
9) 850,000 mg.
10) 23,000 grams
11) 310 liters
12) 28 grams
13) 15 ml.
14) 1/4
15) 27,000 kg.
16) 69,350 kg.
17) 64,000 kg.
18) 1 million mg.
19) .0115 kg.
20) .370 kg.

Temperature (Page 64)
1) 57.2°F Yes
2) 105.8°F Yes
3) -89.2°C
4) 6093.3°C
5) -459.4°F
6) 25 million° F
7) 1947.2°F
8) 5086°C
9) 37°C
10) Same

Level 1   (Page 67)
1) 1814.393 feet
553 meters x 39.372 = 21772.716 inches   21772.716 inches ÷ 12 = 1814.393 feet

2) 5.9 feet
1.8 meters x 39.372 = 70.8696 inches   70,8696 inches ÷ 12 = 5.9 feet

3) 3300 pounds
1500 kilograms x 2.2 = 3300 pounds

4) 1219 cm.
40 feet = 480 inches
Going backwards through the converting machine: 480 ÷ 39.372 = 12.19 meters
12.19 meters x 100 = 1219 centimeters

5) 50,636,905 gallons
7500 liters x 1.057 = 7927.5 quarts per day   7927.5 x 365 = 2,893,537.5 quarts per year.
2,893,537.5 quarts = 723,384.37 gallons
723,384.37 gallons x 70 years = 50,636,905 gallons

6) 99.84 km.
Going backwards through the converting machine: 62 miles ÷ .621 = 99.84 kilometers

7) 176 ounces
5 kilograms x 2.2 = 11 pounds   11 pounds is equal to 11 x 16 = 176 ounces

8) 13 inches (More)
33 centimeters is equal to .33 meters (33 ÷ 100)
.33 meters x 39.372 = 13 inches

9) 180,675 pounds/year
225 kilograms x 2.2 = 495 pounds   495 pounds x 365 = 180,675

10) 39.37 feet
120 decimeters is equal to 12 meters (120 ÷ 10)
12 meters x 39.372 = 472.464 inches which is equal to 39.37 feet

Level 2   (Page 68-69)

1) Truck weighs 18,181.82 kg. (Yes)
Backwards through changing machine: 40,000 ÷ 2.2 = 18,181.18 kg.

2) 56.93 kg.
Backwards through changing machine: 125.25 pounds ÷ 2.2 = 56.93 kg.

3) Buy in United States
If gas cost $1.05 per gallon, then it is $1.05 ÷ 4 = $.2625 per quart
Going backwards through the converting machine: One quart ÷ 1.057 = .946 liters
One quart equals .946 liters, which cost .946 x .38 = 36 cents

4) 1000 kg
A cubic decimeter of water weighs one kilogram.
A cubic meter is equal to 10 x 10 x 10 = 1000 cubic decimeters.
A cubic meter weighs 1000 kilograms.

5) 2200 pounds
1000 kilograms x 2.2 = 2200 pounds.

6) $32
100 liters = 100 x 1.057 = 105.7 quarts.
105.7 quarts = 26.425 gallons.
26.425 gallons x $1.20 = $31.71

7) Yes
180 kilometers x .621 = 111.78 miles

8) 12,211 layers
1/16 = .0625
Going backwards through the conversion machine: .0625 ÷ 39.372 = .0015874 meters
.0015874 meters x 100 = .15874 centimeters
.15874 centimeters ÷ .000013 centimeters = 12,210.769   (rounded: 12,211)

9) 10.76 sq. ft.
A meter is equal to 39.372 inches
39.372 x 39.372 = 1550.1543 square inches in a square meter.
144 square inches are in a square foot so divide 1550.1543 by 144 = 10.76 square feet

10) 6400 meters
8.848 kilometers are equal to 8,848 meters
8000 feet = 96,000 inches from the summit.
Backwards through the changing machine: 96,000 ÷ 39.372 = 2438.281 meters
2438.281 meters from the summit is 8848 - 2438.281 = 6410 meters (rounded: 6400)

Einstein Level   (Pages 70 -71)

1) 3973.5 grams
30,000 gallons x 4 = 120,000 quarts   120,000 quarts ÷ 1.057 = 113,528.85 liters
Grace needs 35 grams per 1000 liters.
113,528.85 liters ÷ 1000 equals 113.53 groups of 1000 liters.
113.53 x 35 = 3973.5 grams of chlorine.

2) $2265

Find the volume in cubic feet. Because a meter is equal to 39.372 inches, a meter is equal to 39.372 ÷ 12 = 3.281 feet.

The length of each side of the meter cube is 3.281 feet.

The volume is 3.281 x 3.281 x 3.281 = 35.32 cubic feet.

$80,000 ÷ 35.32 = $2265

3) $220.75

Christine needs 3000 ÷ 18 = 166.67 gallons of gas.

166.67 gallons of gas are equal to 666.68 quarts of gas.

Change quarts to liters by going in reverse through the changing machine:

666.68 ÷ 1.057 = 630.73 liters.   Cost: 630.73 liters x .35 = $220.75

4) 1159 grams

85% of 3 pounds: .85 x 3 = 2.55 pounds

Go in reverse through changing machine: 2.55 pounds ÷ 2.2 = 1.159 kilograms

Because there are 1000 grams in each kilogram: 1.159 x 1000 = 1159 grams

5) 3 adults

16.5 tons are equal to 33,000 pounds.

33,000 ÷ 2.2 = 15,000 kilograms

600 + 4800 + 4800 + 4800 = 15,000 kilograms

6) 394/10,000,000

A micron is 1/1000 of a millimeter and there are 1000 millimeters in a meter, so there must be 1,000,000 microns in one meter.   (1000 x 1000)

Because 1 meter is equal to 1,000,000 microns, 1,000,000 microns are equal to 39.372 inches.

1 micron is therefore equal to 39.372 ÷ 1,000,000 = .000039372 inches (Rounded: .0000394)

7) 1/299,792,458,000 of a second

If light travels one meter in 1/299,792,458 of a second, then light will travel 1 millimeter in 1/1000 of that amount of time.

$$\frac{1}{299,792,458} \ x \ \frac{1}{1000} = \frac{1}{299,792,458,000} \text{ of a second}$$

8) 30,400 pounds

We need to find the volume in cubic decimeters because we know that one cubic decimeter of water is equal to one kilogram.

6' x 8' x 10' is the same as 72" x 96" x 120". Change inches to meters by going in reverse through the changing machine.   1.829 meters x 2.438 meters x 3.048 meters = 13.591 cubic meters.

Because there are 1000 cubic decimeters in a cubic meter, there are 13.591 x 1000 = 13,591 cubic decimeters of water in the pool. (13,591 kilograms)

13,591 x 2.2 = 29,900 pounds plus the 500 pound weight of the tank is equal to 30,400 pounds.

9) -40°

The formula is F = 1.8 x C + 32

If the temperature is the same for both Fahrenheit and Centigrade (F = C), then you can change the formula to C = 1.8 x C + 32

Solve: C = 1.8C + 32

Subtract C from both sides: 0 = .8C + 32

Subtract 32 from both sides: -32 = .8C

Divide each side by .8:   -40 = C

10) 10,900 kg

How many 10 second parts are in 8 hours? 8 hours has 3600 x 8 = 28,800 seconds.

28,800 ÷ 10 = 2880   10-second parts

Because it takes 10 seconds to fill one gallon, there must be 2880 gallons in the pool.

2880 gallons are equal to 11,520 quarts.

11,520 ÷ 1.057 = 10,899 liters or 10,899 kilograms (Each liter of water weighs one kilogram.)

Chapter 5: Decimals

Adding and Subtracting (Page 73)
1) 268.92
2) 23.9995
3) 577.995
4) 1.765
5) 15,679.9
6) 15.36
7) 10.63°
8) 635.678 sq. ft.
9) $47.04
10) 100.28 feet

Multiplying Decimals (Page 75)
1) 43.848
2) .014722
3) .05336
4) 40.64 miles
5) 28 septillion
6) 297.18 inches
7) 17 years
8) $117.45
9) 236.25 miles
10) $117.82

Division (Page 77)
1) 2.01
2) .51
3) 2000.3
4) 12.2 feet
5) 7.85 feet
6) 38 miles
7) 47 jars
8) $56.32
9) 81 pumpkins
10) $103.70

Level 1   (Page 78-79)

Note: It is often very difficult for students to figure out what numbers to multiply or divide when problems contain decimals. If students substitute the number "2" for the smaller number in the problem and a "10" for the larger number, it makes the steps to solving the problem much easier to see.

1) 98 coins

2.94 high ÷ .03 thick = 98 coins

2) 18.25 miles

264.625 miles ÷ 14.5 bars = 18.25 miles

3) $24.60

379 ÷ 18.95 = 20 gallons   20 gallons x $1.23 per gallon = $24.60

4) 491.67°
The temperature must climb 459.67 degrees to reach zero. It must then climb another 32 degrees to reach the freezing point of water. 459.67 + 32 = 491.67

5) 200,000
4 inches ÷ .00002 = 200,000

6) $0.00
$1240 ÷ 100 = $12.40 for each student at School A
School B split the $12.40 into 100 parts: $12.40 ÷ 100 = $0.124 or 12.4 cents
School C split the 12.4 cents into 100 parts: .124 ÷ 100 = $0.00124 (Rounds to "0" cents)

7) $55.30
One pen cost $64.78 ÷ 82 = $.79   70 pens cost 70 x .79 = $55.30

8) 248.53 Earth years
90,777.6 days ÷ 365.26 days = 248.5287

9)   (a) 9.6 pounds
160 pounds x .06 pounds = 9.6 pounds
          (b) 12.8 pounds
80 pounds x .16 pounds = 12.8 pounds
          (c) 94,500 pounds
3500 pounds x 27 pounds = 94,500 pounds

10) 8
I f 4/10 of a number is 32, then 1/10 of the number is 8. (32 ÷ 4)
The mystery number must be 80 because 1/10 of 80 is 8.
The problem asks for 1/10 of the number. 1/10 of the mystery number is 8.

Level 2   (Page 80-81)
1) 51.6 feet
To find the length of the carpeted part of the room, the two 2.4 foot wide sections must be subtracted from the 20.8 foot length. (20.8 - 2.4 - 2.4 = 16)
To find the width of the carpeted part of the room, subtract the 2.4 foot wide sections from the 14.6 foot width of the room. (14.6 - 2.4 - 2.4 = 9.8)   (16 + 16 + 9.8 + 9.8 = 51.6)

20.8'

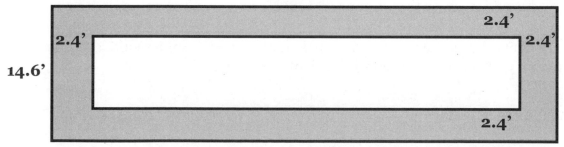

2) 1.25 miles

Chantelle will hike 8.25 hours x 8 days = 66 hours of hiking
82.5 miles ÷ 66 hours = 1.25 miles

3) 2" wide roll

The 2" wide roll is 55 x 36 inches in a yard = 1980 inches long
The area of the 2" roll is 2 inches x 1980 inches= 3960 square inches
The cost for each square inch is $5.75 ÷ 3960 = .001452 cents

The 1.75" wide roll is 48 x 36 inches in a yard = 1728 inches long
The area of the 1.75" roll is 1.75 inches x 1728 = 3024 square inches
The cost for each square inch is $5.25 ÷ 3024 = .0017362 cents

4) 35 hours and 25 minutes

How many .4 gallon parts are in 50 gallons?   50 ÷ .4 = 125 parts
17 minutes for each part to leak out. 125 x 17 minutes per part = 2125 minutes for the tank to empty. 2125 ÷ 60 = 35 hours and 25 minutes

5) 312.5 blood cells

How many .125 second parts are in one minute?   60 seconds ÷ .125 seconds = 480 parts
.125 of a second is 1/480 of a full minute.
150,000 ÷ 480 = 312.5 red blood cells in .125 seconds.

6) 24 hours

The year 16,001,998 is 16,000,000 years from 1998. There are 16,000,000 ÷ 100 = 160,000 centuries in that time.
160,000 centuries x .0015 seconds = 240 seconds longer in a year in the year 16,001,998
240 seconds are equal to 4 minutes.   23 hours 56 minutes + 4 minutes = 24 hours.

7) 1000 feet

A millionth of a second is 1000 times longer than a billionth of a second. Therefore light travels 1000 feet in a microsecond.

8) 372,000 femoseconds

A femosecond is 1000 times smaller than a picosecond. In one picosecond there are 1000 femoseconds. There are 372 x 1000 = 372,000 femoseconds in 372 picoseconds.

9) 5,280,000 picoseconds

Because light travels one foot in a nanosecond, it takes 5280 nanoseconds for light to travel a mile (5280 feet). A picosecond is 1000 times smaller than a nanosecond, therefore it takes 5280 x 1000 = 5,280,000 picoseconds for light to travel a mile.

10) .82 inches of rain

$$\frac{one\ inch\ of\ rain}{10.65\ inches\ of\ snow}=\frac{n}{8.75\ inches\ of\ snow}$$

Divide both sides by 10.65:   n = .82 inches

(cross-multiplying) 10.65n =8.75

Einstein Level   (Page 82-83)

1) $371.05

If an average salary is $248.95 for five weeks, then the total amount earned for the five weeks
is 5 x $248.95 = $1244.75
Emily has already earned: $182.40 + $621.00 + $52.10 + $18.20 = $873.70
$1244.75 - $873.70 = $371.05

2) .08 inches

A circle with a 4.5 inch radius has a 9 inch diameter. The formula for the circumference of a
circle is pi x diameter: 9 x 3.14 = 28.26 inch circumference.
Because there are 360 degrees in a circle, the length of one degree is
28.26 inches ÷ 360 = .0785 inches

3) 5

The piece of paper has a volume of 10.5 x 8 x .0025 = .21 cubic inches
The radius of a quarter is .9375 ÷ 2 = .46875
The volume of a quarter is 3.14 x .46875 x .46875 x .0625 = .0431 cubic inches
.21 (volume of paper) ÷ .0431 (volume of quarter) = 4.872 quarters per piece of paper.

4) 12.75 inches

When the paper is folded in half, its short sides are equal to half of the original side of the
square.
Add up the sides of the folded rectangle: 3n = 38.25   n = 12.75 inches

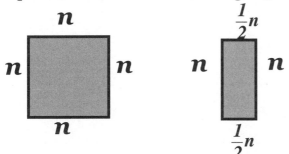

5) 14.45 cents

If ten 100 watt bulbs use 1 kilowatt, then one 100 watt bulb would use .1 kilowatts of electricity. Because a 75 watt bulb is .75 of a 100 watt bulb, a 75 watt bulb would use .75 x .1 kilowatts
= .075 kilowatts of electricity.
A 40 watt bulb is .4 of a 100 watt bulb so it would use .4 x .1 = .04 kilowatts of electricity.
.1 kilowatts + .075 kilowatts + .04 kilowatts = .215 kilowatts per hour
.215 kilowatts per hour x 8 hours = 1.72 kilowatts   1.72 kilowatts x 8.4 cents = 14.448

6) 28.75 inches

When the triangle is folded in half, its perimeter is 23.75 inches. Because the height is known, the remaining two sides of the triangle must equal 23.75 - 9.375 = 14.375 inches. The original triangle was twice this length: 2 x 14.375 = 28.75 inches.

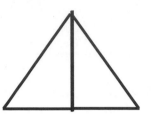
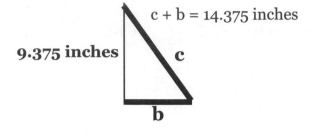

7) 134,000 miles

The cost difference is $2600

Cost per mile for gas in expensive car: $1.35 ÷ 27.3 = .0494505

Cost per mile for less expensive car: $1.35 ÷ 19.6 = .0688775

Savings per mile in expensive car: .068875 - .0494505 = .019427

How many miles must Nancy drive to make up the $2600 of extra cost?

$2600 ÷ .019427 = 133,834.35 miles

8) $153.98

How many 19.21 mile segments fit into 3000 miles?   3000 ÷ 19.21 = 156.17

Travis will use .85 gallons of gas for each of the 156.17 segments: .85 x 156.17 = 132.7445 gallons.

132.7445 gallons x $1.16 per gallon = $153.98

9) 754 years

Each year is .242 days "too long"

The problem is really asking how many .242 day pieces would it take to add up to half of a year (365 ÷ 2 = 182.5 days)

182.5 ÷ .242 = 754 pieces or 754 years.

10) 1.61 kilometers

$$\frac{1 \ kilometer}{.621 \ miles} = \frac{n \ kilometers}{1 \ mile}$$

Cross-multiplying: .621n =1

Divide both sides by n: n = 1.61

Chapter 6: Fractions

(Page 86)
1) 5/6
2) 5/6
3) 5/10 = 1/2
4) $17/12 = 1\dfrac{5}{12}$
5) 23/30
6) 13/20
7) 5/8
8) 7/8 of the pie
9) $5\dfrac{11}{15}$ pounds of gold
10) $2\dfrac{1}{4}$ miles

(Page 89)
1) $2\dfrac{2}{3}$
2) $7\dfrac{3}{4}$
3) 7/20
4) $1\dfrac{7}{16}$
5) $4\dfrac{2}{3}$
6) $4\dfrac{11}{12}$
7) $3\dfrac{14}{15}$
8) $7\dfrac{3}{8}$
9) $3\dfrac{2}{5}$
10) $1\dfrac{19}{24}$

(Page 90)
1) $3\dfrac{1}{2}$
2) $2\dfrac{2}{3}$
3) 5
4) 15
5) 4

(Page 91)
1) 37/7
2) 25/3
3) 27/4
4) 43/2
5) 110/9

(Page 92)
1) 4/5
2) 1/4
3) 6/7
4) 2/3
5) 3/4
6) 2/9
7) 7/8
8) 1/2

(Page 93)
1) $74\dfrac{3}{8}$
2) 1/16
3) 2/9
4) 12
5) $7\dfrac{14}{15}$
6) $4\dfrac{3}{4}$
7) 16
8) $77.90
9) 12 pies
10) 120 miles

(Page 94)
1) 45
2) 2/9
3) $4\dfrac{14}{25}$

(Page 95)
1) 8
2) 10
3) 26
4) 4
5) 9
6) 6
7) 25
8) 82
9) 8

(Page 98)
1) $12\dfrac{1}{2}$
2) $15\dfrac{9}{25}$
3) 1/200
4) 17
5) 144
6) 1/144
7) 1/14 pie
8) 30 miles
9) $1\dfrac{8}{15}$ feet
10) $6.50 per hour

Level 1   (Page 99-100)
Note: It is often very difficult for students to figure out what numbers to multiply or divide when problems contain fractions. If students substitute the number "2" for the smaller number in the problem and a "10" for the larger number, it makes the steps to solving the problem much easier to see.

1) 80 minutes
If you substitute 2 and 10, the problem becomes: Emily needs to read 10 pages and reads 2 pages per minute, how long will it take her? Now it is obvious that division is the correct operation.

$$\frac{85}{1} \div \frac{17}{16} \text{ is the same as } \frac{85}{1} \, x \, \frac{16}{17} = 80$$

2) $104.84

$$7\frac{5}{8} \, x \, 13\frac{3}{4} \text{ is the same as } \frac{61}{8} \, x \, \frac{55}{4} = \frac{3355}{32} = 104.84$$

3) 2 hours
In one hour, Jay can paint 1/6 of the car while Mike can paint 1/3 of the car.
Together they can paint 1/3 + 1/6 = 1/2 of the car in one hour.
It will take them 2 hours to paint the whole car.

4) $2\frac{29}{40}$ pies

$$8\frac{1}{8} - 5\frac{2}{5} = 2\frac{29}{40}$$

5) 1/6 pizza
7 pizzas ÷ 42 people = 7/42 = 1/6

6) 2.44 miles
If thunder travels at 2 miles per second, how far will it travel in 10 seconds?
Now it is obvious that you need to multiply to get the answer: 2 x 10 = 20 miles

$$\frac{1}{5} \, x \, 12\frac{1}{5} \text{ is the same as } \frac{1}{5} x \frac{61}{5} = \frac{61}{25} = 2.44 \text{ miles}$$

7) $150,000
If a store spends 1/5 of its income on salaries ($180,000), then its total income must be 5 x $180,000 = $900,000
1/6 of $900,000 is equal to $150,000

8) 240 pounds
If 7/12 of his dad's weight is 140 pounds, then 1/12 is 140 ÷ 7 = 20 pounds
If 1/12 is equal to 20 pounds, then 12/12 must equal 12 x 20 = 240 pounds.

9) 60 pounds
n = weight of the brick

$$\frac{1}{2}n + 20 = \frac{1}{3}n + 30$$

Subtract $\frac{1}{3}n$ from both sides: $\frac{1}{6}n + 20 = 30$

Subtract 20 from both sides: $\frac{1}{6}n = 10$

Multiply both sides by 6: n = 60

10) 6 hours
If it takes 5 hours to paint 5/6 of a truck, it must take one hour to paint only 1/6 of the truck. 6/6 of the truck would therefore take 6 hours.

Level 2   (Page 101-102)

1) 74,948,114.5 meters
Change numbers to 2 and 10 to help the brain understand the problem: If light travels a meter in 2 seconds, how far does it travel in 10 seconds? Here it is easy to see that you would divide 10 by 2 = 5 meters.
Changing the process to the real problem: 1/4 ÷ 1/299,792,458 = 74,948,114.5

2) $4\frac{3}{5}$ feet

Add the fractions and divided by 5: $6 + 5\frac{7}{8} + 4\frac{3}{4} + 3\frac{1}{4} + 3\frac{1}{8} = 23$ $23 ÷ 5 = 4\frac{3}{5}$

3) 1/4

1st Step	2nd Step	3rd Step

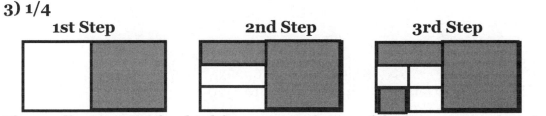

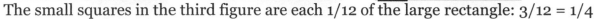

The small squares in the third figure are each 1/12 of the large rectangle: 3/12 = 1/4

4) 9 days

If one worker finished the tunnel: $8 \ x \ 2\frac{1}{4} = 18 \ days$ 2 workers: 18 ÷ 2 = 9 days

5) $2\frac{1}{4}$

$\frac{1}{8}$ x $\frac{3}{11}$ x $\frac{66}{1}$ (Cross reduce) $\frac{1}{8}$ x $\frac{3}{1}$ x $\frac{6}{1}$ = $\frac{18}{8}$ = $\frac{9}{4}$ = $2\frac{1}{4}$

6) $\frac{7}{18,250}$

$\frac{White\ blood\ cell:\ 14\ days}{Nerve\ cell:\ 365\ x\ 100\ years\ =\ 36,500\ days}$ = $\frac{14}{36,500}$ (Reduce) $\frac{7}{18,250}$

7) 320 pounds
Sara's weight: 105 pounds
Luke's weight is twice as much as Sara's weight: 210 pounds

Luke's weight of 210 pounds is 3/4 of Dan's weight. If 3/4 is 210, then 1/4 must be
210 ÷ 3 = 70 pounds. If 1/4 = 70 then 4/4 (or all) must equal 280 pounds
Dan's weight: 280 pounds

Dan's weight of 280 pounds is 7/8 of Ed's weight. 1/8 of Ed's weight must be
280 ÷ 7 = 40 pounds. If 1/8 = 40 pounds, then 8/8 = 8 x 40 = 320 pounds
Ed's weight: 320 pounds

8) $3,125
If 7/8 of Claire's money is $43,750, then 1/8 of her money must be $43,750 ÷ 7 = $6250
If 1/8 is equal to $6250, then 8/8 (or all) of Claire's money must be equal to
$6250 x 8 = $50,000
$50,000 - $43,750 = $6250 remaining   Half of $6250 = $3125

9) 2/49 of a box
2 boxes ÷ 7 people = 2/7 of a box for each person for the whole trip.
Because the trip is a 7 day trip, the 2/7 of a box must be divided by 7 to find the amount for

each day. $\frac{2}{7} \div \frac{7}{1}$ $\frac{2}{7} x \frac{1}{7} = \frac{2}{49}$

10) 1/20
Ben gave away 1/3 + 1/4 + 1/5 + 1/6 = 57/60 of his company.
Ben had 3/60 of his company left.   3/60 reduces to 1/20

Einstein Level   (Page 103-104)

1) $52.61
Area of plywood: 4.5 feet x 8.25 feet = 37.125 square feet
Area of round table top: 3.14 x 1.5 x 1.5 = 7.065 square feet

(Area of circle is $pi \ x \ r^2$)

Amount of leftover wood is found by subtracting: 37.125 - 7.065 = 30.06 square feet
Cost: 30.06 square feet x $1.75 = $52.605

2) 21.25 seconds
720 miles in one hour (3600 seconds) is the same as 3600 ÷ 720 = 5 seconds per mile)
A jet traveling at 720 miles per hour takes 5 seconds to travel one mile.
Sound takes 5 seconds to travel one mile.

Because the jet and the sound are traveling towards each other, they get a mile closer every 2.5 seconds.
Two miles would take 5 seconds; three miles would take 7.5 seconds; four miles would take 10 seconds. They need to cover 8.5 miles, so it will take them 8.5 x 2.5 = 21.25 seconds

3) $5670

After Child A and Child B are given their money, there is $1 - \dfrac{1}{6} - \dfrac{1}{7} = \dfrac{29}{42}$ of the money

left.   (The number one in the subtraction problem stands for the whole amount.)

If 29/42 are equal to $23,490, then 1/42 is equal to $23,490 ÷ 29 = $810
If 1/42 is equal to $810, then 42/42 (all the money) is equal to 42 x $810 = $34,020

1/6 of $34,020 = $5670

4) 6 minutes later (12:06)
If Luke hiked a 10 mile trail at a speed of 2 miles per hour, it is obvious that it would take him
10 ÷ 2 = 5 hours   This tells us that we must divide.

Luke: $\dfrac{9}{2} \div \dfrac{15}{7}$ *is the same as* $\dfrac{9}{2} x \dfrac{7}{15} = \dfrac{21}{10}$ *or* $2\dfrac{1}{10}$ *hours*

Dad: $\dfrac{9}{2} \div \dfrac{9}{4}$ *is the same as* $\dfrac{9}{2} x \dfrac{4}{9} = \dfrac{4}{2}$ *or* 2 *hours*

Luke took 1/10 of an hour longer to climb the mountain. 1/10 of an hour is 6 minutes

5) 3/14 mile
 How far will Luke travel in 1/10 hour?

Because he travels $2\dfrac{1}{7}$ miles in an hour, he will travel $2\dfrac{1}{7} \ x \ \dfrac{1}{10} = \dfrac{3}{14}$ miles in 1/10 of an hour.

6) $128

The remaining 5 white squares are 1/32 each. If 5/32 are equal to $20, then 1/32 is equal to
$20 ÷ 5 = $4   If 1/32 is equal to $4, then 32/32 are equal to 32 x 4 = $128

7) 2 hours and 24 minutes
Kyle will paint 1/4 of the fence in one hour.
Gabe will paint 1/6 of the fence in one hour.
Together they will paint 1/4 + 1/6 = 5/12 of the fence in one hour. If 5/12 are equal to 60
minutes, then 1/12 is equal to 60 minutes ÷ 5 = 12 minutes.

If 1/12 is equal to 12 minutes, then 12/12 are equal to 12 x 12 = 144 minutes

8) 1 hour and 12 minutes
Hose A fills 1/6 of the pool in one hour.
Hose B fills 1/2 of the pool in one hour.
Hose C fills 1/6 of the pool in one hour.
Together they fill 1/6 + 1/2 + 1/6 = 5/6 of the pool in one hour.
If 5/6 are equal to 60 minutes, then 1/6 is equal to 60 minutes ÷ 5 = 12 minutes.
If 1/6 is equal to 12 minutes, then 6/6 are equal to 6 x 12 = 72 minutes.

9) $150,000

Sister	Brother	Brother
	Brother	Brother

From the drawing, it is easy to see that each brother had 1/6 of the total.
Sister's 1/3 + brother's 1/6 = 1/2 of the total = $75,000
If 1/2 the total is equal to $75,000, then the total is equal to $150,000

10) 45 sandwiches
Adults: 5/8 of a sandwich   56 x 5/8 = <u>35 sandwiches</u>

School children: The problem states that $1\frac{3}{4}$ of the children's amount = 5/8 $1\frac{3}{4}n = 5/8$

Divide both sides by 7/4   n = 5/14 of a sandwich   5/14 x 14 children = <u>5 sandwiches</u>

Babies: Babies eat half as much as school children, but there are twice as many babies.
Therefore, the babies also need <u>5 sandwiches.</u>

35 + 5 + 5 = 45 sandwiches

Chapter 7: Perimeters

(Page 106)	**(Page 107)**	**(Page 109)**
1) 28 feet	1) 21.98	1) 13 feet
2) 26 feet	2) 26.69	2) 10 feet
3) 50 feet	3) 314 inches	3) 4.47 feet
	4) 39 inches	

Level 1   (110)

1) $423.90
Circumference = diameter x pi: 30 feet x 3.14 = 94.2   94.2 x $4.50 = $423.90

2) 60 inches

$$a^2 + b^2 = c^2$$ (10 x 10) + (24 x 24) = c^2 100 + 576 = c^2 c = 26 inches
Perimeter: 10 + 24 + 26 = 60 inches

3) 36 feet

$$a^2 + b^2 = c^2$$ (9 x 9) + (12 x 12) = c^2 225 = c^2 c = 15
Perimeter: 9 + 12 + 15 = 36 feet

4) 240 inches

$$a^2 + b^2 = c^2$$ a^2 + (96 x 96) = (104 x 104) a^2 + 9216 = 10,816

Subtract 9216 from both sides: a^2 = 1600   a = 40
Perimeter: 40 + 96 + 104 = 240 inches

5) 42 feet

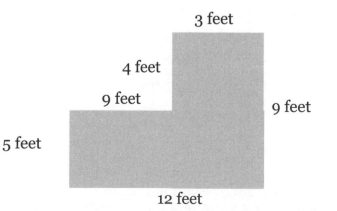

3 feet
4 feet
9 feet
9 feet
5 feet
12 feet

Finding the lengths of the missing sides. Perimeter = 3+9+12+5+9+4=42 feet

6) 70 feet

Circumference = Diameter x pi: 219.8 feet = D x 3.14

Divide both sides by 3.14:   D = 70 feet

7) 25.12 feet

Circumference = Diameter x pi: If the radius is 4 feet, then the diameter is 8 feet.

8 x 3.14 = 25.12 feet

8) 160 feet

Find the length of the missing side by using the Pythagorean Theorem.

$$a^2 + b^2 = c^2$$

$$30^2 + 40^2 = c^2$$

$$2500 = c^2$$

c = 50

9) 1425 feet

Distance around the field: 2500 x 3.14 = 7850   Walking around field: 7850 ÷ 2 = 3925

3925 - 2500 = 1425 feet

10) 36 feet

Find hypotenuse by making a triangle and then using the Pythagorean Theorem.

$$9^2 + 12^2 = c^2$$

$$225 = c^2$$

c = 15

6 + 5 + 3 + 7 + 15 = 36 feet

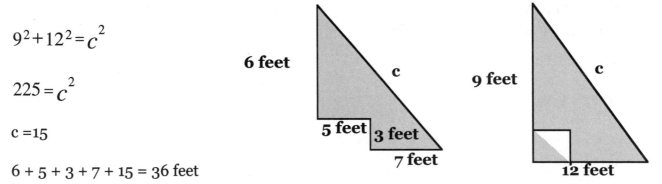

Level 2   (Page 112)

1) 537,568 miles

The diameter of the orbit is 280 + 8000 + 280 = 8560 miles.

The circumference is 3.14 x 8560 = 26,878.4   26,878.4 x 20 orbits = 537,568 miles

2) Running is faster
The circumference of the lake is 2 x 3.14 = 6.28 miles   Halfway around is 3.14 miles.
If Jayme runs at a speed of 7 miles per hour, it will take him 3.14 ÷ 7 = .45 hours
Canoeing 2 miles at a speed of 4 miles per hour would take half an hour.

3) 75.36 feet
The first runner will run 4000 feet.
The diameter of the track is 1000 ÷ 3.14 = 318.47 feet. Because the second runner will run 3 feet outside of the circle, the diameter of her circle is 318.47 + 6 = 324.47 feet.

The circumference of the second circle is 324.47 x 3.14 = 1018.84   1018.84 x 4 = 4075.36

4) 22 times
Each end of the track is half of a circle with a 100 foot diameter and a 314 foot circumference. The distance around the track is 200 + 200 + 314 = 714 feet.

3 miles is 5280 x 3 = 15,840 feet.   15,840 ÷ 714 feet per lap = 22.18 laps

5) 50.24 inches
The hour hand will sweep two circles with 8 inch diameters.
The circumference of each circle is 25.12   2 x 25.12 = 50.24 inches

6) 1130.4 inches
The hour hand has a diameter of 12 inches and a circumference of 37.68 inches.
The hour hand makes two revolutions in 24 hours, so it travels 2 x 37.68 = 75.36 inches

The minutes hand has a 16 inch diameter and a 50.24 inch circumference.
The minute hand makes 24 revolutions in 24 hours, so it travels 50.24 x 24 = 1205.76 inches.
1205.76 - 75.36 = 1130.4 inches.

7) 28.56 inches
If the radius is 8 feet, the diameter is 16 feet and the circumference is 50.24 feet.
1/4 of the circumference is 50.24 ÷ 4 = 12.56 feet
8 feet + 8 feet + 12.56 feet = 28.56 feet

8) 125.6 feet
Runner A's circle is 400 x 3.14 = 1256 feet   4 laps: 1256 x 4 = 5024 feet.

Runner B's circle is 410 feet in diameter. Circumference: 410 x 3.14 = 1287.4 feet
4 laps: 1287.4 x 4 = 5149.6 feet
5149.6 - 5024 = 125.6 feet

9) 8408
Circumference: 3 x 3.14 = 9.42 feet   15 miles: 5280 feet per mile x 15 = 79,200 feet
79,200 ÷ 9.42 = 8407.64 revolutions

10) 30 times farther

The hour hand has a circumference of 8 inches x 3.14 = 25.12 inches.
In three hours, the hour hand will travel 1/4 of the full circle: 25.12 ÷ 4 = 6.28 inches.

The minute hand has a circumference of 20 inches x 3.14 = 62.8 inches.
In three hours, the minute hand will make three revolutions: 3 x 62.8 = 188.4 inches.
188.4 ÷ 6.28 = 30   The minute hand travels 30 times the distance the hour hand travels.

Einstein Level   (Page 114-115)

1) 1345.2 feet

Total distance Ben ran in feet: 8 miles x 5280 feet = 42,240 feet
The distance on one trip around the track: 42,240 ÷ 10 = 4224 feet
Circumference ÷ π = diameter   4224 ÷ 3.14 = 1345.2 feet

2) 1.27 feet

The wheel turns 1320 times during a 5280 foot trip, so each turn is 5280 ÷ 1320 = 4 feet.
A wheel with a circumference of 4 feet has a diameter of: 4 ÷ 3.14 = 1.27 feet

3) 15 inches

Using the Pythagorean Theorem:

$$a^2 + b^2 = c^2 \qquad 9^2 + 12^2 = C^2 \qquad 225 = C^2 \quad C = 15 \text{ inches}$$

4) 2.79 inches

If the radius is 8", then the diameter is 16 inches. Circumference: 16 x 3.14 = 50.24 inches

Because there are 360 degrees in a circle, 20° is $\dfrac{20}{360}$ of the circumference. $\dfrac{20}{360} = \dfrac{1}{18}$

50.24 ÷ 18 = 2.79 inches

5) 48 feet

The length of the dotted line can by found by
using the Pythagorean Theorem:

$$a^2 + b^2 = c^2 \qquad 6^2 + 8^2 = c^2 \qquad c = 10 \text{ feet}$$

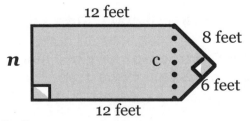

If the dotted line is equal to 10 feet, then the left end of
the figure labeled *n* must be equal to 10 feet.   12+12+8+6+10=48 feet

6) 5 miles
How many revolutions does the tire make in 10 miles?
Change the 10 miles to inches: 10 miles = 52,800 feet = 633,600 inches

Circumference of the tire: 16 x 3.14 = 50.24 inches
633,600 inches traveled ÷ 50.24 inches in the circumference = 12,611 revolutions

Because the bug is halfway between the center and the outside of the tire, it is spinning in an 8 inch diameter circle. Circumference: 8 x 3.14 = 25.12 inches

During the 10 mile trip, the bug travels 12,611 x 25.12 inches = 316,788 inches
316,788 inches ÷ 12 = 26,399 feet   26,399 feet ÷ 5280 = 5 miles

7) 20 feet

The distance from the building can by found by
using the Pythagorean Theorem:

$$a^2 + b^2 = c^2 \qquad a^2 + 48^2 = 54^2$$

$$a^2 + 2304 = 2704$$

Subtract 2304 from both sides: $a^2 = 400$ $a = 20$

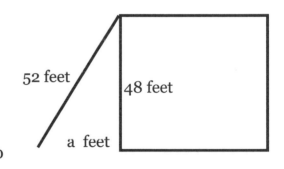

52 feet

48 feet

a feet

8) $\sqrt{8}$ or $2\sqrt{2}$
Because the area of the large square is 16, the length of each is 4 inches. Each half-side is then 2 inches.

The length of BC can by found by
using the Pythagorean Theorem:

$$a^2 + b^2 = c^2 \qquad\qquad 2^2 + 2^2 = c^2 \qquad\qquad c = \sqrt{8}$$

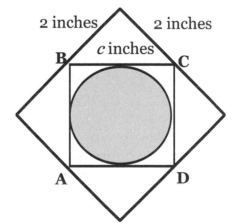

2 inches   2 inches

B   c inches   C

A   D

9) 2512 km.
Change all measurements to millimeters.
8 decimeter diameter = 800 millimeters
2 centimeters = 20 millimeters
Circumference = 800 millimeters x 3.14 = 2512 millimeters
One kilometer = 1,000,000 millimeters

How many revolutions will it take before half the rubber (10 millimeters) are worn away?
10 millimeters ÷ .00001 = 1,000,000 revolutions.

1,000,000 revolutions x 2512 millimeters(circumference) = 2,512,000,000 millimeters
2,512,000,000 millimeters = 2,512 kilometers

10) 41.78 miles

Odometer set:
1.5 feet in diameter = 4.71 feet in the circumference.
47 miles = 248,160 feet
248,160 feet ÷ 4.71 feet in circumference = 52,688 revolutions

Adam's tires:
1.33333 feet in diameter = 4.187 feet in the circumference
52,688 revolutions x 4.187 feet = 220,605 feet really traveled
220,605 feet ÷ 5280 feet in a mile = 41.78 miles.

Chapter 8: Areas

(Page 117)

1) 90 square inches
2) 48 square inches
3) 64 square inches
4) 40 square feet

(Page 118)

1) 60 square feet
2) 750 square inches
3) 28 square inches
4) 5 inches
5) 4 feet

(Page 119)

1) 706.5 square inches
2) 153.86 square feet
3) 200.96 square feet
4) 3 inches
5) 5 inches

Level 1 (120 - 121)

1) $550
Area of the carpet: 5 x 22 = 110 square yards
110 square yards x $5 per square yard = $550

2) $1099
Radius is 10 feet   Area of the room :   3.14 x 10 x 10 = 314 square feet
314 square feet x $3.50 = $1099

3) 126 square feet
Figure can be broken into two rectangles:
5 feet x 12 feet = 60 square feet
6 feet x 11 feet = 66 square feet
60 + 66 = 126 square feet

4) 60 square feet
Figure can be cut into a triangle and a rectangle.
Area of rectangle: 4 x 10 = 40 square feet
Area of triangle: 10 x 4 x .5 = 20 square feet
20 + 40 = 60 square feet

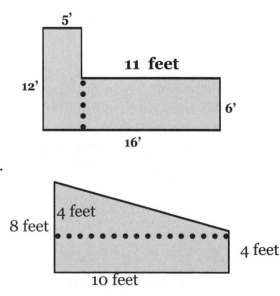

5) 46 square feet
Rectangle's area is 4 x 8 = 32 square feet.

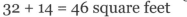

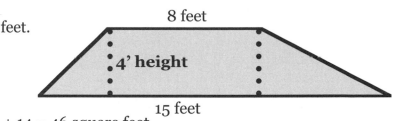

Push the two triangles together.
The height will be 4 feet and
the base will be 15 - 8 = 7 feet
Area = 4 x 7 x .5 = 14   32 + 14 = 46 square feet

6) 15 packages
The area of the ruined lawn is 3.14 x 30 x 30 = 2826 square feet
2826 square feet ÷ 200 square feet per package = 14.13   Needs to buy 15 packages.

7) 37.5 square feet
Make a triangle by extending the sides.
The area of the triangle is 9 x 11 x .5 = 49.5 square feet.
The area of the white rectangle is 3 x 4 = 12 square feet.

The area of the shaded part is 49.5 - 12 = 37.5 square feet.

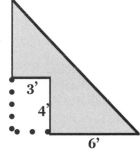

8) 359 square feet
The area of the large figure including the white inset is 19 x 20 = 380 square feet.
The area of the white inset is 7 x 3 = 21 square feet.
The area of the shaded part is 380 - 21 = 359 square feet.

9) 81 square yards
The area of the large figure including the two white insets
is 9 x 11 = 99 square yards.

The areas of the white insets are:
3 x 5 = 15 square yards
1 x 3 = 3 square yards

The area of the shaded part is 99 - 18 = 81 square yards.

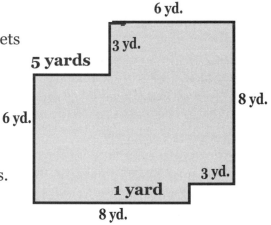

10) 540 square feet
The area of the entire room is 28 x 36 = 1008 square feet.

The dimensions of the bare floor are 26 feet x 18 feet
because Rick has 5 feet of carpet around the entire room.
Area: 26 x 18 = 468 square feet

Area of rug: 1008 - 468 = 540 square feet.

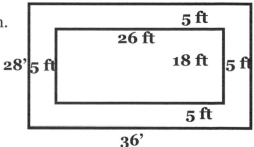

Level 2   (122 - 124))

1) 2 gallons

The area of her entire room is 3.14 x 10 x 10 = 314 square feet
The diameter of the remaining unpainted floor is 16 feet.
      The area of the remaining unpainted floor is 3.14 x 8 x 8 = 200.96 square feet.

The area of the part that has been painted is the whole floor minus the unpainted part.
      314 square feet - 200.96 square feet = 113.04 square feet

We now know that one gallon will paint 113.04 square feet. Kristin needs to buy two more gallons because the part that remains is 200.96 square feet.

2) 344 square feet

The area of the lawn is 40 x 40 = 1600 square feet.
The area of the circle that the sprinkler reaches is 3.14 x 20 x 20 = 1256 square feet.
The area of the parts that the sprinkler does not reach is 1600 - 1256 = 344 square feet.

3) 16.75 square feet

The area of the entire circle is 3.14 x 8 x 8 = 200.96 square feet
The shaded part is 30/360 (Because there are 360 degrees in a circle) or 1/12 of the circle.
200.96 ÷ 12 = 16.75 square feet

4) 28.5 square feet

The area of the circle is 3.14 x 5 x 5 = 78.5 square feet
The diagonal across the square is 10 feet. (Diameter of the circle)
The height of each triangle is 5 feet.
Each triangle therefore has an area of 10 x 5 x .5 = 25 square feet.
78.5(area of the circle) - 50(area of the two triangles) = 28.5 square feet

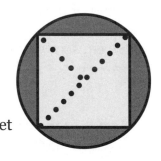

5) 32 square inches

If the area of the outside square is 64 square inches,
then the length of each side is 8 inches.
      The diameter of the circle must then be 8 inches,
      as is the diagonal across the smaller square.

The height of each triangle is 4 inches, so the
area of each triangle must be 8 x 4 x .5 = 16 square inches.
16 + 16 = 32 square inches

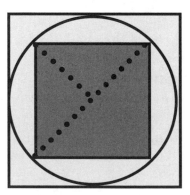

6) 800,000 red blood cells

The area of a circle with a 1/4 inch diameter: 3.14 x 1/8 x 1/8 = .0490625
The area of a circle with a one inch diameter: 3.14 x 1/2 x 1/2 = .785
How many small circles will fit into the large circle? .785 ÷ .0490625 = 16
16 x 50,000(red blood cells in the small circle) = 800,000 red blood cells

7) 34.24 square feet
The area of the circle is 3.14 x 4 x 4 = 50.24 square feet
The area of the triangle is 8 feet(base) x 4 feet(height) x 1/2 = 16 square feet
50.24 - 16 = 34.24 square feet

8) 3 days
The small circle has an area of 3.14 x 1 x 1 = 3.14 square inches.
The large circle has an area of 3.14 x 5 x 5 = 78.5 square inches
The white part of the circle has an area of 78.5 - 3.14 = 75.36 square inches.

If 25.12 square inches are removed each day,
the white part will be gone in 75.36 ÷ 25.12 = 3 days

9) 6.88 square inches
Because four diameters are equal to 8 inches, the diameter of each circle is 2 inches and the width of the rectangle is 4 inches.

The area of the rectangle is 8 inches x 4 inches = 32 square inches.
The area of each circle is 3.14 x 1 x 1 = 3.14   8 circles have an area of 25.12 square inches

The area of the shaded part is 32 square inches(rectangle) - 25.12 square inches(8 circles) = 6.88 square inches.

10) 1 million times as much
The area of the telescope mirror is 3.14 x 100 x 100 = 31,400 square inches.
The area of the pupil of an eye is 3.14 x .1 x .1 = .0314 square inches

How many of the .0314 area pupils will fit into 31,400 square inches?
31,400 ÷ .0314 = 1,000,000

Einstein Level   (125 - 127))

1) 1326.65 square feet
The area of the grass that is ruined is half of a circle with a 26 foot radius. In addition, as the leash catches on the corner of the barn, two quarter circles are formed that each have a radius of 13 feet.

Area of large half circle:
(3.14 x 26 x 26) ÷ 2 = 1061.32 square feet.

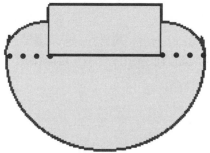

Area of quarter circles:
(3.14 x 13 x 13) ÷ 4 = 132.665 square feet.

Total area: 1061.32 + 132.665 + 132.665 = 1326.65 square feet

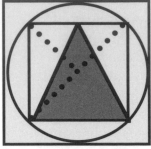

2) 20.25 square feet

The length of each side of the large square is 9 inches.
The diameter of the circle is therefore 9 inches, as is the
diagonal across the small square.
Because the height of the triangle is 4.5 inches,
the area of each triangle is 4.5 x 9 x .5 = 20.25 square feet.

Each triangle is equal to half the area of the square. The shaded Isosceles triangle is also equal
to half the area of the square.

3) 160 pancakes

The area of one of the large pancakes is 3.14 x 4 x 4 = 50.24 square inches.
The area of 10 pancakes is 10 x 50.24 = 502.4 square inches
The area of one of the small pancakes is 3.14 x 1 x 1= 3.14 square inches.
How many small pancakes can be made from 502.4 square inches? 502.4 ÷ 3.14 = 160

4) 25 square feet

The area of the rectangle: 5 x 10 = 50 square feet
The area of the upper half circle: 3.14 x 5 x 5 x .5 = 39.25 square feet
Total area: 50 + 39.25 = 89.25 square feet
The area of the white half circle: 3.14 x 5 x 5 x .5 = 39.25 square feet
The area of the white triangle: 10 x 5 x .5 = 25 square feet
 Area of shaded part: 89.25 - 39.25 - 25 = 25 square feet

5) $1311.60

Wendy's profit per square foot: $1500 ÷ 10,000 = $.15 per square foot.
Part destroyed: 3.14 x 20 x 20 = 1256 square feet   Lost money: 1256 x $.15 = $188.40
Wendy's projected profits: $1500 - $188.40 - $1311.60

6) 251.2 square inches

The area of the top and bottom: 3.14 x 4 x 4 = 50.24 square inches.
The circumference of the cylinder: 3.14 x 8 = 25.12 inches.
The curved part of the cylinder can be cut out and turned into a rectangle with an area
of 25.12(length) x 6(height) = 150.72 square inches
50.24(top) + 50.24(bottom) + 150.72(curved part) = 251.2 square inches

7) $96\sqrt{3}$

Each triangle has an 8 foot base and sides that are also 8 feet.
The height of the triangle can be found by using the

Pythagorean Theorem: $8^2 - 4^2 = b^2$ $b^2 = 48$

$b = \sqrt{48}$ or $b = \sqrt{16}$ x $\sqrt{3}$ $b = 4\sqrt{3}$

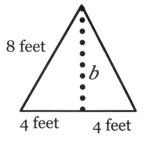

The area of each triangle is the 8(base) x $4\sqrt{3}$ (height) x .5 = $16\sqrt{3}$

If each triangle's area is $16\sqrt{3}$, the area of six triangles is $96\sqrt{3}$

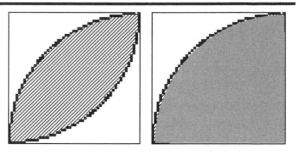

8) 57 square feet

The area of one white section can be found by finding the area of the quarter circle and subtracting it from the total area of the square.

Area of square: 100 square feet
Area of circle: 3.14 x 10 x 10 = 314 square feet
Area of 1/4 circle: 314 ÷ 4 = 78.5 square feet

Area of one white part: 100 - 78.5 = 21.5 square feet   2 white parts: 43 square feet
Area of the shaded part: 100 - 43 = 57 square feet

9) 25.12 square inches

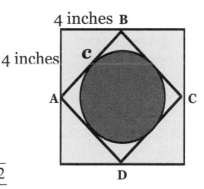

Each side of the large square is 8 inches.
Each half side is 4 inches.

The hypotenuse of each corner triangle can be found by using the Pythagorean Theorem.

$$4^2 + 4^2 = c^2 \qquad c^2 = 32 \qquad c = \sqrt{32}$$

The diameter of the circle is also $\sqrt{32}$ and the radius is $\dfrac{\sqrt{32}}{2}$

The area of the circle is $3.14 \ x \ \dfrac{\sqrt{32}}{2} x \dfrac{\sqrt{32}}{2} - 3.14 \ x \dfrac{32}{4} - 3.14 \ x \ 8 - 25.12$ square inches.

10) 67.875 square inches

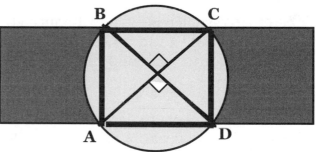

The radius of the circle is $\dfrac{\sqrt{50}}{2}$

The area of the circle is $\dfrac{\sqrt{50}}{2} x \dfrac{\sqrt{50}}{2} x \ 3.14 =$

$\dfrac{50}{4} x \ 3.14 = 12.5 \ x \ 3.14 \ = 39.25$ square inches

The area of a quarter of the circle is 39.25 ÷ 4 = 9.8125 square inches

The area of each of the 4 triangles is $\dfrac{\sqrt{50}}{2} x \dfrac{\sqrt{50}}{2} x \ .5 = 12.5 \ x \ .5 \ = \ 6.25$ *square inches*

AB (Width of the rectangle) can be found using the Pythagorean Theorem.

$\dfrac{\sqrt{50}}{2} x \dfrac{\sqrt{50}}{2} + \dfrac{\sqrt{50}}{2} x \dfrac{\sqrt{50}}{2} = c^2 \qquad c^2 = 25 \quad c = 5$ Rectangle's area = 5 x 20 = 100 sq. in.

Area of rectangle (100) - 2 triangles(12.5) - 2 quarter circles(19.625) = 67.875 square inches

Chapter 9: Volume

(Page 129)

1) 343 cubic feet
2) 3/4 of a cubic foot
3) 27 cubic cm.

(Page 130)

1) 753.6 cubic inches
2) 28.26 cubic inches
3) 56.52 cubic inches

(Page 131)

1) 33.49 cubic inches
2) 904.32 cubic inches
3) 4,186,666,666 cubic miles

Level 1   (133)

1) 5000 cubic feet
10 feet x 25 feet x 20 feet = 5000 cubic feet

2) 502.4 cubic feet
Area of circular top: 3.14 x 4 x 4 = 50.24 square feet.   50.24 x 10 = 502.4 cubic feet

3) 267,946,650,000 cubic miles

Volume = $\frac{4}{3}$ x 3.14 x 4000 x 4000 x 4000 = 267,946,650,000 cubic miles (approximately)

4) 1000 kg
A cubic meter of water is equal to 1000 cubic decimeters of water (10 x 10 x 10 = 1000)

5) 125,600 liters
Because each cubic decimeter of water is equal to a liter, change all measurements to decimeters.
Diameter: 40 decimeters   Radius: 20 decimeters   Height: 100 decimeters
Area of circular top: 3.14 x 20 x 20 = 1256 square dm.
Volume: 1256 x 100 = 125,600 cubic decimeters (125,600 liters)

6) 80,000 kg.
Change measurements to decimeters because each cubic decimeter of water weighs one
kilogram.   40 x 50 x 40 = 80,000 cubic decimeters (80,000 kg.)

7) 2332 kg
The volume of the air is 20 x 30 x 3 = 1800 cubic meters.
The weight of the air is 1800 x 1.29 = 2322 kilograms
2322 + 10 kilograms (container) = 2332 kg.

8) 1,620,000 fossils
Because a cubic yard is 3 feet x 3 feet x 3 feet, there are 27 cubic feet in a cubic yard.
27 x 60,000 fossils per cubic foot = 1,620,000 fossils

9) 113.04 cubic feet
The metal sphere will cause an amount of water to overflow that is equal to its volume.

Radius of the sphere: 3 feet   Volume: $\frac{4}{3}$ x 3.14 x 3 x 3 x 3 =113.04 cubic feet

10) 1728 cubic inches
A cubic foot is 12 inches high, 12 inches long, and 12 inches wide.
The volume of the cube is 12 x 12 x 12 = 1728 cubic inches.

Level 2   (134 - 135)

1) 1884 cubic inches
Change measurements to inches: Radius is one inch   Height is 600 inches
Area of circular top: 3.14 x 1 x 1 = 3.14 square inches
Volume: 3.14 x 600 = 1884 cubic inches.

2) 100.48 cubic feet
Area of circular top: 3.14 x 2 x 2 = 12.56 square feet
Volume: 12.56 x 8 feet = 100.48 cubic feet

3) 1000 kg.
A cubic meter is 10 dm. x 10 dm. x 10 dm. = 1000 cubic decimeters. (1000 kg)

4) 18 yards
Change all measurements to yards
12 feet = 4 yards   81 feet = 27 yards   6 inches are equal to 6/36 = .1666 yard
Volume: 4 x 27 x .1666 = 18 cubic yards

5) $3,465,000
Change all measurements to yards.
45 feet = 15 yards   9 inches = 1/4 yard
15 miles: 15 x 1760 yards per mile = 26,400 yards
Volume of cement needed for road: 15 x .25 x 26,400 = 99,000 cubic yards
99,000 x $35 = $3,465,000

6) 64 times

Volume of Earth: $\frac{4}{3}$ x π x 4000 x 4000 x 4000 =

Volume of the moon: $\frac{4}{3}$ x π x 1000 x 1000 x 1000 =

When you reduce, the $\frac{4}{3}$'s cancel. The π's cancel. The rest reduces to 64.

7) 5,451,776,000 cubic yards

Because there are 1760 yards per mile, the volume of one mile is equal to
1760 x 1760 x 1760 = 5,451,776,000 cubic yards

8) 48,385 cubic inches

Change all to inches.
Volume of 1 inch cube: 1 x 1 x 1 = 1 cubic inch
Volume of 1 foot cube: 12 x 12 x 12 = 1728 cubic inches
Volume of 1 yard cube: 36 x 36 x 36 = 46,656 cubic inches
46,656 + 1728 + 1 = 48,385 cubic inches

9) 3,153,600,000 cubic yards

There are 3 feet x 3 feet x 3 feet = 27 cubic feet in a cubic yard
2700 ÷ 27 = 100 cubic yards per second.
Seconds in one year:
60 seconds x 60 minutes/hour x 24 hours/day x 365 days/year = 31,536,000 seconds/year
31,536,000 seconds x 100 cubic yards per second = 3,153,600,000

10) $81.67

Change measurements to yards:
36 feet: 12 yards
21 feet: 7 yards
One inch thickness: 1/36 or .0277777
     Volume of one inch of thickness: 12 x 7 x .0277777 = 2.3333268
     Cost: 2.3333268 x $35 = $81.67

Einstein Level   (136 - 137)

1) $529\frac{7}{8}$ cubic inches

The diameter of a hose with a 1" outside diameter and 1/8 inch walls is 1 -1/8 -1/8 = 3/4 inch

Radius: $\frac{3}{4} \div 2 = \frac{3}{8}$ inch

Height: 1200 inches

Area of circular top: 3.14 x $\frac{3}{8}$ x $\frac{3}{8}$ = .4415625 square inches

Volume = .4415625 x 1200 = 529.875 cubic inches

2) 7 feet

Maximum load: 80,000 pounds - 6500 pounds = 73,500 pounds
Volume of box: 25 x 12 x 8 = 2400 cubic feet.
Weight of full load: 2400 cubic feet x 35 pounds = 84,000 pounds
Weight per foot in height: 84,000 ÷ 8 = 10,500 pounds.
73,500 allowable ÷ 10,500 per foot = 7 feet high

3) 750,000 cubic centimeters

Go in reverse through the meter/inch changing machine: 36 inches ÷ 39.372 = .914 meters

.914 meters = 91.4 centimeters

Volume: 91.4 x 91.4 x 91.4 = 763,552 cubic centimeters

4) .04 centimeters

The volume of the sheet must equal 1 cubic centimeter.

1.25 x 20 x n = 1 cubic centimeter

25n = 1 cubic centimeter n = .04 centimeters thick

5) 4 cans

Because a liter is a cubic decimeter, change all measurements to decimeters.

.05 mm thick: .0005 dm.   10 meters high: 100 dm.   24 meters long: 240 dm.

Volume: .0005 x 100 x 240 = 12 cubic decimeters   (12 liters)

Each can holds 3 liters, so 4 cans must be bought.

6) 7:04 P.M.

Change measurements to decimeters: Radius 2.5 decimeters   Height: 15 decimeters

Area of top circular part: 3.14 x 2.5 x 2.5 = 19.625 square decimeters

Volume: 19.625 square decimeters x 15 (height) = 294.375 cubic decimeters

If it takes 6 seconds to fill one liter, it takes 6 x 294.375 = 1766.25 seconds to fill the tank.

1766.25 seconds ÷ 60 seconds in a minute = 29.4375 minutes

6:35 + 29 = 7:04

7) 8 pounds

4 quarts are equal to .946 x 4 = 3.784 liters

3.784 liters are equal to 3.784 kilograms

3.784 kilograms x 2.2 pounds = 8.32 pounds

8) 47.1 cubic inches

The radius of the entire washer, with the hole included is 2 inches.

The area of the washer top with the hole included is: 3.14 x 2 x 2 = 12.56 square inches.

The volume is 12.56 x .125 (1/8) = 1.57 cubic inches.

The area of the hole top is 3.14 x 1 x 1 = 3.14 square inches.

The volume of the hole is 3.14 x .125 inches high = .3925 cubic inches.

Volume of one washer excluding the hole: 1.57 - .3925 = 1.1775 cubic inches.

Volume 40 washers excluding the holes: 1.1775 x 40 = 47.1 cubic inches

9) 230 feet

The radius of Don's water heater is .75 feet

Change all measurements to inches: Height is 48 inches   Radius is 9 inches

Area of circular part of water heater: 3.14 x 9 x 9 = 254.34 square inches

Volume: 254.34 x 48 = 12,208.32 cubic inches

1/10 volume of water heater = 1220.832 cubic inches.

Radius of garden hose: 3/8 or .375 inches

Area of circular part of hose: 3.14 x .375 x .375 = .4415625 square inches

Volume of needed hose: .4415625 square inches x n inches in length = 1220.832 cubic inches

.4415625n = 1220.832   Divide both sides by .4415625: n = 2764.8 inches

2764.8 inches = 230.4 feet

10) 1/4 of the box

The sand in the box is allowed to weigh 708 pounds - 4 pounds = 704 pounds

The volume of the box: 8 x 4 x 4 = 128 cubic feet

The weight of a full box is 22 pounds per cubic foot x 128 cubic feet = 2816 pounds

704 is what part of 2816?   704/2816 reduces to 1/4

Chapter 10: Percents

(Page 139)   **(Page 140)**   **(Page 141)**   **(Page 141)**

(Page 139)	(Page 140)	(Page 141)	(Page 141)			
1) .65	1) 78%	1) 50%	1) 1/5	50%	.5	1/2
2) 1.5	2) 115%	2) 80%	2) 14/25	15%	.15	3/20
3) .02	3) 5%	3) 10%	3) 3/100	35%	.35	7/20
4) .24	4) 23%	4) 37.5%	4) 1/100	18.75%	.1875	3/16
5) .05	5) .5%	5) 5%	5) 1 1/10	5%	.05	1/20
6) .542	6) 500%	6) 250%	6) 4	6%	.06	3/50
		7) 66.67%		1/2%	.005	1/200
		8) 1%		250%	2.5	2 1/2
		9) 2.5%		480%	4.8	4 4/5
		10) 320%		.0006%	.000006	3/500,000

(Page 143)	**(Page 144)**	**(Page 145)**	**(Page 147)**
1) 42	1) 32	1) 2.5%	1) 50%
2) 28	2) 50	2) 4000%	2) 50%
3) 15	3) 90	3) 34.72%	3) 10%
4) 69	4) 1700	4) 288%	4) -35%
5) 1	5) $84	5) 1388.89%	5) -80%
6) 320	6) 190,833,330	6) 71.43%	6) 25%
7) $85.60	square miles	7) 7%	7) -25%
8) $51		8) 300%	8) 1400%
9) $12,400		9) 33.33%	9) 20%
10) $88.20		10) 25%	10) 50%

Level 1   (Page 148)

1) $24

Percent of number problem: 20% of 120   .20 x 120 = $24

2) 30%

Comparing problem: 27 out of 40 have a pet   Change 27/40 to a decimal
$27 \div 40 = .675$ 67.5%

3) 50%

Percent of increase problem: Amount of increase over the original: $\dfrac{\$40 \ (increase)}{\$80 \ (original)}$

Reduces to 1/2 = 50%

4) $157.50

Percent of number problem: 5% of $150   .05 x 150 = 7.5
$7.50 interest + the $150 = $157.50

5) $8.80

Percent of number problem: 10% of $8   .1 x 8 = $.80   New allowance: $8.80

6) 20%

Comparing problem: 60 compared to 300   60/300 = .2 = 20%

7) 63

Percent of number problem: 75% of 84   .75 x 84 = 63

8) 95%

Percent of increase or decrease problem: $\dfrac{\$190 \ (decrease)}{\$200 \ (original)}$ reduces to 19/20 = 95%

9) 800%

Comparing problem: $400 compared to $50   400/50 = 8   8 is equal to 800%

10) $620

Backwards problem: Paycheck is called n $.22n = 136.40

Divide both sides by .22: $n = 620$

Level 2   (Page 149)

1) 87,273 people

Backwards problem: 55% of $n = 48,000$ $.55n = 48,000$

Divide both sides by .55: n = 87,272.7

2) 180 students

Backwards problem: 90% of the students don't like the color purple. 90% of $n = 162$

$.9n = 162$ Divide both sides by .9: $n = 180$

3) $267.96

Percent of number problem: If 3% interest is paid annually, 1.5% is paid in 6 months

1.5% of 264   .015 x 264 = $3.96 $264 + $3.96 = $267.96

4) $64

Percent of number problem:

Kristin: $200   Megan: 80% of 200 .8 x 200 = $160

Ellen: 40% of $160   .4 x 160 = $64

5) $82.68

Percent of number problem: 35% of $120   .35 x 120 = $42   Discount is $42

New price: $120 - 42 = $78

Sales tax: 6% of 78   .06 x 78 = $4.68   Total cost: $78 + $4.68 = $82.68

6) $185,420.95

Percent of number problem: 1.229% includes money and interest.

18th birthday: $3000

19th birthday: 122.9% of $3000   1.229 x 3000 = $3687

20th birthday: 122.9% of $3687   1.229 x 3687 = $4531.32

21st birthday: 122.9 of $4531.32 = $5569

And so on

38th birthday owes $185,420.95

7) 650%

Percent of increase or decrease problem: $\dfrac{\$13{,}000 \; (increase)}{\$2000 \; (original)}$ reduces to 6.5 = 650%

8) $37,500
Backwards problem: Luke's salary is n $.32n = \$12,000$
Divide both sides by .32: $n = \$37,500$

9) $300
Zach's starting money: n
If he spent 40% of n, then he has 60% of n left over: $.60n$

Zach's remaining money is $.6n$. If he spends 25% of $.6n$, he has 75% of $.6n$ left over.
75% of $.6n$ $.75 \times .6n = .45n$

Zach's remaining money is $.45n$. If he spends all but 20%, then he has 20% of $.45n$ left over.
$.2 \times .45n$ is left over. $.2 \times .45n = \$27$ $.09n = 27$
Divide both sides by .09: $n = \$300$

10) .33%
Comparing problem: 1/2 pound compared to 150 pounds $.5/150 = .003333$
$.003333 = .33\%$

Einstein Level   (Page 150 - 151)
1) 129%

Percent of increase problem: $\dfrac{45 \ square \ feet \ (increase)}{35 \ square \ feet \ (original)}$ reduces to $9/7 = 1.29 = 129\%$

2) $4679.43
Percent of number problem: Multiply by 104% each year to get total money.
1st year: $1.04 \times 4000 = 4160$
2nd year: $1.04 \times 4160 = \$4326.40$
3rd year: $1.04 \times \$4326.40 = \$4499.46$
4th year: $1.04 \times \$4499.46 = \$4679.43$

3) $8861.34
Percent of number problem: Multiply by 122% each year to get total money owed.
1st year: $1.22 \times 4000 = \$4880$
2nd year: $1.22 \times 4880 = \$5953.60$
3rd year: $1.22 \times \$5953.60 = \$7263.39$
4th year: $1.22 \times \$7263.39 = \$8861.34$

4) Thursday
Percent of number problem: When an item is 15% off, it is 85% of the regular price. When an item is 25% off, it is 75% of the regular price. 35% off is 65% of the regular price. etc.
Monday: 85% of $40 $.85 \times 40 = \$34$
Tuesday: 75% of $34 $.75 \times 34 = \$25.50$
Wednesday: 65% of $25.50 $.65 \times 25.50 = \$16.58$
Thursday: 55% of $16.58 $.55 \times 16.58 = \$9.12$

5) 27
Sara's age: n
Daniel's age: 15% of n   .15n
Luke's age: 75% of n   .75n
Rachel's age: 300% of .15n   3 x .15n = .45n

Equation: n + .15n + .75n + .45n = 141   2.35n = 141
Divide both sides by 2.35   n = 60   Rachel = .45n or .45 x 60 = 27

6) 18.78%
The area of each set's screen can be found by drawing diagonals.
The 30 inch set has two triangles. Both have a base of 30 inches
and heights of 15 inches.
Area: 30 x 15 x .5 = 225   Two triangles: 450 square inches

The 13 inch set has two triangles. Both have a base of 13 inches
and height's of 6.5 inches.
Area: 13 x 6.5 x .5 = 42.25 Two triangles: 84.5 square inches

Comparing problem: 84.5/450 = .1878   18.78%

7) 3.7%   .058%
There are 3 x 3 x 3 = 27 cubic feet in a cubic yard.
Comparing problem: 1/27 = .037   3.7%

There are 12 x 12 x 12 = 1728 cubic inches in a cubic foot.
Comparing problem: 1/1728 = .00058   .058%

8) $1213.70
Amount sold: n
Amy charged people 5% tax.   105% of n = $1202.25   1.05$n$ = 1202.25
Divide both sides by 1.05: n = $1145   The amount sold was $1145.
106% of $1145   1.06 x $1145 = $1213.70

9) 300%
Original area: 4 x 4 = 16 square inches
New area: 8 x 8 = 64 square inches

Percent of increase problem: $\dfrac{48 \ (increase)}{16 \ (original)} = 3 = 300\%$

10) 75%
Original radius we will call 4 inches. Area =3.14 x 4 x 4 = 50.24 square inches
Radius cut in half. Area: 3.14 x 2 x 2 = 12.56 square inches

Percent of decrease problem: $\dfrac{37.68 \ (decrease)}{50.24 \ \ (original)} = .75 = 75\%$

Super Einstein Problem: 30 centimeter cube

Because a meter cube is 100 centimeters on each side, there are 100 x 100 x 100 = 1,000,000 cubic centimeters in a cubic meter.

2.7 % of these: 2.7% x 1,000,000   .027 x 1,000,000 = 27,000 cubic centimeters
What number cubed is equal to 27,000?   The answer is 30

Chapter 11: Ratio and Proportion

(Page 156)   **(Page 159)**

1) 24   6) 102.5 feet   1) 22.5 cups
2) 11.25   7) $4.44   2) 63 pounds
3) 21.6   8) 95 feet   3) 360 pennies
4) 14.64   9) 56 2/3 inches   4) 85 ounces
5) 387.5   10) 2990 miles   5) 136 pounds

Level 1   (160)

1) 6 feet 3 inches

$$\frac{5 \ feet \ (Mark's \ height)}{8 \ feet \ (Shadow)} = \frac{n \ (Dad's \ height)}{10 \ (Dad' shadow)}$$ Cross-multiply: 8n = 50   n = 6.25 feet

2) 230.4 feet

$$\frac{32 feet}{10 \ seconds} = \frac{n \ feet}{72 \ seconds}$$ Cross-multiply: 10n = 2304   n = 230.4 feet

3) 140 students

$$\frac{13 \ boys}{15 \ girls} = \frac{65 \ boys}{n \ girls}$$ Cross-multiply: 13n = 975   n = 75 girls   75 girls + 65 boys = 140 students

4) 186 2/3 million

$$\frac{2 \ know}{3 \ people} = \frac{n}{280 \ million}$$ Cross-multiply: 3n = 560 million   n = 186 2/3 million

5) 8.75 inches

$$\frac{7(shortest)}{40 \ (perimeter)} = \frac{n}{50 \ perimeter}$$ Cross-multiply: 40n = 350   n = 8.75 inches

6) $5,200,000

$$\frac{4 \ (star's \ salary)}{3 \ (next \ highest)} = \frac{n}{3,900,000}$$ Cross-multiply: 3n = 15,600,000   n = $5,200,000

7) 2321 pounds

$$\frac{11\ parts\ copper}{15\ total\ parts} = \frac{n}{3165\ weight\ of\ statue}$$ Cross-multiply: 15n = 34,815   n = 2321 pounds

8) 36 home runs

$$\frac{2\ (home\ runs)}{13\ (strikeouts)} = \frac{n}{234\ (strikeouts)}$$ Cross-multiply: 13n = 468   n = 36 home runs

9) 6.8 centimeters

$$\frac{1\ cm\ (on\ map)}{14.7\ (real\ miles)} = \frac{n}{100\ miles}$$ Cross-multiply: 14.7n = 100   n = 6.8 centimeters

10) 31 feet 8 inches

$$\frac{5\ feet\ (Lindsey's\ height)}{6\ feet\ (Lindsey's\ shadow)} = \frac{n\ (tree's\ height)}{38\ feet\ (tree's\ shadow)}$$ Cross-multiply: 6n = 190 n = 31 2/3

Level 2   (161-162)

1) 17,850 smokers

Break the 100 down into 15 and 85: $\dfrac{85\ lung\ cancer(smokers)}{15\ lung\ cancer(non-smokers)} = \dfrac{n\ (smokers)}{3150\ (non-smokers)}$

Cross-multiply: 15n = 267,750   n = 17,850 smokers who are lung cancer victims

2) 2210 miles

Change $\dfrac{1}{8}$ and $1\dfrac{1}{16}$ to decimals: $\dfrac{.125}{260\ miles} = \dfrac{1.0625}{n}$ Cross-multiply: .125n = 276.25

Divide both sides by .125: n = 2210 miles

3) 1/10 pound

$$\frac{1500\ pounds\ (adult\ bear)}{1\ pound\ (baby\ bear)} = \frac{150\ pounds\ (adult\ human)}{n\ (baby)}$$ We call baby n because we already

know a typical baby weighs 7 pounds, but we want to know what it would weigh if it was proportionally the same as brown bears. Cross-multiply: 1500n = 150   n = .1 pounds

4) 900 feet

Change fractions to decimals: $\dfrac{.0625\ (flea\ height)}{9.375\ (jump)} = \dfrac{6\,feet\ (person's\ height)}{n\ (jump)}$

Cross-multiply: .0625n = 56.25   n = 900 feet

5) 25 inches

$$\frac{.125 \ inches \ (globe)}{125 \ miles \ (real)} = \frac{n \ (globe \ circumference)}{25{,}000 \ miles \ (real \ circumference)}$$

Cross-multiply: 125n = 3125

n = 25 inches

6) Plane

The fatality rate per mile for cars is 4 times the rate for airplanes. The trip to London by plane is 16 times the distance by car to Chicago, so the trip by plane would be more dangerous.

7) Same chances

If the driver was under the influence of alcohol, his trip would be four times as dangerous. This would be like driving 800 miles instead of 200 miles. Because 800 miles is 1/4 the miles of the plane trip (3200 miles to London), each trip would be equally dangerous. (Because air travel is 4 times as safe as car travel)

8) 93 feet

$$\frac{62 \ inches \ (Nancy's \ height)}{35 \ inches \ (Nancy's \ shadow)} = \frac{n \ (tree's \ height)}{52.5 \ feet \ (tree's \ shadow)}$$

Cross-multiply: 35n = 3255

n = 93 feet

9) 198.375 pounds

$$\frac{200 \ pounds \ (recipe \ lye)}{138 \ pounds \ (Diane's \ lye)} = \frac{287.5 \ pounds \ (recipe \ coconut \ oil)}{n \ (reduced \ coconut \ oil)}$$

Cross-multiply: 200n = 39,675   n = 198.375 pounds

10) 3.14   3.14   Ratio is always 3.14

$$\frac{circumference: \ 81.64}{diameter: \ 26} = 3.14$$

$$\frac{circumference: \ 276.32}{diameter: \ 88} = 3.14$$

The ratio of circumference to diameter is always pi (3.14). π is the ratio of the circumference to the diameter.

Einstein Level   (163-164)

1) 10 ounces

Compare Mark's weight to the total weight of his family.

$$\frac{80 \ pounds \ (Mark's \ weight)}{512 \ pounds \ (Family)} = \frac{n \ (ounces \ of \ ice \ cream)}{64 \ (total \ ounces \ of \ ice \ cream)}$$

Cross-multiply: 512n = 5120

Divide both sides by 512: n = 10 ounces

2) 78.5:50 or 1.57
Each side of the large square is 10 units because we will make the area of the square 100 square units. The area of the circle is 3.14 x 5 x 5 = 78.5 square units. (Diameter must be 10)

A diagonal of the small square is the diameter of the circle, which is 10 units.
The area of each triangle is 10 (base) x 5 (height) x .5 = 25
The area of the two triangles is 50. (So the area of the square is 50)

Ratio: $\dfrac{78.5}{50}$

3) 12:8
If the blue and red dye are in a ratio of 7:8, then there are 15 parts to the ratio. (7+8)
Because the cup is **3/4** full, there must be 5 parts to each quarter. (15 ÷ 3)
If you fill the container with blue dye, you are adding 1/4 or 5 parts to the blue.
New ratio: (7+5):8   12:8

4) 5:3:2.66
 If the blue and red dye are in a ratio of 5:3, then there are 8 parts to the ratio. (3+5)
Because the cup is **3/4** full, there must be 8÷3 = 2.66 parts to each quarter.
If green dye fills the container, it must be a quarter of the container or 2.66.
New ratio: 5:3:2.66

5) $5:13\dfrac{2}{3}:2\dfrac{2}{3}$

If the container is half emptied, the ratio is still the same: 5:3:2.66 or 10.66 parts (5+3+2.66).
Half the container has 10.66 pieces, so when half a container of red is added, you are adding
10.66 parts of red. 3 + 10.66 = 13.66
New ratio: 5:13.66:2.66

6) 180 cars
Bikes: n
Motorcycles: 2n
Trucks: 4n
Cars: 12n
Equation: 19n = 285   n=15   12n = 180

7) 44 feet
Meagan height: n   Mark: n+5
Meagan's shadow: 127.5 inches   Mark's shadow: 140 inches

$$\frac{n\ (Meagan's\ height)}{127.5\ (Meagan's\ shadow)} = \frac{n+5\ (Mark's\ height)}{140\ (Mark'shadow)}$$ Cross-multiply: 140n = 127.5n + 637.5

Get the *n*'s on one side of the equation: 12.5n = 637.5   n = 51   Meagan is 51 inches

$$\frac{51 \; inches \; (Meagan's \; height)}{127.5 \; inches \; (Meagan's \; shadow)} = \frac{n \; (Tree's \; height)}{110 \; (Tree's \; shadow)}$$ Cross-multiply: 127.5n = 5610

Divide both sides by 127.5: n = 44 feet

8) 562 pounds 1 ounce
There are 6+8+1+4 = 19 total parts to the ratio. (Gold has 1 part)

Change weight to all ounces: (10,679 x 16) + 3 ounces = 170,867 ounces

$$\frac{1 \; part \; gold}{19 \; total \; parts} = \frac{n}{170,867 \; total \; weight}$$ Cross-multiply: 19n = 170,867   n = 8993 ounces

8993 ounces = 562 pounds 1 ounces

9) 270/7
6 snakes:7 turtles

1 snake:3 parrots

So we know that 6 snakes:18 parrots (Multiply both by 6 to get to 6 snakes.)

18 parrots:6 snakes

2 parrots:15 dogs

So we know that 18 parrots:135 dogs (Multiply both by 9 to get to 18 parrots.)

18 parrots:135 dogs

2 cats:1 dog

So we know that 135 dogs:270 cats (Multiply both by 135 to get to 135 dogs)

Now we know that 7 turtles:6 snakes:18 parrots:135 dogs:270 cats

10) Fraction: 1/1601   Ratio: 1/1600
100 gallons of water contains 1600 cups. If one cup of milk is placed in the tub, then the tub contains 1601 cups of liquid.

There are now 1601 total parts with one part being milk.   Fraction: 1/1601

There is one part milk and 1600 parts water.   Ratio: 1:1600

Chapter 12: Trigonometry

Tangents   (Page 175)
1) 3.28 feet
2) 25°
3) 6.93 feet

$$\frac{a}{12} = \text{tangent } 30° \qquad \frac{a}{12} = \frac{.5774}{1} \quad \text{Cross-multiply: } a = 6.93$$

4) 15 feet

$$\frac{a}{15} = \text{tangent } 45° \qquad \frac{a}{15} = \frac{1}{1} \qquad \text{Cross-multiply: } a = 15$$

5) 3.53 feet

Continue to use opposite over adjacent: $\dfrac{a}{20} = \text{tangent } 10° \qquad \dfrac{a}{20} = \dfrac{.1763}{1} \qquad a = 3.53$

6) 56.71 feet

$$\frac{a}{10} = \text{tangent } 80° \qquad \frac{a}{10} = \frac{5.6713}{1} \qquad \text{Cross-multiply} \qquad a = 56.71$$

7) 10°

$$\frac{3}{17.016} = \text{tangent } A \qquad \frac{3}{17.016} = .1763 \qquad \text{The angle with a tangent of .1763 is } 10°$$

8) 34°

$$\frac{14}{20.756} = \text{tangent } A \qquad \frac{14}{20.756} = .6745 \qquad \text{The angle with a tangent of .6745 is } 34°$$

9) 31.18 feet

$$\frac{a\ (Height\ of\ building)}{18} = \text{tangent } 60° \qquad \frac{a}{18} = \frac{1.7321}{1} \qquad a = 31.18$$

10) 57 feet

$$\frac{6\ (height\ off\ ground)}{b} = \text{tangent } 6° \qquad \frac{6}{b} = \frac{.1051}{1} \qquad .1051b = 6 \quad b = 57.08$$

11) Approximately 600 feet

$$\frac{150\ (height\ of\ lighthouse)}{b} = \text{tangent } 14° \qquad \frac{150}{b} = \frac{.2493}{1} \qquad .2493b = 150 \quad b = 602$$

Sines   (Page 179)
1) 50 feet
2) 105.65 feet
3) 35.36 feet

$$\frac{opposite\ side}{hypotenuse}: \quad \frac{a}{50} = \text{sine } 45° \qquad \frac{a}{50} = \frac{.7071}{1} \qquad a = 35.36$$

4) 27.05 feet
The side we are trying to find is opposite an unknown angle. We must first find its measure by remembering that there are 180 total degrees in a triangle.
The unknown angle is equal to 180 - 15 - 90 = 75°

$$\frac{opposite\ side}{hypotenuse}: \quad \frac{a}{28} = \text{sine } 75° \qquad \frac{a}{28} = \frac{.9659}{1} \qquad a = 27.05$$

5) 11,468 feet

$$\frac{opposite\ side}{hypotenuse}: \quad \frac{1000}{c} = \text{sine } 5° \qquad \frac{1000}{c} = \frac{.0872}{1} \qquad .0872c = 1000 \qquad c = 11,467.89$$

6) 161.81 feet

$$\frac{opposite\ side}{hypotenuse}: \quad \frac{50}{c} = \text{sine } 18° \qquad \frac{50}{c} = \frac{.3090}{1} \qquad .3090c = 50 \qquad c = 161.81$$

7) 26.6 feet
Because there are 180 degrees in a triangle, we know that the base angles are 70°.

$$\frac{opposite\ side}{hypotenuse}: \quad \frac{25}{c} = \text{sine } 70° \qquad \frac{25}{c} = \frac{.9397}{1}$$

$$.9397c = 25 \qquad c = 26.6$$

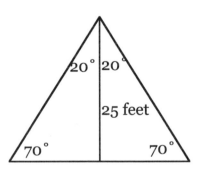

8) 18.2 feet
We know the measurements of two sides of a right triangle.   Use the Pythagorean Theorem.

$$a^2 + b^2 = c^2$$

$$a^2 + (25 \times 25) = (26.6 \times 26.6)$$

$$a^2 + 625 = 707.56$$

$$a^2 = 82.56$$

$$a = 9.1 \qquad \text{The base is } a + a = 18.2$$

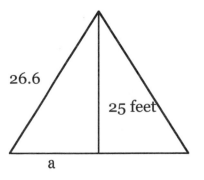

9) 72.5 feet

$\dfrac{opposite\ side}{hypotenuse}: \dfrac{a}{80} = \text{sine } 65°$ $\dfrac{a}{80} = \dfrac{.9063}{1}$ $a = 72.5$

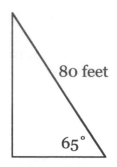

80 feet

65°

10) Yes; angle is between 4° and 5°

$\dfrac{opposite\ side}{hypotenuse}: \dfrac{1800\ feet\ (Height)}{23,760\ feet\ (length\ of\ road)}$ must be less than sine 6° or .1045

$1800 \div 23,760 = .075$ The angle than has a sine of .075 is between 4° and 5°.

11) 17.4 miles

$\dfrac{opposite\ side}{hypotenuse}: \dfrac{8000}{c} = \text{sine } 5°$ $\dfrac{8000}{c} = \dfrac{.0872}{1}$ $.0872c = 8000$

$c = 91,743$ feet   91,743 feet = 17.4 miles

Cosines   (Page 184)
1) 96.59 feet
2) 82.82 feet
3) 25°

$\dfrac{adjacent\ side}{hypotenuse}: \dfrac{36.252}{40} = \text{cosine } A$ .9063 is the cosine for 25°

4) 13.59 feet

$\dfrac{adjacent\ side}{hypotenuse}: \dfrac{b}{15} = \text{cosine } 25°$ $\dfrac{b}{15} = \dfrac{.9063}{1}$ $b = 13.59$

5) 29.56 feet

$\dfrac{adjacent\ side}{hypotenuse}: \dfrac{19}{c} = \text{cosine } 50°$ $\dfrac{19}{c} = \dfrac{.6428}{1}$ $.6428c = 19$ $c = 29.56$

6) 50°

$\dfrac{adjacent\ side}{hypotenuse}: \dfrac{51.424}{80} = \text{cosine } A$ .6428 is the cosine for 50°

7) 21 feet
The angles in an equilateral triangle
are all 60°, so the top angle must be 30°.

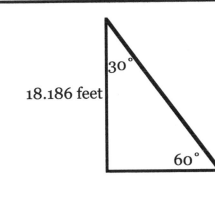

$$\frac{adjacent\ side}{hypotenuse} : \frac{18.186}{c} = \text{cosine } 30°$$

$$\frac{18.186}{c} = \frac{.8660}{1} \qquad .8660c = 18.186 \qquad c = 21$$

8) 63.39 feet

$$\frac{adjacent\ side}{hypotenuse} : \frac{b}{150} = \text{cosine } 65°$$

$$\frac{b}{150} = \frac{.4226}{1} \qquad b = 63.39$$

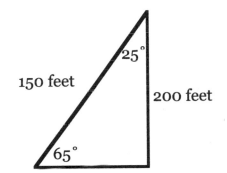

9) No, the pitch is between 27° and 28°
Angle A must be greater than 40°.

$$\frac{adjacent\ side}{hypotenuse} : \frac{16}{18} = \text{cosine A}$$

.89 is the cosine of an angle of about 28°.

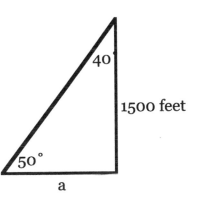

10) 1258.65 feet

$$\text{Tangent} = \frac{opposite\ side}{adjacent\ side} : \frac{1500}{a} = \text{tangent } 50°$$

$$\frac{1500}{a} = \frac{1.1918}{1} \qquad 1.1918a = 1500 \qquad a = 1258.6$$

Einstein Level   (Page 187)

1) 199 feet

$$\sin e: \frac{Opposite}{hypotenuse} : \quad \frac{180}{c} = \text{sine } 65° \qquad\qquad \frac{180}{c} = \frac{.9063}{1}$$

$$.9063c = 180 \qquad\qquad c = 198.6$$

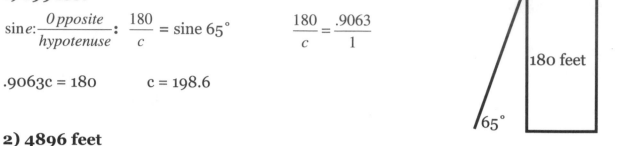

180 feet

65°

2) 4896 feet

$$\frac{adjacent\ side}{hypotenuse} : \quad \frac{height\ of\ plane}{5280\ feet} = \text{cosine } 22° \qquad \frac{height\ of\ plane}{5280\ feet} = \frac{.9272}{1} \qquad \text{height} = 4895.6$$

3) 2.72 miles
Because sound takes 5 seconds to travel one mile, the distance to the thunderstorm is 3 miles.

$$\frac{Distance\ off\ ground}{15,840\ feet\ (3\ miles)} = \text{sine } 65°$$

$$\frac{Distance\ off\ ground}{15,840\ feet\ (3\ miles)} = \frac{.9063}{1} \qquad \text{Distance} = 14,355 \text{ feet}$$

$$14,355 \div 5280 = 2.72$$

4) 102.47 feet

$$\frac{opposite}{adjacent} = \text{tangent } 18° \qquad\qquad \frac{height}{300} = \frac{.3249}{1}$$

height = 97.47 feet + Greg is 5 feet tall = 102.47

5) 2 miles
The avalanche is 4 miles away because
it takes sound 20 seconds to travel 4 miles.

$$\sin e: \frac{Opposite}{hypotenuse} : \quad \frac{height}{4\ miles} = \text{sine } 30°$$

$$\frac{height}{4\ miles} = \frac{.5}{1} \qquad\qquad \text{height} = 2 \text{ miles}$$

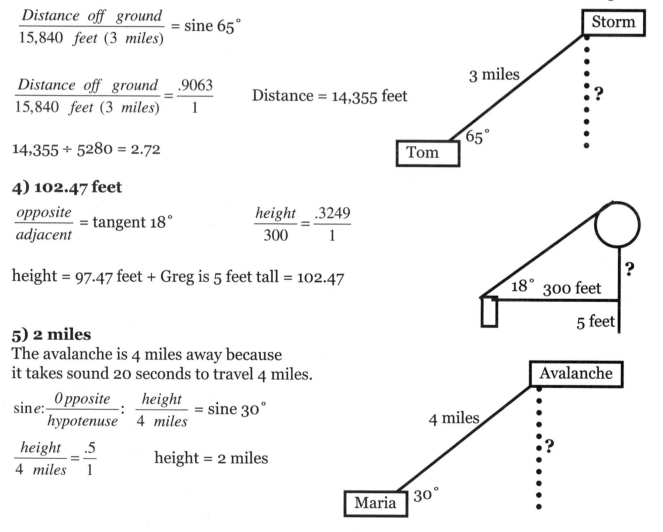

6) 188 feet

$$\frac{opposite}{adjacent} = \text{tangent } 20°$$

$$\frac{height}{500 \ feet} = \text{tangent } 20°$$

$$\frac{height}{500 \ feet} = \frac{.3640}{1}$$

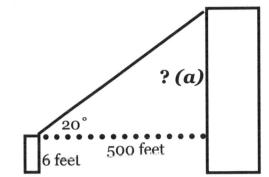

? (a)

20°

6 feet   500 feet

height = 182 + 6 feet in height = 188 feet

7) 5615 feet

$$\frac{opposite}{adjacent} = \text{tangent } 10°$$

990 feet

10°

distance away (b)

$$\frac{990 \ feet}{b} = \text{tangent } 10°$$

$$\frac{990 \ feet}{b} = \frac{.1763}{1} \qquad .1763b = 990 \qquad b = 5615$$

8) 120 feet

Height of top part of tree: $\frac{opposite}{adjacent} = \text{tangent } 23°$ $\frac{height}{120} = \frac{.4245}{1}$ height = 50.94

Height of bottom part of tree: $\frac{opposite}{adjacent} = \text{tangent } 30°$ $\frac{height}{120} = \frac{.5774}{1}$ height = 69.29

Add two parts together = 120 feet

9) 1423 feet
If the angle of depression is 8°, then the remaining angle is 82°.

$$\frac{opposite}{adjacent} = \text{tangent } 82°$$

$$\frac{distance}{200} = \text{tangent } 82°$$

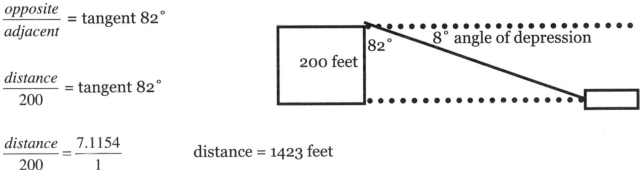

82°   8° angle of depression

200 feet

$$\frac{distance}{200} = \frac{7.1154}{1} \qquad \text{distance} = 1423 \text{ feet}$$

10) 125 feet

$$\frac{opposite}{adjacent} = tangent\ 72°$$

$$\frac{height}{39\ feet} = \frac{3.0777}{1}$$ height = 120 feet

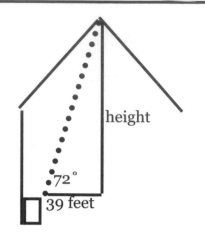

Chapter 13: Probability

(Page 195)
1) P(Heads) = 1/2
2) P(Double 1's or 2's) = 1/18
3) P(T,T) = 1/4
4) P(12) = 1/36
5) P(Guess month) = 1/12
6) P(Guess Birthday) = 1/31
7) P(T,T,T) = 1/8
8) P(Going to mall) = 1/1,000,000

(Page 197)
1) 1/12
2) 3/52
3) 1/10
4) 28/85

(Page 198)
1) 7/26
2) 5/7

(Page 201)
1) 1/32
2) 1/7776
3) 1/104,976
4) 1/169
5) 1/624
6) 1/17   1/221

(Page 203)
1) 4651/7776
2) 1023/1024
3) 26/27
4) 6095/20,736
5) 7351/125,000

(Page 205)
1) 22
2) 19,231
3) 258
4) 39
5) Mathematical probability is the expected outcome. Experimental probability is the actual outcome when an experiment is done.

Level 1   (Page 206)
1) 1/128

$$\frac{1}{2}x\frac{1}{2}x\frac{1}{2}x\frac{1}{2}x\frac{1}{2}x\frac{1}{2}x\frac{1}{2} = \frac{1}{128}$$

2) 166 2/3
There are 36 possible outcomes for a roll of two dice. (6 outcomes from one die times 6 outcomes = 36)

Of those 36 outcomes, there are 6 that are equal to 7: (3,4) (4,3) (1,6) (6,1) (2,5) (5,2)
The probability of rolling a 7 is therefore 6 out of 36 rolls or 1/6. 1000 ÷ 6 = 166.67

3) 50 nickels and 50 pennies
There are 100 nickels and 100 pennies. If you picked 100 coins, the expected outcome is an equal amount of each.

4) 7/26
Because there are 13 diamonds and one ace of spades in a deck of 52 cards, the probability would be 14 out of 52.

5) 494 students
2/3 of 741 = 494

6) 1/216
There are 216 different outcomes when three dice are rolled. (6 x 6 x 6 = 216) Only one of those possibilities has all three dice being one.

7) Yes; the probability is still 1/2

8) No

The probability of getting three heads is $\frac{1}{2} x \frac{1}{2} x \frac{1}{2} = \frac{1}{8}$. The probability of rolling two dice and getting a seven is 1/6. (36 outcomes, and six of those are a seven.)

9) Yes
The probability of rolling a three is 1 in 6. The probability of rolling a seven is also 1 in 6.

10) 1/32
$$\frac{1}{2} x \frac{1}{2} x \frac{1}{2} x \frac{1}{2} x \frac{1}{2} = \frac{1}{32}$$

Level 2   (Page 207)
1) 25/31
There are 1240 coins. (40 quarters, 200 nickels, and 1000 pennies) You have a 1000 out of 1240 chance of picking a penny. 1000/1240 reduces to 25/31

2) 4/13
There are 13 spades and 3 additional kings besides the spade king. 16/52 reduces to 4/13

3) 3/4
There are four possible outcomes for the two additional children: (B,B) (G,G) (B,G) (G,B) When you look at the four possible outcomes, you can see that three have a girl.

4) 1/64

Each time they have a child, the probability of having a child with Tay-Sachs is 1 in 4. If they have three children, the probability that all three children will have Tay-Sachs is $\frac{1}{4} x \frac{1}{4} x \frac{1}{4} = \frac{1}{64}$.

5) 27/64

Each time they have a child, the probability of having a child **without** Tay-Sachs is 3 in 4. If they have three children, the probability of no child having Tay-Sachs will be $\frac{3}{4} x \frac{3}{4} x \frac{3}{4} = \frac{27}{64}$.

6) 37/64

We know from problem #5 that the probability of no child having Tay-Sachs is 27 out of 64. This means that the remaining 37/64 are outcomes where at least one child has Tay-Sachs.

7) 1/4

Identical triplets have the same genetic makeup. If one child has Tay-Sachs, they all do. The probability is therefore 1/4.

8) 1/64

This situation would be the same as having three children: $\frac{1}{4} x \frac{1}{4} x \frac{1}{4} = \frac{1}{64}$

9) 1/1461

In four years there are 365 + 365 + 365 + 366 = 1461 days. There is only one February 29th in those 1461 days.

10) 40.5 cases

.00003 x 1,350,000 = 40.5

Einstein Level   (Pages 208-209)

1) 781/1024

This is a problem that must be solved by asking what the probability is of not picking a spade. Each time you pick, the probability of not picking a spade is 3 out of 4. For five picks the probability is: $\frac{3}{4} x \frac{3}{4} x \frac{3}{4} x \frac{3}{4} x \frac{3}{4} = \frac{243}{1024}$ If the probability of not picking a spade is 243/1024, then the probability of picking at least one spade is all that is left. 1024 - 243 = 781/1024

2) 1/1,906,884

A player picks 5 numbers. The winning ping pong balls pop up at the end of the week. The player has a 5/49 chance of matching the first ball. Because he has four numbers left and there are 48 ping pong balls left, he has a 4/48 chance of matching the second ball; a 3/47 chance of matching the third ball; a 2/46 chance of matching the fourth and a 1/45 chance of matching the last.

$\frac{5}{49} x \frac{4}{48} x \frac{3}{47} x \frac{2}{46} x \frac{1}{45}$ reduces to 1/1,906,884 (Cross reduce)

3) 1/93,437,316

$\dfrac{5}{49} \times \dfrac{4}{48} \times \dfrac{3}{47} \times \dfrac{2}{46} \times \dfrac{1}{45} \times \dfrac{1}{49}$ reduces to 1/93,437,316 (cross reducing)

4) 1/649,740
When the player picks the first card, there are 20 "good" cards in the deck: 10, jack, queen, king and ace of the four suits.

After the first pick, there are only four "good" cards left because he has committed to one

suit. $\dfrac{20}{52} \times \dfrac{4}{51} \times \dfrac{3}{50} \times \dfrac{2}{49} \times \dfrac{1}{48}$ reduces to 1/649,740 (Cross reduce)

5) $\dfrac{30{,}024{,}751}{312{,}500{,}000}$

This is a problem that must be solved by asking what the probability is of not being involved in a car accident each year. The answer is 49/50. The probability of not being in an accident

in five years is $\dfrac{49}{50} \times \dfrac{49}{50} \times \dfrac{49}{50} \times \dfrac{49}{50} \times \dfrac{49}{50}$ = 282,475,249/312,500,000.

If the probability of not getting in an accident is 282,475,249/312,500,000, then the probability of getting in an accident is all that is left. 312,500,000 - 282,475,249 = $\dfrac{30{,}024{,}751}{312{,}500{,}000}$.

6) 62/64
The only way these conditions will not be met is if the couple has all girls or all boys. The

probability of each happening is: $\dfrac{1}{2} \times \dfrac{1}{2} \times \dfrac{1}{2} \times \dfrac{1}{2} \times \dfrac{1}{2} \times \dfrac{1}{2} = \dfrac{1}{64}$ The probability of having all boys

is 1/64. All girls is 1/64. The probability of this **not** happening is the remainder: 62/64

7) 1/11
If 1000 people are tested, on average, 10 people will have false positives because the probability of getting a false positive is 1 out of 100. If 1000 people are tested, on average, one out of the thousand will really have the disease.

1000 people are tested, eleven test positive, but only one of those has the disease.
If you test positive, your probability of really having the disease is 1/11.

8) 453,000
The research shows that if the 11,037 men had taken aspirin, they would have had 100 fewer heart attacks. There are 50,000,000 ÷ 11,037 = 4530 groups of 11,037 men in a 50 million man population. Each one of those groups would save 100 heart attacks by taking aspirin.
4530 x 100 = 453,000

9) 1/425
The first pick is always successful. (You are always on your way to getting three of a kind.) After your first pick, there are only three "good" cards left in the deck - which has 51 remaining cards.

After your second pick, there are only two "good" cards remaining in the 50 remaining cards. $\frac{52}{52} \times \frac{3}{51} \times \frac{2}{50}$ reduces to 1/425.

10) 1/5525
Your first pick has a 4/52 probability of being successful. Your second pick has a 3/51 chance of being successful. Your third pick has a 2/50 chance of being successful.

$\frac{4}{52} \times \frac{3}{51} \times \frac{2}{50}$ reduces to 1/5525.

Chapter 14: Statistics

(Page 218)
1) $2-$5
2) 54 students; 21 students
3) No

(Page 221)
1) 20,000,000
2) 453,145 lives saved
3) 360 suicides

(Page 226)
1)
       a) Cell phones
       b) 2500
       c) No, it does not show a significant difference in brain cancer cases between users and non-users of cell phones
2)
       a) about 24.5
       b) 1/3 of a case (No cases)
       c) 1/10 of a case (No cases)
       d) No; 21 times the expected rate

Occam's Razor (Page 229 - 230)
Abducted by aliens
The man was walking near an airport. While he was looking up at the lights of a low flying plane, he didn't hear an approaching car. He was struck by the car and knocked unconscious.

Clever Hans
Clever Hans was able to tell when he had stomped his foot the correct number of times. Nervous viewers would not breathe deeply until he had tapped the right answer. When he hit the correct number, the audience exhaled with relief. Clever Hans was able to detect this.

Sir Edmund Digby and the Healing Salve
The fact that he put salve on enemy guns obviously didn't help his patients heal. What helped them heal was the fact that the bacteria infested salve was no longer being put on the patient's wounds.

Crop Circles
Pranksters enjoyed the attention they were getting in the news. This encouraged them to continue with more and more complicated designs.

(Page 232)
1) A form of selection where everyone in the studied population has an equal chance of being picked for the experiment.

2) Have a 25-plant control group that is exposed to the exact conditions that the 25-plant experimental group is exposed to. The only difference would be that one group of plants would be talked to.

3) Two cases of cancer because this type of cancer is rare. You would also need to know the rate of tongue cancer in the general population.

4) The design of the experiment influences the results.

5) A prank by a neighbor. (Could be several other simple explanations,)

6) Using small samples to make predictions.

7) Mean is the average while the median is the middle number.

8) With a control group, the only difference between the groups is the factor that is being studied.

9) No; there is a 1/4 chance of picking a heart anyway.

10) Meteors or man-made objects.

Chapter 15: Distance = Speed x Time

(Page 237)
1) 3 hours 36 minutes
Distance = Speed x Time   180 miles = 50 x n 180 = 50n
n = 3.6 hours   (Each 1/10 of an hour is 6 minutes.)

2) 5 hours 15 minutes
252 miles = 48 x n 252 = 48n n = 5.25 hours

3) 2880 miles
Distance = 60 x 48   Distance = 2880

4) 90 mph
405 miles = Speed x 4.5 hours   405 = 4.5n n = 90 mph

5) 435 miles
Train A's distance = 80 mph x 3 hours-----------240 miles
Train B's distance = 65 mph x 3 hours-----------195 miles   240 + 195 = 435

(Page 240)
1) 6 mph
3 blocks of 4 mph   1 block of 12 mph
Add and divide by the number of blocks: 4 + 4 + 4 + 12 = 24   24 ÷ 4 = 6 mph

2) 6 2/3 mph
5 blocks of 4 mph   1 block of 20 mph
Add and divide by the number of blocks: 4 + 4 + 4 + 4 + 4 + 20 = 40   40 ÷ 6 = 6.6667

3) 2.86 mph
Main block is 10.   5 blocks of 2 mph   2 blocks of 5 mph
Add and divide: 2 + 2 + 2 + 2 + 2 + 5 + 5 = 20   20 ÷ 7 = 2.86 mph

4) 3.2 mph
4 blocks of 2 mph   1 block of 8 mph
Add and divide by the number of blocks of time: 2 + 2 + 2 + 2 + 8 = 16   16 ÷ 5 = 3.2 mph

5) 16 mph

12 mph	12 mph	48 mph

8 blocks of 12 mph   1 block of 48 mph   (Because Claire spent 4 times as much time going 12 mph as 48 mph for each 1/3 of her travels)
Add and divide: (12 + 12 + 12 + 12)+ (12 + 12 + 12 + 12) + 48 = 144   144 ÷ 9 blocks = 16

Level 1   (Page 241)
1) 210 miles
Distance = 60 mph x 3.5 hours   Distance = 210 miles

2) 31.2 hours
Distance = Speed x Time $1716 = 55 \times n$ $55n = 1716$ $n = 31.2$

3) 24 mph
204 miles = Speed x 8.5 hours $204 = 8.5n$ $n = 24$ mph

4) 12.9 hours
The distance from Chicago to New York is 721 miles.
First part of trip: 450 miles = 65 x Time $450 = 65n$ $n = 6.9$ hours
Second part of trip: 271 miles = 45 x Time $271 = 45n$ $n = 6$ hours

5) 59.2 hours
Round trip between Denver and New York is 1627 x 2 = 3254 miles
3254 miles = 55 x Time $3254 = 55n$ $n = 59.2$ hours

6) 640 miles
First train: Distance = 35 mph x 8 hours   Distance = 280 miles
Second train: Distance = 45 mph x 8 hours   Distance = 360 miles

7) 4.8 mph
4 blocks of 3 mph   1 block of 12 mph
Add and divide by the number of blocks: 3 + 3 + 3 + 3 + 12 = 24   24 ÷ 5 = 4.8 mph

8) Same time
Mark's time: 2 miles = 4 mph x Time $2 = 4n$ $n = 1/2$ hour
Sister's time: 2 miles = 8 mph x Time $2 = 8n$ $n = 1/4$ hour
Mark arrives at 8:30   Sister arrives at 8:30

9) 16 2/3 mph

5 blocks of 10 mph   1 block of 50 mph

Add and then divide by the number of blocks:

10 + 10 + 10 + 10 + 10 + 50 = 100   100 ÷ 6 = 16.667

10) May 1999

51,000,000 miles = 17,500 mph x Time $51{,}000{,}000 = 17{,}500n$ $n = 2914$ hours

2914 hours ÷ 24 = 121 days   121 days is equal to approximately 4 months.

Level 2   (Page 243)

1) 2 miles

Younger brother's distance: Distance = 5 mph x 2.5 hours   Distance = 12.5 miles

Older brother's distance: Distance = 7 mph x 1.5 hours   Distance = 10.5 miles

2) 30 minutes

Child 1: Distance = 4 mph x Time   Distance = 4t

Child 2: Distance = 6 mph x Time   Distance = 6t

We want to know when the distance apart is equal to 5 miles.

Equation: 5 miles = 4t + 6t   5 = 10t   t = 1/2 hour

3) 8:15

Martha's distance = 4 mph x Time   Distance = 4t

Kristin's distance = 12 mph x Time   Distance = 12t

We want to know when their total distance is equal to 4 miles because that is where they will meet.

4 miles = 4t + 12t   4 = 16t   t = 1/4 hour

4) $34

If she travels 8 hours per day and food is $8 per day, then her cost is $1 per hour.

We must find out how many hours the trip will take her.   Distance = Speed x Time.

408 = 12 mph x Time $408 = 12n$ $n = 34$ hours

5) 2057 seconds

2 miles = 3.5 mph x Time $2 = 3.5n$ Divide both sides by 3.5 $n = .5714$ hours

Because there are 3600 seconds in an hour, we change .57 hours into seconds by multiplying by 3600.   .57 x 3600 = 2057 seconds

6) 29 1/3 mph

Because the formula Distance = Speed x Time is more easily used with hours, 9 minutes must be changed to hours. Because there are 60 minutes in an hour, divide 9 by 60:

9/60 = .15 hours.

4.4 miles = Speed x .15 hours $4.4 = .15n$ $n = 29.3333$ mph

7) 8:20
We need to find how long it takes Michelle to ride her bike to the soccer field.

20 miles = 12 mph x Time   20 = 12n $n = 1\frac{2}{3}$ hours = 1 hour and 40 minutes

1 hour and 40 minutes before 10:00 is 8:20

8) No, it will take her 16.43 minutes
6.3 miles = 23 mph x Time   6.3 miles = 23n   n = .27 hours
.27 hours is longer than the 15 minutes or 1/4 hour that she has to make it to school.

9) 17.78 mph

Trip to School   Trip home

4 blocks of 10 mph   1 block of 40 mph   2 blocks of 20 mph   Another 2 blocks of 20 mph

Add and divide by the number of blocks: 10 + 10 + 10 + 10 + 40 + 20 + 20 + 20 + 20 = 160
160 ÷ 9 = 17.78 mph

10) Route 1-------------6 minutes   Route 2----------------6.6 minutes
Time for choice#1: 6 miles = 60 mph x Time   6 = 60n n = 1/10 hour or 6 minutes

Time for choice #2: 5.5 miles = 50 mph x Time   5.5 = 50n
n = .11 hours   .11 hours x 60 minutes in an hour = 6.6 minutes

Einstein Level   (Page 245)
1) 3/4 mile
Change the 3 minutes to hours: 3/60 or 3÷60 = .05 hours
Distance train travels in 3 minutes: Distance = 75 mph x .05 hours   Distance = 3.75 miles
Distance car travels in 3 minutes: Distance = 60 mph x .05 hours   Distance = 3 miles

The length of the train is the extra distance the train had to go to pass the car:
3.75 miles - 3 miles = .75 miles

2) 4.5 seconds
Change 1320 feet to miles: 1320/5280 reduces to 1/4 mile.
Distance = Speed x Time   .25 mile = 200 x Time   .25 = 200n n = .00125 hours

Change .00125 hours to seconds: If you wanted to change 3 hours into seconds, you would
multiply by 3600 because there are 3600 seconds in an hour. This is the same situation:
Multiply .00125 hours by 3600.   .00125 x 3600 = 4.5 seconds.

3) Two hours after Dad starts, or 3 hours after Gabe starts
After 1 hour, Gabe has gone 48 miles, his dad 0 miles
After 2 hours, Gabe has gone 2 x 48 = 96 miles; his dad has gone 1 x 72 = 72 miles
After 3 hours, Gabe has gone 3 x 48 = 144 miles, his dad has gone 2 x 72 = 144 miles

4) 48 mph
Block of time will be 120 mph
Going up the river: 3 blocks of 40 mph   Going down the river: 2 blocks of 60 mph each.
Add and divide by the number of blocks: 40 + 40 + 40 + 60 + 60 = 240   240 ÷ 5 = 48 mph

5) 7/12 mile
Change 20 seconds to hours: 20 seconds ÷ 3600 seconds in an hour = .005555 hours
Pretend Warren was standing still. The distance the train traveled in those 20 seconds is:
Distance = 90 mph x .005555 hours   Distance = .5 miles

Warren is not standing still, but riding in the opposite direction as the train. He is therefore making the train pass him more quickly than if he is standing still. The distance Warren traveled must be added to the train's length.

Warren's distance = 15 mph x .005555 hours   Distance = .08333   or 1/12 mile
Train's distance traveled + Warren's distance traveled = 7/12 mile

6) One inch
The second place finisher must have had a time of 26.81 seconds in the 50-yard race.
We must first find the speed of the second place finisher in inches per second.
Change yards into inches: 50 x 36 = 1800 inches.
Speed in inches per second: 1800 ÷ 26.81 = 67.14 inches per second.

Now we must find out how far the second place swimmer swam when the 1800 inch race ended at 26.80 seconds.

Distance = 67.14 inches per second x 26.80 seconds   Distance = 1799.35 inches
Second place finisher was less than 1 inch from the finish line when the 1800 inch race ended.

7) 40 miles
Time it took to get to school at 60 mph will be called: t hours
The time it took to get to school at 40 mph was 20 minutes or 1/3 hour longer than at 60 mph so it will be called: $t + 1/3$ hours

60 mph trip equation: Distance = 60 mph x t Distance = $60t$
40 mph trip equation: Distance = 40 mph x (t + 1/3)   Distance = 40t + 40/3

Because the distances are equal, we can set them equal to each other:
$60t = 40t + 40/3$ $20t = 40/3$ $t = 2/3$ hour
Now that we know the time: Distance to school = 60 mph x 2/3 hour   Distance = 40 miles

8) 1/2 yard
What is the speed of the second place finisher in yards per second?
100 yards ÷ 9.92 seconds = 10.08 yards per second.

What distance had the second place finisher traveled when the winner crossed the finish line at 9.87 seconds? (Distance = Speed x Time)

Distance = 10.08 yards per second x 9.87 seconds   Distance = 99.49 yards
The second place finisher was 100 yards - 99.49 yards = 1/2 yard behind the winner when the race ended.

9) .48 miles
Change 2 minutes 24 seconds into hours: 144 seconds ÷ 3600 = .04 hours
Distance train traveled: Distance = 24 mph x .04 hours   Distance = .96 miles
Distance Susan traveled: Distance = 12 mph x .04 hours   Distance = .48 miles

Because Susan is traveling with the train, her distance must be subtracted from the distance that the train traveled.
Train's distance - Susan's distance = .48 miles

10) Impossible
Distance = Speed x Time

The distance that Mack will travel is 2 miles total. The average speed we want is 60 mph.
2 miles = 60 x Time $2 = 60n$ $n = 1/30$ of an hour, which is equal to 2 minutes.

How long did it take Mack to get to work at 30 mph?
1 mile = 30 x Time $1 = 30n$ Time = 1/30 of an hour or 2 minutes

To average 60 mph on his round trip, Mack must have a total traveling time of 2 minutes. Unfortunately, when Mack traveled the one mile to work at a speed of 30 mph, it took him 2 minutes. He has no time left.

Chapter 16: Simultaneous Equations

(Page 250)

1) x = 10   y = 5

Subtract:
$$4x + 3y = 55$$
$$\underline{4x + y = 45}$$
$$2y = 10 \qquad y = 5 \qquad \text{x must equal 10}$$

2) x = 9   y = 2

Subtract up:
$$3x + y = 29$$
$$\underline{7x + y = 65}$$
$$4x = 36 \qquad x = 9 \qquad \text{y must equal 2}$$

3) Hat = $22

Equations:
$$2H + C = 92$$
$$\underline{2H + 2C = 140}$$

Subtract up: $\qquad C = 48 \qquad\qquad$ Hats must be 22

4) Pencil = $.59

Equations:
$$Pen + Pencil = 158$$
$$\underline{Pen - Pencil = 40}$$

Add: $\qquad 2\ Pens = 198 \qquad Pen = 99 \qquad$ Pencil must be 59

5) x = 1/2   y = 8

Subtract:
$$4x + y = 10$$
$$\underline{2x + y = 9}$$
$$2x = 1 \qquad x = 1/2 \qquad \text{y must equal 8}$$

(Page 253)

1) x = 7   y = 3

(Multiply by 3): x + y = 10
$$3x + 3y = 30$$
$$\underline{3x + 5y = 36} \qquad \text{(Subtract up)}$$
$$2y = 6 \qquad y = 3 \qquad x = 7$$

2) x = 5   y = 15

(Multiply by 9): 2x + 3y = 55
(Multiply by 2): 9x + 4y = 105
$$18x + 27y = 495$$
$$\underline{18x + 8y = 210} \qquad \text{(Subtract)}$$
$$19y = 285 \qquad y = 15 \qquad x = 5$$

3) Socks $4.50

(Multiply by 2): 3 Shoes + 2 Socks = 123
(Multiply by 3): 2 Shoes + 3 Socks = 89.5
$$6\ Shoes + 4\ Socks = 246$$
$$\underline{6\ Shoes + 9\ Socks = 268.5} \qquad \text{(Subtract up)}$$
$$5\ Socks = 22.5 \qquad Socks = 4.5$$

4) x = 8   y = 9
(Multiply by 3): $x + 3y = 35$ $3x + 9y = 105$
                    $3x + y = 33$ $\underline{3x + y = 33}$ (Subtract)
                                          $8y = 72$ $y = 9$ $x = 8$

5) Nik is 14
(Multiply by 2): $M + 3N = 54$ $2M + 6N = 108$
                    $2M + 4N = 80$ $\underline{2M + 4N = 80}$ (Subtract)
                                          $2N = 28$ $N = 14$

(Page 255)
1) x = 4   y = 12
If $x + y = 16$, then $x = 16 - y$ Substitute $(16 - y)$ for x in the equation $2x + 3y = 44$

$2(16 - y) + 3y = 44$ $32 - 2y + 3y = 44$ $32 + y = 44$ $y = 12$

2) x = 10   y = 1
If $x + 2y = 12$, then $x = 12 - 2y$ Substitute $(12 - 2y)$ for x in the equation $2x + y = 21$

$2(12 - 2y) + y = 21$ $24 - 4y + y = 21$ $24 - 3y = 21$
Add 3y to each side: $24 = 21 + 3y$ Subtract 21 from each side: $3 = 3y$ $y = 1$

3) x = 14   y = 18
If $2x + 4y = 100$, then $2x = 100 - 4y$ Divide by 2 to get one x: $x = 50 - 2y$
Substitute $(50 - 2y)$ for x in the equation $6x + 10y = 264$ $6(50 - 2y) + 10y = 264$

$300 - 12y + 10y = 264$ ⟶ $300 - 2y = 264$
Add 2y to each side: $300 = 264 + 2y$ ⟶ Subtract 264 from each side: $2y = 36$ $y = 18$

4) x = 10   y = 0
If $x + y = 10$, then $x = 10 - y$
Substitute $(10 - y)$ for x in the equation $7x + 9y = 70$ $7(10 - y) + 9y = 70$

$70 - 7y + 9y = 70$ $70 + 2y = 70$ Subtract 70 from both sides: $2y = 0$ $y = 0$

5) x = 6 5/7   y = -4/7
If $2x - y = 14$, then $2x = 14 + y$ Divide by 2 to get one x: $x = 7 + .5y$
Substitute $(7 + .5y)$ for x in the equation $3x + 2y = 19$ $3(7 + .5y) + 2y = 19$

$21 + 1.5y + 2y = 19$ ⟶ $21 + 3.5y = 19$ ⟶ Subtract 21 from each side: $3.5y = -2$
divide both sides by 3.5: $y = -2/3.5$ or $-4/7$

(Page 257)

1) Dog = 5 Cats

Because 2 Horses are equal to 3 snails, we know that one Horse is equal to 1.5 snails.
In the second equation, substitute 1.5 snails for the Horse: 1.5 Snails = Dog + Cat

Now write the top two equations: Dog = Cat + Snail

1.5 Snails = Dog + Cat

Switch the first equation around because we want to get rid of the snails.

Cat + Snail = Dog   (Multiply by 3)
1.5 Snails = Dog + Cat   (Multiply by 2)

3 Cats + 3 Snails = 3 Dogs
3 Snails =2 Dogs + 2 Cats   (Subtract to remove Snails)
3 Cats = Dog - 2 Cats

Add 2 Cats to each side: 5 Cats = Dog

2) 3 Pears = 2 Apples

Because 3 Bananas are equal to an Apple, one Banana is equal to 1/3 Apple

Substitute 1/3 Apple for the Banana in the first equation: 1/3 Apple + Pear = Apple
Subtract 1/3 Apple from both sides: Pear = 2/3 Apple

We want 2 Apples so we must multiply the equation by 3: 3 Pears = 2 Apples ($\frac{2}{3} x 3 = 2$)

3) Car = 8 Bikes

Because Bike = 2 Unicycles, we can change the 8 Unicycles in the second equation to 4 Bikes.

Car - Truck = 2 Bikes
2 Trucks = Car + 4 Bikes

We need to get rid of the trucks, so we will multiply the top equation by 2:

2 Cars - 2 Trucks = 4 Bikes

Add equations: 2 Trucks = Car + 4 Bikes

2 Cars = Car + 8 Bikes   Subtract 1 car from both sides: Car = 8 Bikes

4) Square = 2 Circles

Because 2 Squares = Triangle, we can put 2 Squares in place of the Triangle in the first equation:

2 Squares - Square = 2 Circles   Square = 2 Circles

5) English = 2 1/3 SS

2 M = 3 S

E = SS + S

M = 2 SS

Because one Math = 2 Social Studies, we can replace the 2 Math in the first equation with 4 SS.

4 SS = 3 S

E = SS + S   Now multiply the bottom equation by 3 to get rid of the Science.

4 SS = 3 S

<u>3 E = 3 SS + 3S</u>   Now subtract the equations

4 SS - 3E = - 3 SS

Add 3 E to both side: 4 SS = - 3 SS + 3 E

Add 3 SS to both sides: 7 SS = 3 E

Divide both sides by 3: $\dfrac{7}{3}$ SS = E

(Page 258)

1) x = 11   y = 7

3x + y = 40

<u>5x - y = 48</u>   Add the equations

8x = 88   x = 11

2) x = 3.5   y = -7.5

9x - y = 39

2x - 2y = 22   Multiply top equation by -2

-18x + 2y = -78

<u>2x - 2y = 22</u>   Add equations

-16x = -56   Divide both sides by -16: x = 3.5

3) $.58

3P + 2 R = 230   (Multiply by 3 to get rid of rulers)

2 P + 3 R = 200   (Multiply by 2 to get rid of rulers)

9 P + 6 R = 690

<u>4 P + 6 R = 400</u>   (Subtract)

5 P = 290

P = 58

4) $.65

9 G + 3 A = 870   (Multiply by two to get rid of the angelfish)
4 G + 6 A = 830

18 G + 6 A = 1740
<u>4 G + 6 A = 830</u>   (Subtract)
14 G = 910   G = 65

5) 1st number = 2   2nd number = 7

x + 4y = 30   (Multiply by 4 to get rid of the x's)
4x + y = 15

4x + 16y = 120
<u>4x + y = 15</u>   (Subtract)
     15y = 105   y = 7

6) $15.50

6B - 2S = 70.50
<u>4B + 2S = 84.50</u>   (Add)
10B = 155   B = 15.50

7) 2.5 hours

Carol's pay: 6x + 5 = y
June's pay: <u>4x + 10 = y</u>   (Subtract)
          2x - 5 = 0

Add 5 to each side: 2x = 5   x = 2.5

8) Cat = 4 Dogs

We want to get rid of the hamsters, so multiply the top equation by 3.

C = 2D + H (x 3) ⟶ 3C = 6D + 3H ⟶ 3C = 6D + 3H
3H = C + 2D   3H = C + 2D (Turn equation around)   C + 2D = 3H

3C = 6D + 3H
<u>C + 2D = 3H</u>   (Subtract)
2C - 2D = 6D ⟶

Add 2D to each side: 2C = 8D   C = 4D

9) Dog = 5 cats

Because two horses are equal to 3 mice, one horse is equal to 1.5 mice. Change horse in the second equation to 1.5 mice.

D = C + M   D = C + M   (Multiply by 3 to get rid of mice)
1.5 M = D + C   (Turn equation around) D + C = 1.5 M (Multiply by 2 to get rid of mice)

3D = 3C + 3M
2D + 2C = 3M_____ (Subtract)
3D - 2D -2C = 3C + 3M - 3M   D - 2C = 3C   Add 2C to both sides: D = 5C

10) Math = Social Studies

Because 2 English books are equal to one Math book, 1.5 Math books can be substituted for the 3 English books in the third equation.

4 Science - Social Studies = Math
1.5 Math = Science + Social Studies (Flip second equation)

4 Science - Social Studies = Math
Science + Social Studies = 1.5 Math   (Multiply second equation by 4 to get rid of Science)

4 Science - Social Studies = Math
4 Science + 4 Social Studies = 6 Math   (Subtract equations)

- 5 Social Studies = - 5 Math   Math = Social Studies

Chapter 17: Graphing Equations

(Page 262)   **(Page 263)**

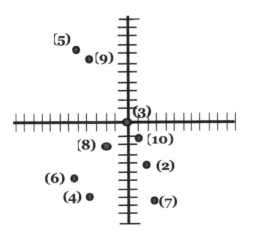

A. (3,2)
B. (8,-8)
C. (-1,-7)
D. (-8,3)
E. (-3,7)
F. (-1,-1)

(Page 265)

1)

2)

3)

4)

5)

6)

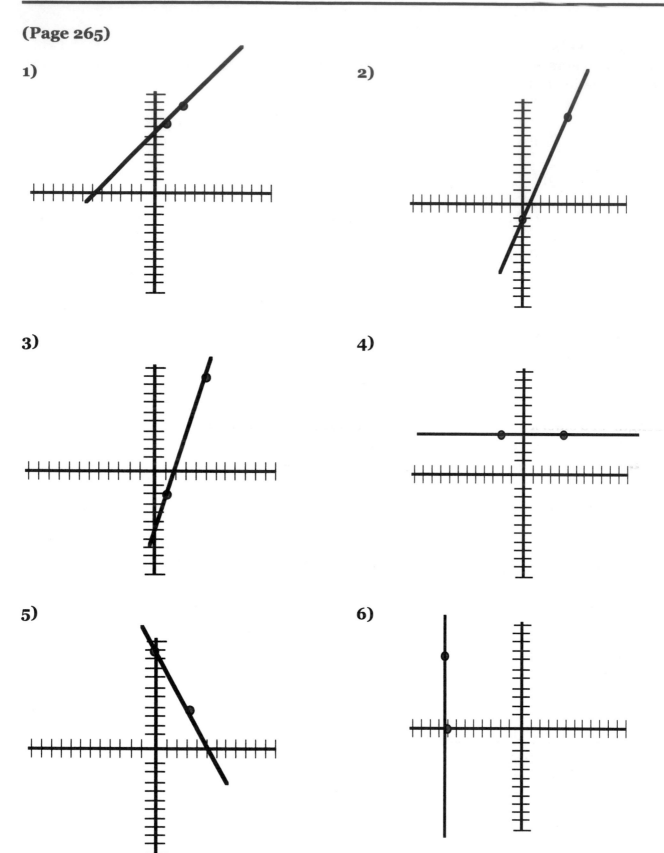

(Page 270)

2) Equation: y = 5x
Hours worked: x
Money earned: y

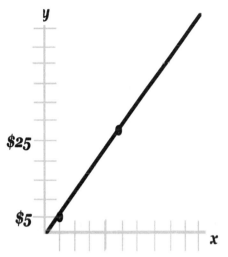

3) Equation: 2x = y
Brother's allowance: x
Nik's allowance: y

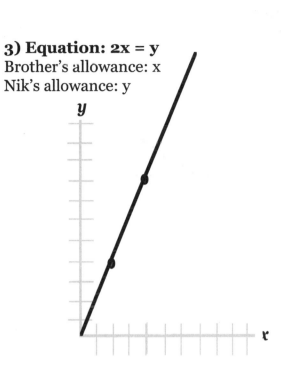

4) Equation: $x^2 = y$
Length of a side: x
Area: y

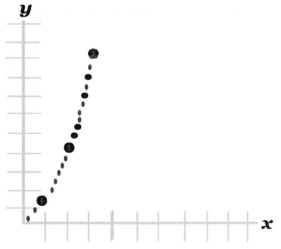

5) 25x = y
Number of square yards: x
Price of carpet: y

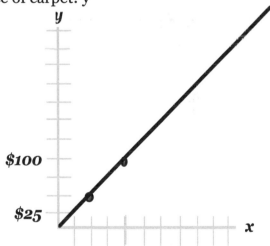

6) Equation: xπ = y
Diameter: x
Circumference: y

7) 8x + 25 = y
Hours worked: x
Pay: y

8) Equation: $x^3 = y$

Length of one side: x
Volume: y

9) $\left(\dfrac{1}{2}\right)^2 \pi = y$ (Area = radius x radius x pi)

Diameter: x
Area: y

10) $y = \dfrac{900}{x}$

Distance from body: x
Amount of weight that can be held: y

xy is always equal to 900,
so y is equal to 900/x

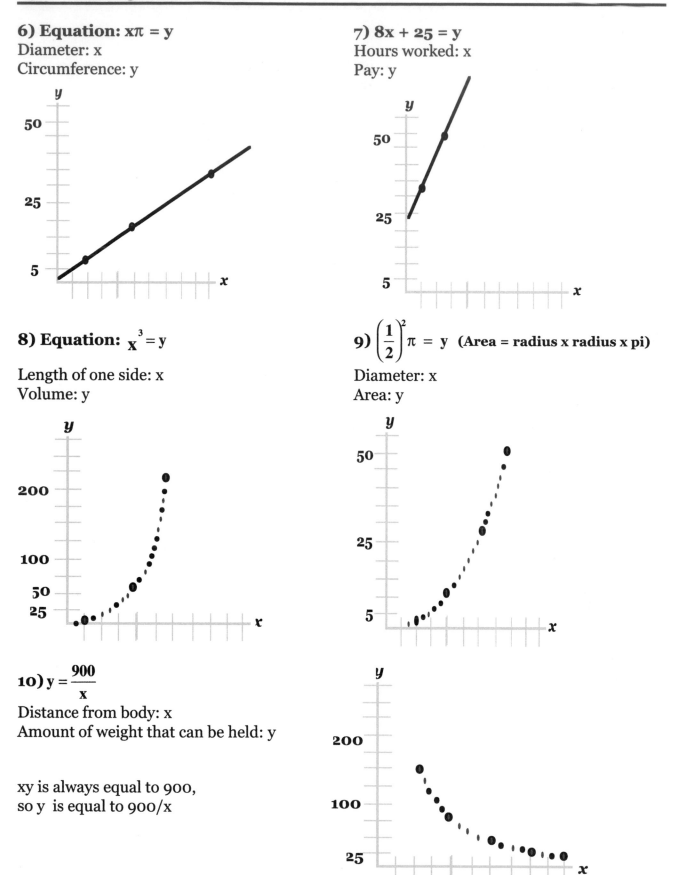

(Page 277-279)

1) 1   **2) 3**   **3) 2**   **4) 1**   **5) 6**

6) 20 mph
The average speed is the distance traveled divided by the number of hours traveled.

Pick two numbers for "x", say 1 and 2. Now we can easily find "y" for those two numbers:
When x is 1:   20 x 1 + 15 = y   y =35
When x is 2:   20 x 2 + 15 = y   y = 55

Average speed is distance traveled--subtract the y's divided by the number of hours--subtract the x's

$$\frac{55-35}{2-1} = 20$$ (Average speed is the slope of the line)

7) No slope...........................**5th**
Steep positive slope...............**2nd**
0 slope...................................**1st**
Very steep negative slope........**4th**
Gradual negative slope...........**3rd**
Gradual positive slope.............**6th**
Medium negative slope............**7th**

8) About 20 mph
Average speed is the slope of the line: The graph goes up about 100 on the y-axis for every 5 on the x-axis.   100/5 = 20 mph

9) 10 mph per second
Acceleration is the slope of the line: The graph goes up about 50 on the y-axis for every 5 on the x-axis.   50/5 = 10 miles per hour per second

10) y = 60   Acceleration = 0
Because the vehicle is traveling at a constant speed, the acceleration is 0. The slope of the graph must therefore be zero. The slope of a horizontal line through 60 mph shows a constant speed of 60 mph.

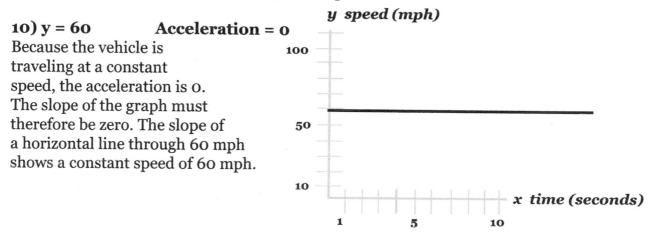

Chapter 18: Acceleration

(Page 282)
1) 5 mph per second
How much did the car increase its speed each second?
65 mph total increase ÷ 13 seconds = An increase of 5 mph for each second

2) 6 mph per second
What speed did the car lose each second?
A total of 30 mph of lost speed ÷ 5 seconds = 6 mph per second of lost speed

3) 32 feet per second per second
The rock went from a speed of 64 feet per second to a speed of 160 feet per second. It gained 96 feet per second in speed in 3 seconds.

The amount of speed the rock gained each second is 96 feet per second ÷ 3 seconds = 32 feet per second of speed for each second it traveled.

(Page 286)
1) 44 feet per second
Speed in feet per hour: 5280 feet x 30 miles = 158,400 feet per hour
Because there are 3600 seconds in an hour, the car's speed is 158,400 ÷ 3600 = 44 feet per second.

2) 22 feet per second
Because 15 mph is half of 30 mph, the answer would be half of the previous answer (#1).

3) 225 feet per second
450 feet ÷ 2 seconds = 225 feet per second

4) $\dfrac{\textbf{7 feet per second}}{\textbf{per second}}$
The increase of speed is 100 feet per second - 44 feet per second = 56 feet per second
Acceleration: 56 feet per second ÷ 8 seconds = 7 feet per second of speed increase for every second.

5) 0
If a speed does not change, there is no acceleration.

6) $\dfrac{\textbf{15 miles per hour}}{\textbf{per second}}$
Change in speed: 60 mph   Time the change took place: 4 seconds
Acceleration: 60 mph ÷ 4 seconds = 15 mph of speed increase for every second traveled.

7) $\dfrac{21\frac{2}{3}\ \text{mph}}{\text{per second}}$

Change in speed: 65 mph   Time: 3 seconds
Deceleration: 65 mph (Change in speed) ÷ 3 seconds (Time) = 21.66 mph per second

8) $\dfrac{\textbf{Change in speed}}{\textbf{Change in time}}=\dfrac{50-50}{1\ \text{minute}}=0$

9) $\dfrac{\textbf{22 feet per second}}{\textbf{per second}}$

60 miles per hour (3600 seconds) is the same as 60 x 5280 = 316,800 feet in 3600 seconds.   Speed in feet per second: 316,000 feet ÷ 3600 = 88 feet per second

Change in speed: 88 feet per second (From 0 to 88 feet per second)
Time: 4 seconds
Acceleration: 88 ÷ 4 = 22 feet per second for every second

10) $\dfrac{\textbf{-352 feet per second}}{\textbf{per second}}$

Speed in feet per hour: 80 miles x 5280 = 422,400 feet
Speed in feet per second: 422,400 ÷ 3600 = 117.33 feet per second
Change in speed: Drop of 117.33 feet per second (From 117.33 to zero)
Time: 1/3 second
Acceleration: 117.33 ÷ 1/3 = -352 feet per second for every second

(Page 291)

1) $\dfrac{\textbf{55 feet per second}}{\textbf{per second}}$

Acceleration = g (32 feet per second per second) x tangent of 60°
A = 32 x 1.7321   A = 55 feet per second per second

2) 18 feet per second/per second
A = 32 x tangent 30°   A = 32 x .5774   A = 18.4768 or 18

3) Approximately 2.5°
Acceleration = 5 (change in speed)÷ 5 (Time) = 1 mile per hour per second
Change acceleration to feet per second per second: 5280 feet ÷ 3600 seconds in an hour = 1.466 feet per second per second.
1.466 (Acceleration) = 32 (g) x tangent of angle   Tangent = 1.466 ÷ 32 = .046
        The angle with a tangent of .046 is between 2° and 3°

!

4) $\dfrac{\text{32 feet per second}}{\text{per second}}$ **is the acceleration of objects near the surface of the Earth.**

Acceleration = g x tangent of 45°   A = 32 x 1   A = 32 feet per second per second

5) Approximately 66.5°

Acceleration is 250 ÷ 5 = 50 miles per hour per second.
Change acceleration to feet per second per second: 50 miles = 264,000 feet ÷ 3600 seconds in an hour = 73.333 feet per second per second.

73.33 (A) = 32 (g) x tangent of angle   tangent = 73.33 ÷ 32   tangent = 2.29
The angle with a tangent of 2.29 is between 66° and 67°

6) 13° angle

The water will act as an acceleration meter.   Acceleration = 5 mph per second
Change to feet per second per second: 26,400 feet ÷ 3600 seconds = 7.33 feet per second per second.
7.33 (A) = 32 (g) x tangent of angle   tangent = 7.33 ÷ 32   tangent = .229
The angle with a tangent of .229 is approximately 13°. The water will be at a 13° angle.

7) $\dfrac{\text{4.4 feet per second}}{\text{per second}}$

Acceleration: 30 mph (change in speed) ÷ 10 seconds (time) = 3 mph per second
Change to feet per second per second:
15,840 feet (number of feet in 3 miles) ÷ 3600 seconds (number of seconds in 1 hour) = 4.4 feet per second per second.

8) 2/3 mph is equal to .98 feet per second per second

40 mph (change in speed) ÷ 60 seconds (time) = 2/3 mph per second
Change to feet per second per second:
3520 feet in 2/3 mile ÷ 3600 seconds in an hour = .98 feet per second per second

9) No

The angle of the water would need to be over 45° to spill. This would be an acceleration of 32 feet per second per second. The acceleration of the car works out to 29.33 feet per second per second.

10) 63 mph

A = 32 (g) x tangent 30°   A = 32 x .5774   A = 18.48 feet per second per second
If the car slows at 18.48 feet per second per second, then before it started slowing down for 5 seconds, it was traveling at a speed of 18.48 feet per second x 5 = 92.4 feet per second.

Change 92.4 feet per second to miles per hour: 92.4 feet in one second is equal to 92.4 feet x 3600 (seconds in an hour) = 332,640 feet per hour.
332,640 feet ÷ 5280 feet in one mile = 63 miles in an hour

Chapter 19: Calculus

(Page 305)
1) 20 mph

The slope of the tangent line, or the derivative of $y=x^2$ is 2x. 2 times 10 = 20 mph

2) 11 mph

The slope of the tangent line, or the derivative of $y=x^2$ is 2x. 2 times 5.5 = 11 mph

3) 30 hours
2 times n hours = 60 mph n must equal 30

4) 1 mph

The slope of the tangent line, or the derivative of $y=x^2$ is 2x. 2 times .5 hours = 1 mph

5) $x^2 = y$

6) 49 mph
Speed is equal to the time squared.   Speed = 7 x 7   Speed = 49 mph

7) 14 mph per second

The acceleration is the slope of the tangent line, which is the derivative of $y=x^2$ or 2x.
When x is 7 seconds, 2x is equal to 14 mph per second.

8) 10 seconds
If speed is equal to the amount of time squared, then we need to ask ourselves what number multiplied by itself is equal to 100? The answer of course is 10.

9) 25 seconds
This is asking the following question: When is the slope of the tangent line equal to 50 mph per second or what is the value of x when 2x is equal to 50? The answer is 25 seconds.

10) 48

If x is equal to 4 in the equation $y=3x^2$, then y is equal to 3 x 4 x 4 = 48.

(Page 306)

1) $4x^3$

2) 14x

3) $15x^2$

4) $60x^5$

5) $9x^2$

6) 5

Chapter 20: Math Contests

Math Contest 1: Page 307
1) 150 miles
Pythagorean Theorem

$$90^2 + 120^2 = c^2$$

$$8100 + 14400 = c^2 \quad 22500 = c^2 \qquad c = 150$$

Northbound 90 miles

Eastbound 120 miles

2) 73.75 feet

$$\frac{5 \ (Mary)}{6 \ (Shadow)} = \frac{n \ (tree)}{88.5 \, feet \ (tree's \ shadow)}$$

Cross-multiply: 6n = 442.5   n = 73.75

3) 77.04 square inches
Because each side of the square must be 12 inches, the diameter of the circle must be 12 inches. The radius then must be 6 inches.

Area of circle: 6 x 6 x 3.14 = 113.04 square inches
Area of triangle: 12 inches (base) x 6 inches (height) x .5 = 36 square inches
Area of shaded part: 113.04 - 36 = 77.04 square inches

4) $9.50
Ball: n
Glove: n + 9
Equation: 2n + 9 = 10   n = .5   n + 9 = 9.5

5) $44
45% of 80: .45 x 80 = 36 $80 - $36 = $44

Math Contest 2: Page 308
1) 99 minutes
If Kristin can read 2 pages per minute, how long will it take her to read 10 pages. It is obvious that this problem is solved by dividing.   123.75 ÷ 1.25 = 99

2) $145
Cost of guitar: n
Tax: .05 n
Equation: n + .05n = 152.25   1.05n = 152.25   n = 145

3) 1/1296

$$\frac{1}{6} x \frac{1}{6} x \frac{1}{6} x \frac{1}{6} = \frac{1}{1296}$$

4) b = 15

$$\frac{8.661}{b} = \tan 30°$$ $$\frac{8.661}{b} = \frac{.5774}{1}$$ Cross-multiply: .5774b = 8.661 b = 15

5) .043 cubic inches

Volume $= \pi r^2 h$
Diameter = 15/16 = .9375 Radius = .9375 ÷ 2 = .46875 Height = .0625

Volume = 3.14 x .46875 x .46875 x .0625 = .0431 cubic inches

Math Contest 3: Page 309
1) 12 years old
Michelle: n
Bob: 4n
Sara: 2n
Equation: 7n = 84 n = 12

2) 44 square inches
Area of entire triangle: 14 inches (base) x 8 inches (height) x .5 = 56 square inches
Area of small rectangle: 3 x 4 = 12 square inches
Area of shaded part: 56 - 12 = 44 square inches

3) 8 million microns
There are 1000 microns in a millimeter and 1000 millimeters in a meter, so there are 1,000,000 microns in a meter.

4) Tuesday 8:15 P.M.
Distance = Speed x Time 1530 = 42.5 x Time Time = 36 hours
36 hours from 8:15 A.M. is the next day at 8:15 P.M.

5) 96.25 ounces

$$\frac{5 \ ounces \ (orange \ juice)}{7 \ ounces \ (mineral \ water)} = \frac{n}{134.75 \ ounces \ (mineral \ water)}$$
Cross-multiply: 7n = 673.75 n = 96.25

Math Contest 4: Page 310
1) $166.50

$$\frac{9 \ (Bill)}{7 \ (Steve)} = \frac{n \ (Bill)}{129.50 \ (Steve)}$$ Cross-multiply: 7n = 1165.5   n = 166.50

2) Yes 3 and 9
You can divide both the top and the bottom by three and nine because when the digits of the top or the bottom are added, the numbers are divisible by 3 and 9.

3) 1/221
First card picked has a 4/52 chance of being a jack. If your first card is a jack, the second card picked has a 3/51 chance of being a jack. (There are 3 jacks left and 51 cards left.)

$$\frac{4}{52} \ x \ \frac{3}{51} = \frac{1}{221}$$

4) 17.875
Diameter: 5 inches   Radius: 2.5 inches   Rectangle is 5 inches wide and 10 inches long
Area of rectangle: 5 x 10 = 50 square inches
Area of circle: 3.14 x 2.5 x 2.5 = 19.625 square inches
Area of triangle: 5 (base) x 5 (height) x .5 = 12.5 square inches
Area of shaded part: (rectangle - circle - triangle)   50 - 19.625 - 12.5 = 17.875 square inches

5) 498,182,400,000 miles
Seconds in December: 60 x 60 x 24 x 31 = 2,678,400 seconds
186,000 miles per second x 2,678,400 = 498,182,400,000

Math Contest 5: Page 311
1) 112 quarters
Number of nickels: n   Value of nickels: 5 x n = 5n
Number of dimes: 2n   Value of dimes: 10 x 2n = 20n
Number of quarters: 16n   Value of quarters: 16n x 25 = 400n

Equation: 5n + 20n + 400n = 2975   425n = 2975   n = 7   16n = 112

2) 1345 times
Circumference of tire: 3.14 x 15 = 47.1 inches   Inches in mile: 5280 x 12 = 63,360
63,360 ÷ 47.1 = 1345

3) 19/34
Chance of first card not being a heart: 39/52
Chance of second card not being a heart: 38/51   (38 non-heart cards left)

39/52 x 38/51 = 19/34

4) 54 mph
Distance = Speed x Time
3000 = Speed x 55.555   Speed = 3000 ÷ 55.555   Speed = 54

5) $.50
98% discount: .98 x 25 = 24.5 $25 - $24.50 = .50

Math Contest 6: Page 312
1) 1 hour   20 minutes
In one hour Bill will paint 1/4 of the fence.
In one hour Molly will paint 1/2 the fence.
In one hour, together, they will paint 3/4 of the fence.
Each 1/4 must be equal to 20 minutes, so it will take them 20 minutes to paint the rest of the fence.

20	20	20	

2) 18.24 square inches

Area of circle: 3.14 x 4 x 4 = 50.24 square inches
Cut square into 2 triangles. Area of each: 8 (base) x 4 (height) x .5 = 16 square inches
50.24 (area of circle) - 32 (area of two triangles) = 18.24 square inches

3) 20 mph
5 blocks of 12 mph   + 1 block of 60 mph = 120   120 ÷ 6 blocks = 20 mph

4) $45.36
Discount: 40% of $84   .40 x 84 = $33.60
New price: $84 - $33.60 = $50.40

Additional discount: 10% of $50.40   .1 x 50.40 = $5.04
New price: $50.4 - $5.04 = $45.36

5) 25 students
2 + 5 + 10 + 8 = 25 students

No vacation

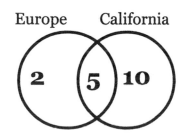

Math Contest 7: Page 313

1) 3493

Function machine:

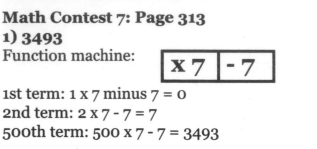

1st term: 1 x 7 minus 7 = 0
2nd term: 2 x 7 - 7 = 7
500th term: 500 x 7 - 7 = 3493

2) 48 years old

Equation: $\dfrac{9n}{12} = 36$ Multiply both sides by 12   9n = 432   n = 48

3) 16 2/3 yards

$$\dfrac{60 \ (Comet's \ distance)}{50 \ (Rudolph's \ distance)} = \dfrac{100 \ (Comet)}{n \ (Rudolph)}$$ Cross-multiply: 60n = 5000   n = 83 1/3

If Rudolph ran 83 1/3 yards, then Comet beat him by 16 2/3 yards

4) 5760 gorgos

Light travels 186,000 miles in one second, so there are 2,790,000 ÷ 186,000 = 15 seconds in a gorgo.
Seconds in 24 hours: 60 x 60 x 24 = 86,400
86,400 seconds ÷ 15 seconds per gorgo = 5760 gorgos in 24 hours

5) 4.36 mph

1 block of 12 mph + 6 blocks of 2 mph + 4 blocks of 6 = 48 ÷ 11 blocks = 4.36 mph

Math Contest 8: Page 314

1) $50.40

Discount: 20% of $60   .2 x 60 = $12

New price: $60 - $12 = $48

Sales tax: .05 x $48 = $2.40   Total cost: $48 + $2.40 = $50.40

2) 13.76 square inches

The shaded part is 1/4 of a circle with a radius that is the length of a side of the square (8).

Area of entire circle: 3.14 x 8 x 8 = 200.96 square inches

Area of 1/4 of the circle: 200.96 ÷ 4 = 50.24 square inches

Area of unshaded part: 64 (area of square) - 50.24 (area of shaded part) = 13.76 square inches

3) 26 children

3 + 5 + 7 + 11 = 26

Neither pet

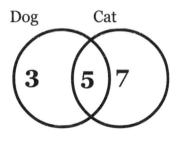

4) 25.98 feet

$\dfrac{b}{15} = \tan 60°$ $\dfrac{b}{15} = \dfrac{1.7321}{1}$ b = 25.98 feet

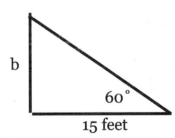

5) 56

Function machine: square the number

1st term: 1 x 1 = 1

2nd term: 2 x 2 = 4

? term = 3136 $\sqrt{3136}$ = 56

Math Contest 9: Page 315

1) 8 days

How long would it have taken for one worker to do half the road?
16 workers took 10 days, so one worker would take 160 days.

1 worker   160 days
2 workers: 160 ÷ 2 = 80 days
20 workers: 160 ÷ 20 = 8 days

2) 2 hours

If Dave runs around the lake to the other side, he is traveling across half of the circumference.
Circumference: 7.6433 x 3.14 = 24 miles   Half circumference: 12 miles
Traveling at 6 mph, it would take Dave 2 hours.

3) 77 quarters

Number of nickels: n   Value of nickels: 5 x n = 5n
Number of quarters: 7n   Value of quarters: 25 x 7n = 175n
Equation: 5n + 175n = 1980   180n = 1980   n = 11   7n = 77

4) 91 squares

6 by 6 squares: 1
5 by 5 squares: 4
4 by 4 squares: 9
Now the pattern is clear---they are all perfect squares.
3 by 3 must equal 16   2 by 2 = 25   1 by 1 = 36   1 + 4 + 9 + 16 + 25 + 36 = 91

5) 1/17

The first card has a 100% probability of being a "good" card. (Because any card will work.)
When you are dealt one card, there are only three of that kind left in the deck, which has 51 cards left.

$$\frac{52}{52} \; x \; \frac{3}{51} = \frac{1}{17}$$

Math Contest 10: Page 316

1) 56

Each number goes up by 1, then 4, then 9, then 16. These are all perfect squares. The next perfect square is 25. The next number must go up by 25: 31 + 25 = 56

2) 5 1/4 mph

7 blocks of 3 mph (Because the time spent going 3 mph was 7 times longer than the time spent going 21 mph.) + 1 block of 21 mph.

Adds up to 42 ÷ 8 blocks = 5.25 mph

3) 8 1/3 miles

It is 93,000,000 miles from the sun to the Earth. Light travels 186,000 miles per second. The time it takes for light to get to the Earth from the sun is: 93,000,000 ÷ 186,000 = 500 seconds. 500 seconds = 8.33 minutes

If a car travels at a speed of 60 mph, it is traveling at a speed of one mile each minute. It will travel 8.33 miles.

4) 1 minute

With each stride, the Tyrannosaurus Rex gains 30 feet or 10 yards.
Because Gabe is 400 yards ahead of the Tyrannosaurus, it will take 400 ÷ 10 = 40 strides before Gabe is caught.

Each stride takes 1.5 seconds, so it will be 40 strides x 1.5 seconds = 60 seconds before Gabe is caught.

5) 15 years old

Dan: n
Dave: 3n
Sara: n - 4
Equation: n + 3n + n - 4 = 91   5n -4 = 91   5n = 95   n = 19   n - 4 = 15

Math Contest 11: Page 317
1) Monday

Sat.					Day before yesterday	Yesterday	Today	

If six days before the day before yesterday is a Saturday, simply count the days forward until you reach tomorrow and you will find that it is a Monday.

2) 4 dimes

Number of dimes: n   Value of dimes: 10 x n = 10n
Number of quarters: 2n   Value of quarters: 25 x 2n = 50n
Number of $5 bills: 2n   Value of $5 bills: 500 x 2n = 1000n

Equation: 10n + 50n + 1000n = 4240   1060n = 4240   n = 4

3) 61,032.675 cubic inches

Each side of the cubic meter is 39.372 inches long.
Volume: 39.372 x 39.372 x 39.372 = 61,032.675 cubic inches

4) $144.64
If Isaac's car gets 28 miles per gallon and he travels 3164 miles, he will use 3164 ÷ 28 = 113 gallons of gas.   113 gallons x $1.28 per gallon = $144.64

5) 16 inches
Use the Pythagorean Theorem to find that the hypotenuse of each triangle is 5 inches.

$3^2 + 4^2 = c^2$ $25 = c^2$ c = 5 inches   Perimeter: 5 + 5 + 6 = 16 inches

Math Contest 12: Page 318
1) 11.16 square feet
Area of the circle: 3.14 x 4 x 4 = 50.24
The two shaded slices of the "pie" total 80°. Because there are 360 ° in a circle, the shaded part is 80/360 or 2/9 of the circle.

2/9 x 50.24 = 11.16 square feet

2) 400,000 liters
A liter is a cubic decimeter. The pool measures 80 decimeters by 50 decimeters by 100 decimeters.

Volume = 80 x 50 x 100 = 400,000 cubic decimeters or 400,000 liters

3) $44.94
Sales tax: 7% of $42   .07 x 42 = $2.94 $42 + $2.94 = $44.94

4) 6 feet 3 inches

$\dfrac{20 \; feet \; pole}{16 \; feet \; (shadow)} = \dfrac{n}{5 \; feet \; (Eric's \; shadow)}$ Cross-multiply: 16n = 100   n = 6.25 feet

5) 42.01 feet

$\dfrac{a}{60} = \tan 35°$ $\dfrac{a}{60} = \dfrac{.7002}{1}$ Cross-multiply: a = 42.01 feet

Math Contest 13: Page 319
1) 1/32

Each baby has a 1 in 2 chance of being a girl.   5 babies: $\dfrac{1}{2} x \dfrac{1}{2} x \dfrac{1}{2} x \dfrac{1}{2} x \dfrac{1}{2} = \dfrac{1}{32}$

2) 120
If Michelle averages 150 for five games, her total score must be 5 x 150 = 750
Michelle has bowled a total of 125 + 155 + 165 + 185 = 630   750 - 630 = 120

3) 36 mph

Distance = Speed x Time $48 = \text{Speed} \times 1\frac{1}{3} \text{ hours}$ Speed = 36 mph

4) 5.4 cm.

$$\frac{2 \ cm. \ (map)}{20 \ miles \ (real)} = \frac{n}{54 \ miles \ (real)}$$ Cross-multiply: 20n = 108   n = 5.4

5) x = 3   y = 4
Add both the equations and the y's will disappear.
New equation: 13x = 39   x = 3

Math Contest 14: Page 320
1) 34.54 feet
If the area of the square is 121 feet, then each side must be 11 feet. The diameter of the circle is then 11 feet.

Circumference: 3.14 x 11 = 34.54 feet

2) 3.75 mph
Use 15 mph as big block of time.
With current: 3 blocks of 5 mph
Against current: 5 blocks of 3 mph

Total: 30   Number of blocks: 8   Average speed: 30 ÷ 8 = 3.75 mph

3) 4
Slope is the difference in y's divided by the difference in x's

When x is 1, then y must be 13   When x is 2, y must be 17

$$\frac{17 - 13 \ (difference \ in \ y's)}{2 - 1 \ (difference \ in \ x's)} = 4/1 = 4$$

4) 6 mph/second
The car increased its speed 54 ÷ 9 = 6 miles each second.

5) 2/77 square inches

πr^2 $\dfrac{22}{7} \ x \ \dfrac{1}{11} \ x \ \dfrac{1}{11} = \dfrac{2}{77}$

Math Contest 15: Page 321
1) x = 8
The easiest way to solve this problem is guess and check. Try a small value for x, say 4.

$$4^{4-2}=4^2=16 \qquad 8^{4-4}=8^0=1 \qquad \text{Try x = 8: } 4^{8-2}=4^6=4096 \qquad 8^{8-4}=8^4=4096$$

2) 90 square inches
The area of the bottom part is a rectangle: 10 x 6 = 60 square inches.
The top part is a triangle with a base of 10 and a height of 6: 10 x 6 x .5 = 30 square inches.

3) π (3.14 to 1)
Every circle has a circumference to diameter ratio of π.

4) 37.5%

Percent of increase is the change divided by the original: $\dfrac{1.5 \ feet \ (change)}{4 \ feet \ (original)}$ = .375 or 37.5%

5) 9/49

Step 1: Start small and work up: $\dfrac{1}{5\dfrac{1}{2\frac{1}{4}}}=\dfrac{1}{5\dfrac{1}{\frac{9}{4}}}$ Divide shaded part: $\dfrac{1}{5\dfrac{1}{\frac{9}{4}}}=\dfrac{1}{5\dfrac{4}{9}}$

Step 2: $\dfrac{1}{5\dfrac{1}{\frac{9}{4}}}=\dfrac{1}{5\dfrac{4}{9}}$ Turn shaded part into improper fraction: $\dfrac{1}{5\dfrac{4}{9}}=\dfrac{1}{\frac{49}{9}}$

Divide: $\dfrac{1}{1}\div\dfrac{49}{9}=\dfrac{1}{1}x\dfrac{9}{49}=\dfrac{9}{49}$

Math Contest 16: Page 322
1) 158 students

$\dfrac{11 \ (flu)}{30 \ (class)}=\dfrac{n}{432 \ (school)}$ Cross-multiply: 30n = 4752 n = 158.4

2) 506
Step 1: Put in any number for **P** and take the square root: All numbers are around 35 and if **P** were a 5, then 1225 would be a perfect square.
Step 2: **R** must be zero because all multiples of 10 end in zero.

Step 3: To be a multiple of 9, all digits in the number must add up to a number that is a multiple of 9. **M** must then equal 6.

3) Mean: $54,500   Mode: No mode
Median: $50,000   Range: $70,000
Mean: Determined by adding and then dividing by the number of items:
327,000 ÷ 6 = 54,500
Mode: The number that appears the most--------they all appear once.
Median: Line numbers up from smallest to largest and then take the middle number. If there is no middle, then average the two middle numbers. The average of 40,000 and 60,000 is 50,000.
Range: The difference between the smallest and the largest-----90,000 - 20,000 = 70,000

4) 253
Because each row increases by three, part of the function machine is multiply by three.
1st number: 1 x 3 = 3   But you want a 1 because there is 1 box, so you must subtract 2.

Function machine: **X 3 -2**   When 85 goes into the machine: 85 x 3 - 2 = 253

5) 89 students

$$\frac{1 \ (left-handed)}{7 \ (group \ total)} = \frac{n}{623 \ (large \ group \ total)}$$ Cross-multiply: 7n = 623   n = 89

Math Contest 17: Page 323
1) 100
1st number: n   4th number: n + 3
2nd number: n + 1   5th number: n + 4
3rd number: n + 2   6th number: n + 5   Equation: 6n + 15 = 615   n = 100

2) 21 mph
Because it takes sound 5 seconds to go one mile, the storm was 17.5 ÷ 5 = 3.5 miles away.
It traveled 3.5 miles in 10 minutes. There are six 10-minute parts in an hour: 6 x 3.5 = 21

3)$150
Starting price: n
If there is a discount of 10%, then the new price is 90% of the starting price.
If there is a 25% discount, the new price is 75% of the starting price, and so on..........

Monday's price: If there is a 40% discount, then the new price on Monday is 60% of n or .6n

Tuesday's price: If there is a 40% discount off Monday's price, then the new price is 60% of Monday's price or .6 x .6n (Monday's price) = .36n   Equation: .36n = 54   n = 150

4) 33 1/3%

Percent of decrease is change ÷ original: $\dfrac{5000 \ (change)}{15,000 \ (original)} = 1/3 = 33.33\%$

5) 7 inches

Area of Michelle's square: 12.4 x 12.4 = 153.76 square inches

Area = $3.14 \times r^2$　　　　$153.75 = 3.14 \times r^2$　　　　$r^2 = 153.75 \div 3.14$

$r^2 = 48.968$　　　　r = 7

Math Contest 18: Page 324

1) 85 boys

90% of 320 students went to the school dance.　.9 x 320 = 288 students went to the dance. If 220 girls were at the dance, then there must have been 288 - 220 = 68 boys at the dance.

80% of the boys = 68　　　　.8n = 68　　　　n = 85

2) 30 gallons

12 gallons added 2/5 to the tank, so each 1/5 must be equal to 6 gallons. If 1/5 is equal to 6 gallons, the whole tank (5/5) must equal 30 gallons.

3) 7744

The numbers are all perfect squares.　　1st term is 4 x 4　　　　2nd term is 5 x 5 3rd term is 6 x 6　　4th term is 7 x 7, so the 85th term must equal 88 x 88 = **7744**

4) 7:9

The remaining 3/4 is still in a ratio of 7: 5　　　(milk : tomato juice) Because there are 12 total parts, then each quarter of the container must hold 4 parts.

If the remaining 1/4 is filled with tomato juice, then the 5 parts tomato juice jumps to 9 parts. New ratio: 7:9

5) 4 times

Pick any radius, say 5 inches: Area = 3.14 x 5 x 5 = 78.5 square inches Now double it: Area = 3.14 x 10 x 10 = 314 square inches　　　　$314 \div 78.5 = 4$

Math Contest 19: Page 325

1) $15

1st day: n	4th day: n + 30	7th day: n + 60	10th day: n + 90
2nd day: n + 10	5th day: n + 40	8th day: n + 70	
3rd day: n + 20	6th day: n + 50	9th day: n + 80	

Equation: 10n + 450 = 600　　　　10n = 150　　　　n = 15

2) 43.74 square inches

Width: n　　　　Length 2n

Rectangle's area = n x 2n or $2n^2$　　$2n^2 = 72$　　Divide both sides by 2 : $n^2 = 36$　　n = 6 Diameter of circle is 6 inches so the radius is 3.　　　Area of circle: 3.14 x 3 x 3 = 28.26 Area of rectangle (72) - Area of circle (28.26) = 43.74 square inches

3) 3 miles per hour per second
Its speed increases 33 mph in a time of 11 seconds. Its acceleration then must be
33 mph ÷ 11 seconds = 3 mph per second.

4) x = 11   y = 2
Add the equations to make the x's disappear.
New equation: 15y = 30   y = 2

5) 1 billion cubic millimeters
A cubic meter has side measurements of 1000 millimeters on each side.
1000 x 1000 x 1000 = 1,000,000,000 cubic millimeters

Math Contest 20: Page 326
1) P = 9   T = 314
The number Travis ended up with: 3.14 x 10 x 10 x P = 314P
The number Mark ended up with: 3 x 3 x T = 9T

If 9 x T = 314 x P, T must equal 314 and P must equal 9.

2) 3 hours 12 minutes
Think 1:   1 person would unload the 3 trucks in 8 x 6 = 48 hours
                        1 person would unload one truck in 48 ÷ 3 = 16 hours
                        2 people would unload one truck in 16 ÷ 2 = 8 hours
                        10 people would unload one truck in 16 ÷ 10 = 1.6 hours

If it takes 10 people 1.6 hours to unload one truck, it will take them 3.2 hours to unload 2 trucks.

3) 1/1728
A cubic foot is 12 inches by 12 inches by 12 inches. 12 x 12 x 12 = 1728 cubic inches

4) 791 pounds
Nickel and copper are in a ratio of 7:11
Because there are 18 total parts, the ratio of nickel to the whole statue is 7:18

$$\frac{7 \ (nickel)}{18 \ (whole \ statue)} = \frac{n \ (weight \ of \ nickel)}{2034 \ (weight \ of \ statue)}$$ Cross-multiply: 18n = 14,238   n = 791

5) $18.50
Cost of book: n
Tax: 6% of n or .06n
Total cost: n + .06n = 1.06n

Equation: 1.06n = 19.61   n = 18.50